9/08

MAR 3 2008

DATE DUE

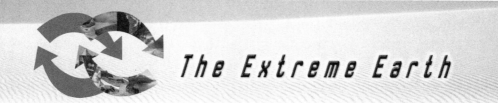

The Extreme Earth

Canyons

Erik Hanson

Foreword by
Geoffrey H. Nash, Geologist

CHELSEA HOUSE
P U B L I S H E R S
An imprint of Infobase Publishing

I dedicate this book to Burton Hanson and to Mathilda.

CANYONS

Copyright © 2007 by Erik Hanson

Chelsea House
An imprint of Infobase Publishing
132 West 31st Street
New York NY 10001

ISBN-10: 0-8160-6435-0
ISBN-13: 978-0-8160-6435-9

Library of Congress Cataloging-in-Publication Data
Hanson, Erik A.
    Canyons / Erik Hanson ; foreword Geoffrey H. Nash.
        p. cm. — (The extreme earth)
    Includes index.
    ISBN 0-8160-6435-0
    1. Plate tectonics. 2. Canyons. I. Title II. Series.
    QE511.4.H36 2007
    551.44'2—dc22   2006015810

Chelsea House books are available at special discounts when purchased in bulk quantities for businesses, associations, institutions, or sales promotions. Please call our Special Sales Department in New York at (212) 967-8800 or (800) 322-8755.

You can find Chelsea House on the World Wide Web at http://www.chelseahouse.com

Text design by Erika K. Arroyo
Cover design by Dorothy M. Preston/Salvatore Luongo
Illustrations by Melissa Ericksen
Photo research by Diane K. French

Printed in the United States of America

VB FOF 10 9 8 7 6 5 4 3 2 1

This book is printed on acid-free paper.

Contents

✧✧✧✧✧✧✧✧✧✧✧✧✧✧✧✧✧✧✧✧✧✧✧

Foreword

The great canyons of the world are like windows into the past. Due to erosion, hundreds of millions of years of the geologic and fossil record in the rocks have been exposed to scientists, hikers, and outdoor enthusiasts. The English term *canyon* comes from the Spanish word *cañón*. In Europe, the term *gorge* is used to describe the same type of landform. Whatever you call them, canyons are variously ranked by length, depth, or overall area, but comparisons can be difficult if using different parameters. They are much more common in arid regions of the world than in wetter areas because erosion of the surrounding rock has a reduced effect in arid climates.

Early explorers of canyons often risked their lives following rivers with unknown rapids, passing through areas with walls so steep that once they set off, the explorers were committed to only exiting the canyon when the river allowed. The canyon generally agreed to be the world's largest is the Grand Canyon of Arizona. It was first explored in the late 1860s, after the Civil War. Today people can follow in the footsteps of these explorers or just peer over the rim of the canyons to get a glimpse of their history. Human beings have made their homes near the water and protection of canyons for millennia. It also seems obvious that today, the reason people want to be near them may be their sheer beauty.

Canyons, a volume in the Extreme Earth set, leads the reader through the geologic growth of 10 canyons that are recognized by scientists as unique. Erik Hanson introduces concepts of tectonic uplift and river erosion that simultaneously raised the plateaus on which the canyons grew and also caused the carving of the channel down through the layers of rock. Rapid uplift of the plateaus produced steeper gradients in the rivers and thus increased erosion by faster-moving water. The Grand Canyon is described in chapter 1 of course, because it is the largest canyon. Other canyons you will read about are the Columbia River Gorge, which was cut down through thousands of feet of basalt that was formerly molten lava, and the limestone mountainous region of the Three Gorges in China. Others include Canyon Diablo in Arizona, which had its development influenced by a meteor crater; Chaco Canyon in New Mexico, which is one of the oldest continually inhabited areas in the United States; and Monterey Canyon off the coast of California, which is interesting because it is a submarine canyon cut by the fast-moving flow of the Salinas River.

Scientists study canyons because their walls reveal the history of the local area all in one place, with the oldest part of the story at the bottom of the stack of layers and the most recent up at the rim. Not every layer of rock may still be present, but even the absence of a rock formation tells a tale if you know how to interpret what remains. Certain canyons like the Grand Canyon are so well studied that the names of the rock formations are as familiar to geologists as the names of old friends.

Canyon formation remains ongoing at all of the areas discussed in this book. Rivers are incising deeper into underlying rock as water seeks a lower level, and many of the plateaus where the canyons are forming are still in the process of being uplifted. Canyon formation is as simple as water flowing downhill and as complex as the 4.5-billion-year history of the Earth.

Erik Hanson's book contains a useful glossary for those unfamiliar with all of the scientific terms. Readers will find this book to be a detailed study of an interesting topic that is relevant to the landscape of some of the most beautiful vistas on the planet.

—Geoffrey H. Nash, geologist

Preface

From outer space, Earth resembles a fragile blue marble, as revealed in the famous photograph taken by the *Apollo 17* astronauts in December 1972. Eugene Cernan, Ronald Evans, and Jack Schmitt were some 28,000 miles (45,061 km) away when one of them snapped the famous picture that provided the first clear image of the planet from space.

Zoom in closer and the view is quite different. Far beneath the vast seas that give the blue marble its rich hue are soaring mountains and deep ridges. On land, more mountains and canyons come into view, rugged terrain initiated by movement beneath the Earth's crust and then sculpted by wind and water. Arid deserts and hollow caves are here too, existing in counterpoint to coursing rivers, sprawling lakes, and plummeting waterfalls.

The Extreme Earth is a set of eight books that presents the geology of these landforms, with clear explanations of their origins, histories, and structures. Similarities exist, of course, among the many mountains of the world, just as they exist among individual rivers, caves, deserts, canyons, waterfalls, lakes, ocean ridges, and trenches. Some qualify as the biggest, highest, deepest, longest, widest, oldest, or most unusual, and these are the examples singled out in this set. Each book introduces 10 superlative examples, one by one, of the individual landforms, and reveals why these landforms are never static, but always changing. Some of them are internationally known, located in populated areas. Others are in more remote locations and known primarily to people in the region. All of them are worthy of inclusion.

To some people, the ever-shifting contours of the Earth are just so much scenery. Others sit and ponder ocean ridges and undersea trenches, imagining mysteries that they can neither interact with nor examine in person. Some gaze at majestic canyons, rushing waterfalls, or placid lakes, appreciating the scenery from behind a railing, on a path, or aboard a boat. Still others climb mountains, float rivers, explore caves, and cross deserts, interacting directly with nature in a personal way.

Even people with a heightened interest in the scenic wonders of the world do not always understand the complexity of these landforms. The eight books in the Extreme Earth set provide basic information on how individual landforms came to exist and their place in the history of the planet. Here, too, is information on what makes each one unusual, what roles they play in the world today, and, in some cases, who discovered and named them. Each chapter in each volume also includes material on environmental challenges and reports on science in action, with details on field studies conducted at each site. All the books include photographs in color and black-and-white, line drawings, a glossary of scientific terms related to the text, and a listing of resources for more information.

When students who have read the eight books in the Extreme Earth set venture outdoors—whether close to home, on a family vacation, or to distant shores—they will know what they are looking at, how it got there, and what likely will happen next. They will know the stories of how lakes form, how wind and weather work together to etch mountain ranges, and how water carves canyons. These all are thrilling stories—stories that inhabitants of this planet have a responsibility to know.

The primary goal of the Extreme Earth set of books is to inform readers of all ages about the most interesting mountains, rivers, caves, deserts, canyons, waterfalls, lakes, ocean ridges, and trenches in the world. Even as these books serve to increase both understanding of the history of the planet and appreciation for all its landforms, ideally they also will encourage a sense of responsible stewardship for this magnificent blue marble.

Acknowledgments

I want to thank Frank Darmstadt, executive editor, for the editorial assistance and guidance he provided. Without his patience and accommodation, the completion of this book would not have been possible. I also want to thank Diane French, photo researcher, for her patience and skillful help with the acquisition of photographs for this book. Some of the canyons are in very remote or unique locations (such as beneath the Pacific Ocean), and uncovering photographs has been no simple task.

Introduction

Canyons provides geological histories of 10 canyons and the rock layers that form their walls. In many ways, canyons are simple, apparently durable structures that have been formed by the actions of water. However, this structural simplicity belies the powerful and dynamic qualities of the forces that produced the canyons.

The geological histories of these 10 canyons contain numerous contradictions and paradoxes. On the one hand, the sites of many canyons have been subjected to very active and animated cycles of erosion, deposition, and uplift. For a long time, the site of the Grand Canyon was part of a kind of bay, or inlet, of an intracontinental seaway. The canyon has also been influenced by fault activity and by intracanyon lava flows, which dammed the Colorado River in multiple sites. On the other hand, many of the canyons have been preserved, in a kind of quiescent state, by the arid desert climates that surround them. Fish River Canyon, in Namibia, is adjacent to one of the most ancient and profoundly dry deserts in the world. The air in some parts of the Namib Desert, in which Fish River Canyon is located, is dry enough to evaporate, on an annual basis, 100 times the total amount of annual rainfall. In the area around Windjana Gorge, some of the large-scale, terraced structures were created by changes in a reef that existed more than 350 million years ago. More recently, rock layers have been deposited and eroded from above these terraces. The terraces were parts of enormous reefs, and the scale of the terraces has precluded their complete erosion.

Other canyons in this book have been shaped by both rivers and subsurface water. In the case of Peonera Canyon and its neighboring canyons, in northeastern Spain, the paths of rivers may have interacted with underground caverns and tunnels. Similar karstlike formations, formed by water in underground springs or aquifers, exist around Windjana Gorge, the Three Gorges of the Yangtze River, and probably Canyon Diablo. In the land around Peonera Canyon and downstream of Zion Canyon, thermal springs and other groundwater sources have helped shape the topography.

In other cases, unique events have interacted with rivers and helped shape the canyons. Columbia River Gorge has been cut out of thick layers of basalt lava, and early forms of the gorge were filled in by lava flows. In the case of Canyon Diablo, a nearby meteor impact appears to have interacted, in subtle ways, with the ongoing erosion of the canyon.

An attempt has been made to pin down the timing of the incision of each canyon, but this has not always been possible. In the case of Chaco Canyon, for example, the timing of incision has been extrapolated from the times at which other canyons, drained by the same system of rivers and tributaries of which the streambed of the Chaco River is part, were incised. If the timing of incision has not been clearly established in the research, the discussion focuses more on the unique aspects of the regional landforms and climate. For most of the canyons, researchers have more precisely established the times at which the rock layers, in the canyon walls, were deposited. These times are the ages of the canyon walls, the ages of the rock layers that make up the walls.

For most of the canyons in this book, the incision of the canyon walls has occurred much more recently, generally within the last 2 to 5 million years, than the rock walls were formed. The formation of the sedimentary rock layers, layers that comprise the walls of most of the 10 canyons, occurred under very unique conditions. By examining the behavior of groundwater or surface water in the area around some canyons, it is possible to get a sense of the conditions that shaped the canyon. As helpful as it is to know the precise time at which a terrace was incised in a canyon wall, the longer-term histories of the canyon wall may be more rich in unique and compelling details.

The study of canyon formation is, in many ways, still in its infancy. As researchers have noted, the study of the drainage and erosion of mountain ranges has been much more involved than the study of canyon formation. Essentially, the focus of research has been more on rain-soaked mountain ranges and less on the actions of rivers in dry areas. The timing of the incision of a canyon and gorge has, however, often been estimated by considering the time at which the erosion of a mountain range, uphill and upstream of the canyon, was especially intense. The drainage and erosion of mountains tend to be relevant to canyon formation, by a few relatively simple mechanisms. Thus, the predominance of research on the erosion of mountain ranges has clearly helped to advance the understanding of canyon formation.

Hopefully, readers will, at a minimum, get a sense of the factors that are involved in canyon formation. The study of surface landforms and surface water, particularly in desert environments, is growing and evolving. How can intermittent flooding actually maintain and intensify the dry, arid climate of a desert? How could a hypervelocity meteor impact contribute to the formation of canyons and geothermally driven springs? This book, which explores some preliminary answers to these questions, will hopefully stimulate the reader to find additional answers.

Origin of
the Landform

Canyons

The formation of a canyon mainly requires moving water, the right types of rocks, and a climate that is relatively dry. The water in a river tends to erode the banks of the river gradually, and this can both widen the river and help establish new curves or winding turns. Rivers also tend to grind and erode in a downward direction, a process that scientists refer to as downcutting or *incision*. As a result of their incision, many rivers will eventually begin to act on rocky layers of land that would otherwise be covered by soil or sediment. If a river can move across an area of land that is rocky, fairly flat, and relatively free of rainfall, the river will tend to produce downward incision and to expand outward, laterally, into its banks. The river may cut out bluffs in some places where the outward erosion is limited or form a gently sloping river valley in places where incision is balanced by erosion on the banks. If the river can grind downward through rock that is especially hard or exists in special layers, the result can be a canyon that is somewhat broad at the top, very deep, and narrow at the canyon floor.

The tendency of a river to cut downward and form a canyon can also be affected by geological forces acting far beneath the canyon floor. Canyons can be more than a mile deep, but they are still just part of the outermost layer of the Earth, known as the *crust*. The Earth's crust is an average of about 28 times as thick as the depth of the Grand Canyon in Arizona. Compared with the thickness of the molten rock that exists beneath the crust, the crust is fairly thin and can be gradually moved upward or downward or sideways.

Broadly speaking, 99.7 percent of the Earth's mass consists of a dense and spherical core surrounded by a layer of molten rock. Scientists think of the Earth as consisting of four overall layers, and these layers will be discussed, in specific contexts, in subsequent chapters. The solid ground of the continents and the land under the oceans are the outer shell of the Earth. These portions of solid rock are known as the crust. Beneath the crust is the *mantle*, which consists of the *upper mantle* and *lower mantle*.

The crust and outermost portion of the upper mantle are, together, known as the *lithosphere*. Between one-third and two-thirds of the lithosphere is part of the upper mantle. The other fraction is the crust. To avoid confusion, the portion of the lithosphere that is mantle will be referred to as the *mantle lithosphere*. The upper mantle consists of the mantle lithosphere and, beneath it, the *asthenosphere*. The portion of the upper mantle that is not part of the lithosphere is the asthenosphere, which extends down to about 217 miles (350 km). The *continental plates* move, as continuous units of crust and mantle lithosphere, across the asthenosphere. Both the mantle lithosphere and asthenosphere are technically composed of solid rock, but the rock of the asthenosphere is relatively softer than the mantle lithosphere. The lower mantle, beneath the asthenosphere, consists entirely of molten, or semiliquid, rock. Beneath the mantle are the *outer core*, which is liquid, and the *inner core*, which is solid.

The lithosphere varies in thickness but generally ends at about 62 miles (100 km) below the surface of the Earth. The thicknesses of the crust and mantle lithosphere do not necessarily always add up to 62 miles (100 km). For example, the crust and mantle lithosphere may both be thicker in the same place. This can cause the thickness of the overall lithosphere, which is the sum of the crust and mantle lithosphere, to be locally increased. This is the case in China, as discussed in chapter 3. These variations are not often directly relevant to canyon formation, but the thickening of the lithosphere can be accompanied by localized uplift.

SETTING THE STAGE: TECTONIC ACTIVITY

The earliest factor that contributes to canyon formation is *tectonic activity*. This term refers to either the movements of plates, which are distinct blocks of crust and mantle lithosphere, or the deformation of the plates by *orogenic activity* or *fault activity*. The term *plate tectonics* refers to the interactions of blocks of crust and mantle lithosphere. When scientists look at the entire surface of the Earth, they divide its underlying crust and lithosphere into about 35 *plates*. The seven largest of these are the *continental plates*, and the borders of the continental plates tend to correspond approximately to the borders of continents.

When two plates collide or grind against each other over time, the landscape on either plate can be deformed. These tectonic forces that occur when plates interact with each other can produce earthquakes and, over a longer time period, create mountain ranges. When one plate collides with another or undergoes subduction beneath another, the zone or line of interaction is known as a *convergent plate boundary*. A *divergent plate boundary* is formed along the boundaries between two plates as the plates move away from each other. The uplifting of one plate as another is forced to dive under is one way that mountains and plateaus are formed, and this uplift can be important for canyon formation. As you are probably aware, water tends to flow from higher elevations to the lower elevation of sea level. Put another way, even a river that appears to be flowing on flat ground is slowly moving downward to sea level. This downhill flow may or may not be accompanied by downward incision. Given enough time, the water will "find" the best and most direct path to the sea. In a river flowing downward at a fairly steep slope, the water will tend to move faster and amplify both its outward and downward erosive effects.

In the convergence between the continental plate and oceanic plate, in the adjacent diagram, the volcanic arc activity has not yet migrated inland. As this type of plate convergence progresses, the volcanic arc activity can migrate in an inland direction. This can create a *backarc zone, backarc basin,* and backarc *foreland basin,* also known as a *retroarc foreland basin.* Some of the canyons discussed in this book, including Zion Canyon and the Grand Canyon, were carved out of sedimentary rocks that built up in these low-lying basins. Other canyons were incised out of foreland basins that had been formed by the convergence between two continental plates. These canyons include Fish River Canyon and Peonera Canyon.

COOPERATIVE EFFECTS OF ROCKS, WATER, AND TECTONIC ACTIVITY

The water in a river, the small pieces of rock on the bottom of a river, and tectonic events can all interact to help a canyon form. The downward slope that a river follows is known as the river's *gradient.* A river with a steep gradient might have a lot of tiny waterfalls over rocks, and the downhill movement causes rocks on the river's bottom to grind downward more. Water that is moving very fast produces more grinding, by causing rocks to strike both one another and the river's bottom. Rivers also carry very small sediment particles, which are essentially very small pieces of rock, suspended in the water. These sediments can have an abrasive effect, akin to the effect of sandpaper, on the bottom of the river. Rocks that are larger but still small enough to be moved by the current of the river also contribute to incision. The buoyancy of objects in water can make submerged rocks effectively "lighter," because the rocks displace a certain amount of water. This allows rocks to move more easily along the bottom of the river. Fast-moving water can also carry away more of the fine fragments that are ground up.

Incision can also be driven by local increases in the gradient of a river, and some of these local changes can result from sediment deposition. If a river receives a large input of water and sediments at one site, the local deposition of sediments can actually intensify the gradient. This local increase in gradient that results from the deposition of sediments, known as *alluvial sediments,* is known as *aggradation.* Aggradation can promote

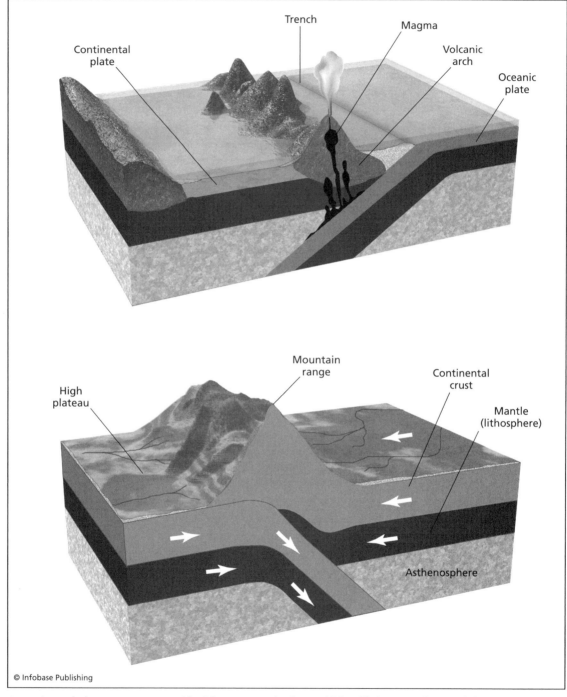

A continental plate can converge with either an oceanic plate, which will always undergo subduction, or another continental plate (or a smaller lithospheric plate with relatively thick continental lithosphere).

incision along portions of the riverbed that are downstream of the site of aggradation. The downstream incision further increases the gradient and speeds up the flow at the site of aggradation, and this can erode the locally deposited sediments that produced the aggradation. In some cases, however, aggradation may be prolonged and may lead to prolonged intervals of incision. In the Grand Canyon, for example, lava dams are thought to have contributed, at times, to the striking differences between the incision rate in the western Grand Canyon and the rate in the eastern Grand Canyon.

Rocks that fall off the walls of a canyon can either help or interfere with the ongoing formation of a canyon. On the one hand, a canyon wall can become less steep when its rocks break off and tumble into the river. On the other hand, these rocks can be broken up and contribute to the incision by the river. This extra incision could help to keep the canyon walls steep, even if some rocks are falling off and smoothing out the tops of the canyon walls.

A river can also produce canyons by interacting with tectonic activity in an ongoing and rather direct manner. When plates of the Earth's crust are interacting to produce uplift, this tectonic activity can enhance the formation of canyons. If the entire canyon is being lifted an inch or millimeter higher each year, compared to sea level or to another part of the continent, the whole river will effectively be flowing downward at a steeper gradient. This will speed up the flow of water in the river and speed up the downcutting, as long as the other canyon-forming conditions are present and are maintained. If a person is cutting a loaf of bread as another person is lifting up the entire loaf, the knife will slice the bread with more force and rapidity. The force of uplift from beneath a canyon can also serve to compress the walls of the canyon, thereby making them more resistant to erosion by wind and rain.

In other cases, uplift along *fault systems* can drive incision in a canyon. Fault-associated uplift almost certainly contributed to the relatively recent phases of incision in the Grand Canyon. Numerous fault systems intersect the Grand Canyon and have produced significant uplift at different times. Sometimes, *fault-associated uplift* can contribute to local differences in the rates of incision. This localized uplift will sometimes produce downstream incision, much as aggradation does. The downstream incision will then dwindle down, as the river erodes the rock that was uplifted along the fault line.

In some cases, uplift from fault lines can interact with other processes and cause one section of a river to be almost cut off from the downstream portions. This can produce complex and sometimes paradoxical effects on sediment transport, making the river behave like two separate rivers. A river will normally respond to a change, such as a change in gradient or sediment delivery, as if the river were a continuous system. In this case, one change is strongly coupled to another change. These *coupling* mechanisms normally allow the river to restore an equilibrium. When the process of sediment transport is uncoupled from the process of sediment delivery or from some other river-mediated process, the river can sometimes produce unusual features in one part of a canyon. Larger rocks and gravel might be deposited in a selective manner, at one downstream site and at no other sites in between. This might produce localized changes in the walls of a canyon.

The details of the different types of coupling are complex, but the general concept is relevant. Researchers have remarked that the Grand Canyon is not as much a single canyon as it is a conglomeration of many canyons, joined into one. At different times, localized lava dams and localized changes in sediment delivery have made the Colorado River behave like two rivers. The incision rate has, at times, been twice as high in one part of the Grand Canyon as in another. The walls of the Grand Canyon also contain different types of rocks in different places. Thus, the Grand Canyon is 10 canyons in the sense that rocks and water, in different parts of the canyon and at different times, have interacted in a multiplicity of ways. The leg bones of a teenager can grow too rapidly to allow his or her muscular reflexes to adjust, a disconnect that can be viewed as an uncoupling of two processes in the body. Similarly, different sections of a canyon can develop at different times and in different ways.

EFFECTS OF RAIN AND CLIMATE ON CANYONS

The erosion of rock by rain and other weather can also influence the formation of canyons. Canyons often form on plateaus, which are large and relatively flat areas of land. Plateaus can result from combinations of *passive uplift* and *active uplift*. In *isostatic uplift*, a form of passive uplift, a large area of land is pushed upward to produce a relatively even terrain. This can result from *erosional exhumation*, which is the erosion of layers of sedimentary rock from a relatively large and uniform area of land. In contrast, mountains are formed through *orogenic uplift*, a form of active uplift. Orogenic uplift is a folding and crumpling of the crust and occurs over smaller areas of land than the plateau-forming isostatic uplift. Plateaus can also be uplifted by active mechanisms, which are discussed in other chapters. Both types of uplift may occur together or at different times. Uplift can also occur beneath a *volcanic arc*, a chain of active or inactive volcanos. A volcanic arc is often created on a continental plate that is converging with an oceanic plate. In this context, the oceanic plate subducts beneath the continental plate. Orogenic uplift and arc-associated uplift will generally produce a low-lying depression of land, known as a *basin*, that is adjacent to the band of uplift. Many of the canyons discussed in this book are located on sites that were once examples of low-lying basins. A basin can take the form of a foreland basin, a backarc basin, or another type of basin. Sediments tend to be transported into these basins, by a river or stream, and accumulate. Over time, the uppermost layers of sediments exert pressure and heat on the thick layers of underlying sediments. This creates thick layers of sedimentary rock in the basin. Later, the erosional exhumation of the sedimentary rocks can cause the crust beneath the surface of the basin to become more buoyant and undergo uplift. This bobbing up of part of a continental plate, in response to the erosion and removal of the dead weight of rock layers, is isostatic uplift. Isostatic uplift is also referred to as isostatic rebound.

As regards the diagram on page 8, it is important to note that erosional exhumation can occur both before and during incision. Outside the context of one specific canyon, erosional exhumation often produces widespread incision of dozens of closely spaced mountain gorges. It is helpful to think of incision as being a result of uplift and of uplift being the result of erosional exhumation. But there can be a back-and-forth interplay between incision and erosion of mountain gorges. When mountain ranges or plateaus are eroded on a large scale by erosional exhumation, isostatic uplift tends to be the result. The three processes tend to reinforce one another in cycles. This interplay may continue until the mountains have been eroded down, as in part 4B of the diagram, and the rivers have nearly incised down to sea level, as in part 3B.

Subsequently, rivers flow across the sedimentary basins and incise canyons. The portions of land are still referred to as backarc basins or foreland basins, even though the orogenic cycles or volcanic arc magmatism have ceased. Even when the basins have accumulated one or two miles of sediments and are no longer low-lying areas, the basins can still be described in terms of the forces that originally produced them.

A number of the canyons discussed in this book were formed at sites that were within a *sedimentary basin* but were higher than other parts of the basin. For example, some of the canyons are located at the margin of a sedimentary basin and are "up-drainage" of the other sites. This location can sometimes allow the canyon to be higher than most of the basin but lower than a nearby mountain range. This is a general feature that applies to the histories of several canyons. As a river exits the mountains and enters a basin, the river will sometimes produce an *alluvial fan.* This preferentially deposits sediments at the margin of the basin, an effect that reinforces the existing differences in elevation. Canyons can nonetheless form without being at a kind of intermediate elevation, on the upstream margin of a sedimentary basin and downstream of a mountain range. It is nonetheless interesting to note. At an intermediate elevation, the site of

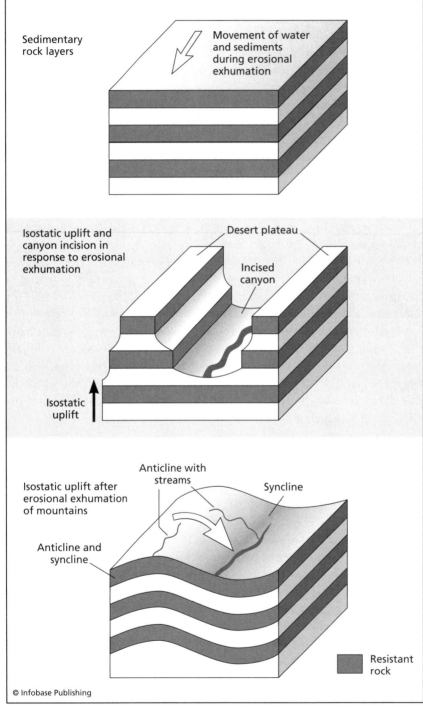

In this diagram, isostatic uplift can be seen as a response to the erosional exhumation of either a flat plateau, as in a sedimentary basin, or a mountain range that is adjacent to a foreland basin or river drainage basin.

developing canyon will receive an input of water and sediments from the mountain range. The site is still higher than other sites in the sedimentary basin, a location that helps to ensure a steep gradient of the river that is flowing out of the canyon.

Gravity, however, can also create rock slides that help canyons form. Some very steep canyon walls can also be the result of periodic landslides or rock slides, rather than just the result of incision. Many canyon walls do not follow a consistent slope down to the river. Canyon walls may be more vertical at the top, more gently sloped about halfway down, and fairly flat at the bottom. When a river is first cutting down, loose rocks are not going to fall very far and are likely to just land in the river. But as the canyon walls become very high, large sections of rock can collapse. Under the influence of gravity, a large slab of rock can be accelerated. These falling slabs of rock can hit the lower parts of a canyon wall with greater force.

In this image of the Grand Canyon, rockslides and differences in the rate of incision may have caused the walls to be steeper in some parts than in others. *(Charles Zachritz/ShutterStock, Inc.)*

THE INFLUENCE OF ROCK LAYERS

If impermeable layers of sedimentary rock exist above more permeable rock layers, this layering pattern can sometimes participate in canyon formation. If the less permeable rock layers are above the more permeable layers, the overlying layers can limit the downward percolation of surface water. This can sometimes prevent the underlying, permeable layers from being eroded away by the downward percolation of surface water.

In some canyons, the existence of permeable layers of rock above impermeable layers appears to have also contributed to canyon formation. Permeable layers can allow surface water to percolate downward and seep into the canyon as groundwater. Sometimes, the groundwater will seep into the canyon at a level that is immediately above the impermeable layers. The permeable layers above the site of *seepage* are to some extent spared the erosive effect of the water. Most of the rainfall that ultimately enters the canyon as groundwater might percolate downward at sites that are distant from the rim of the canyon. The permeable layers at the top of the canyon wall, which is the canyon rim, do not have to bear the brunt of all of the groundwater that enters the canyon. The seepage will then erode the resistant layers and cause the wall to collapse. This process is an example of one type of *groundwater sapping*, and sapping tends to produce U-shaped canyons and channels. Different types of sapping exist, however, and sapping can produce different effects on different layering patterns of rocks. On Earth, the effects of sapping can be difficult to predict or generalize to different canyons.

Sapping is thought to have been involved with the formation of channels and canyons on Mars, a planet on which the liquid water may have been present only, or primarily, below the surface. Some scientists think that volcanic activity warmed the ground of Mars and allowed groundwater to flow, but other scientists think that Mars was once warm enough for rain and the surface flow of water. Sapping does not typically contribute significantly to channel formation on Earth, but it has contributed to the formation of some canyons on the Colorado Plateau. By studying canyons on the Colorado Plateau and other arid regions, researchers have been able to gain insight into the origins of channels and canyons on Mars.

SUBMARINE CANYONS

In some cases, a *submarine canyon* will form offshore of the site at which a river drains into the ocean. Rivers wash a great deal of sediment into the ocean, and this movement of water and sediment can cut out a canyon in the continental shelf. The somewhat shallow water close to the shore of a continent covers the *continental shelf*, which then drops off into deeper water. The continental shelf also slopes downward somewhat as the distance from the shore increases. However, most submarine canyons are not cut out of the continental shelf. In many cases, sediments delivered by a river will bypass the continental shelf almost entirely. The sediments may then produce incision of the continental slope, the land beneath the deeper ocean that is a few miles offshore. In other cases, the sediments will be deposited, in a *submarine fan*, at sites that are more offshore than the continental shelf. In some cases, a submarine canyon will have been incised by sediments from a river that enters the ocean many miles away. For example, river-derived sediments might be transported to the ocean at point A. The sediments may first be transported five miles to the west, reaching point B and largely bypassing the continental shelf. The sediments may then be transported 50 miles north, by an ocean current, to the head of a submarine canyon at point C. The incision of the canyon may be heavily driven by river-derived sediments from point A.

The delivery of sediments to a submarine canyon can occur in the context of several phenomena, including a hyperpycnal flow or a *turbid underflow*. These phenomena are discussed in chapter 6. Suffice it to say that the development of undersea canyons can be heavily driven by onshore flooding events. A flood can cause a river to flow very rapidly, and floods can create various high-energy sediment flows under the ocean. These underflow events transport sediments, events that may interact with undersea fault activity to produce landslides on the walls of submarine canyons. Gravity can drive some underwater sediment movement, but the horizontally directed momentum from onshore floods is a major contributor to underflow events. An undersea plume may, for example, carry water that is warm, low in salinity, and high in sediments.

Tectonic forces on land and at undersea sites can also influence the development of submarine canyons. Uplift on land can increase the gradients of rivers that feed sediment-laden water into the ocean. The increased gradients of these rivers can influence the frequency of turbid underflow events, events that deliver sediments to submarine canyons and could contribute to incision. Undersea fault activity can also strongly influence the locations of meanders in submarine canyons.

TEN CANYONS

This book will discuss the unique features and histories of 10 canyons—the Grand Canyon, Columbia River Gorge, the Three Gorges of the Yangtze River, Peonera Canyon, Windjana Gorge, Monterey Canyon, Zion Canyon, Fish River Canyon, Chaco Canyon, and Canyon Diablo. These canyons are representative of a large variety of different geographic locations and geological origins. In many cases, orogenic cycles and fault activity shaped the delivery of sediments to foreland basins, forearc basins, or basins formed by extensional or oblique-slip fault activity. The canyons were then incised, often at later dates, out of the sediments that had accumulated in these sedimentary basins. In some cases, the primary impact of basin formation and sediment accumulation was to increase the elevation above sea level. This elevation increased the gradients of rivers that flowed, subsequently, across the sedimentary basins. In other cases, incision was driven by a combination of the extra elevation, produced in the past by sediment accumulation, and active tectonic forces. Fault activity can contribute to basin formation, and reactivation of existing faults can then directly drive the incision of canyons out of accumulated sediments. Several of the canyons discussed in this book were influenced by more complex fault movements, which often produced at least some uplift.

Scientists use a variety of different techniques to study canyons and thereby learn about the Earth's past. Learning about canyons may also help scientists predict the ways that climate changes can influence the Earth's topography. For the most part, each of the terrestrial canyons in this book occupies a portion of land that receives very little precipitation. Some of the canyons are in subtropical deserts, in which the climate is truly arid. The sites of the other canyons are characterized by semiarid climates and highly seasonal rainfall patterns. A highly seasonal rainfall pattern, in combination with a low amount of total, annual rainfall, can allow a canyon to persist outside of subtropical latitudes.

Understanding canyons can also help engineers choose sites for hydroelectric dams that provide electricity and allow irrigation. If a canyon becomes a reservoir after a dam is built, what will be the long-term consequences for upstream or downstream parts of the river? Apart from these reasons for learning about canyons, many people enjoy the scenic beauty of canyons. Some canyons in this book are quite inhospitable and are not appropriate for the casual hiker. Fish River Canyon, in the Namib Desert of Namibia, has at times been quite distant from major medical facilities. A doctor who accompanied an expedition to Fish River Canyon noted, in a scientific journal, the potentially perilous aspects of the canyon. After breaking bones in his ankle and tearing ligaments, the doctor was forced to improvise and set the bones in his ankle. At the time of this expedition, the towns in Namibia may not have been as developed as they are now. The town of Ai Ais, near Fish River Canyon, has been enlarged in the past couple of decades to include some cabins and a kind of resort. The town has nonetheless been reported to shut down in the summer, given the extreme and dangerous heat. Similarly, in portions of Zion Canyon, the narrow and steep walls preclude casual hiking. To reach some parts of the canyon, people have to wade through the Virgin River. Peonera Canyon also contains rather perilous rock structures. This rugged environment has actually made Peonera Canyon an attractive destination for canyoneers. Canyoneering has become a kind of extreme sport, and canyons have many different extremes to offer.

The Grand Canyon

Northwestern Arizona, the United States

The Grand Canyon is located in northwestern Arizona and covers an area of roughly 2,000 square miles (5,180 km²). The canyon is 18 miles (29 km) from rim to rim in some places and surrounds the Colorado River for 277 miles (446 km) of its length. The 2,000 square miles of canyon can therefore be regarded as a long rectangle, with an average width of seven miles (11.3 km) and a length of 277 miles, that has been bent and molded around the path of the Colorado River. The canyon is generally about 1.2 miles (2 km) deep, a depth that causes climatological measures to differ significantly between the rim and floor of the canyon.

The walls of the Grand Canyon display rock layers that are as old as 958 million years and as young as about 245 million years. Some of the walls in the western Grand Canyon also contain the remnants of *lava flows* and *lava dams* that were deposited less than a million years ago. However, this *lava* was essentially dumped into the canyon and onto the preexisting terraces and walls. The lava deposits now cover the much older rocks that form the lower parts of the canyon walls.

The Colorado River incised the canyon over the last 6 million years, in response to more than one type of *uplift*. A generalized form of uplift occurred as *sediments* were eroded from large portions of the Colorado Plateau, a process of *erosional exhumation* that made the plateau literally lighter. A buoyant portion of crustal material may have been injected into the *crustal lithosphere* of the Colorado Plateau between 66 and 40 million years ago. This may have contributed to the erosion-driven uplift that subsequently occurred. The erosion-driven uplift that began about 36.6 million years ago and continued through the last 6 million years was, however, strongly driven by the decrease in the sheer weight of sediments. The erosional exhumation of portions of the Colorado Plateau, as a whole, began between 36.6 and 6 million years ago. The incision of the Grand Canyon began 6 million years ago, and the incision was accompanied by erosion-induced uplift of most parts of the Colorado Plateau.

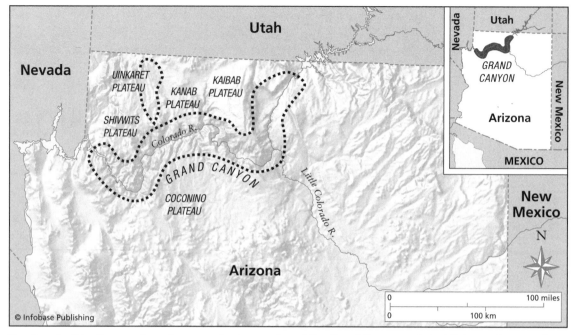

The lines in this diagram show the approximate margins of the Grand Canyon and the Uinkaret Plateau, whose eastern and western margins are, respectively, the Toroweap and Hurricane Faults.

Some of the incision that occurred in the last 600,000 years was driven by the activities of two *fault* lines, which produced uplift and steepened the *gradient* of the Colorado River. These two fault lines cross the Colorado River in the western Grand Canyon. Two fault lines in the eastern Grand Canyon are extremely old and have been periodically reactivated. Several more fault lines appeared more recently in the eastern Grand Canyon and have deformed the land at different times. Three of the ancient faults may have been reactivated about 66 million years ago, and several of the newer faults have produced uplift over the last 5.3 to 23.7 million years. Some of the faults in the eastern Grand Canyon produced significant uplift, but it is not clear that this uplift contributed to the incision of the Grand Canyon.

The walls of the Grand Canyon also provide a long-term record of geological events. The site of the Grand Canyon was submerged beneath an intracontinental seaway at different times, but the deposition of some of the marine sediments in the canyon walls may have been influenced by the actions of both water waves and wind. Researchers think that some of the marine sediments were blown inland from the dry tidal beds or reefs. In some cases, the influences of wind on the deposition, and sedimentation, patterns were mistakenly thought to have been produced by the actions of water waves. Six significant gaps also exist in the ages of the rock layers in the canyon walls (shown in the upper color insert on page C-1). The walls do not contain sediments from every year of geological history, given that various erosional forces varied over time. The more significant gaps are evident as four *disconformities*, one *angular unconformity*, and one *nonconformity*.

A FRAMEWORK FOR UNDERSTANDING UPLIFT

In this discussion of uplift, in relation to the Grand Canyon, the level of detail will be somewhat more complex than in other chapters. An attempt has been made to simplify the discussion of the mechanisms of active and passive uplift. These details will not often be discussed in other chapters, but it is nonetheless interesting to explore them. The Grand Canyon is one of the few canyons in which detailed, mechanistic research has attempted to discern the contribution of *active* v. *passive uplift*. The relative contributions have not been entirely worked out, but the Colorado Plateau exists as a kind of quintessential "laboratory" for the study of canyon formation. With regard to any potential confusion, it is helpful to remember the larger picture. The incision of the canyon was ultimately driven, quite simply, by uplift and steepening of the gradient of the Colorado River.

The active uplift that occurred within the Colorado Plateau, between 66 and 40 million years ago, contributed indirectly to the incision of the Grand Canyon. This uplift, which occurred during the Laramide Orogeny, increased the elevation of the Colorado Plateau above sea level. This uplift did not immediately precede the incision of the canyon, however. The actual incision occurred over the last 6 million years. Thus, the uplift produced by the Laramide Orogeny drove incision by an indirect, delayed mechanism. By increasing the elevation, this early uplift intensified the gradient down which the Colorado River ultimately flowed. The Laramide Orogeny also may have reactivated some of the existing fault lines in and around the Grand Canyon. That said, it is important to note that the Colorado Plateau has been much more *tectonically* stable than the areas surrounding it. As discussed in this chapter, some fault activity and volcanic activity have occurred, at various times, on parts of the plateau. The plateau has, on the whole, been a kind of island of tectonic stability, and the mechanisms underlying this stability are not completely understood.

Additionally, there is evidence that the Laramide Orogeny caused the *lithosphere* beneath the Colorado Plateau to become more buoyant, either by the thinning of the *mantle lithosphere* or other mechanisms. Some of the uplift that occurred during the Laramide Orogeny may have resulted from a temporary increase in the thickness of the crust, as discussed above. This thickening of the crust may have actually made the crust more buoyant, thereby producing uplift during the Laramide Orogeny.

Considerable evidence indicates that the uplift of the Colorado Plateau during, and perhaps even after, the Laramide Orogeny was related to the behavior of the Farallon plate and to its *subduction* beneath the North American plate.

Essentially, the angle of subduction of the Farallon plate appears to have changed, and this has helped to dictate the uplift and fault activity on the Colorado Plateau. The Farallon plate underwent subduction between 70 and 80 million and 40 million years ago. The subduction angle is thought to have first been low for a long time. When a plate dives beneath another at a low subduction angle, the subducting plate extends in a cratonward, or inland, direction below a larger portion of the continental lithosphere. A low angle might be 30 or 45 degrees; a high angle, 70 or 80 degrees. A high angle of subduction is equivalent to a steep dive by the subducting plate. During low-angle subduction, the Farallon plate was sandwiched beneath the mantle lithosphere, the lower portion of the continental plate, of the Colorado Plateau. In general, during low-angle subduction, the overriding plate is like a flat barge that has collided and skidded up and over another boat on a river.

The Farallon plate may have somehow allowed the donation, at first, of a low-density slab of crust to the crust beneath the Colorado Plateau. The initial donation process is thought to have occurred during the time that the Farallon plate was diving, almost straight down, at a steep angle, or high angle. The angle is thought to have then decreased and become sandwiched beneath the Colorado Plateau. During this low-angle "sandwiching phase," the Farallon plate may also have contributed to uplift by thinning the mantle lithosphere. The subducting plate would have essentially stripped off the mantle lithosphere, beneath the Colorado Plateau, from below. Both the crustal thickening and stripping of mantle lithosphere would have made the rock beneath the plateau more buoyant, thereby contributing to active uplift during the Laramide Orogeny. The low-angle subduction is also thought to have shielded the Colorado Plateau from the asthenosphere, thereby limiting much of the volcanic activity. Some parts of the Colorado Plateau did experience some volcanic eruptions, but the volcanic activity could have been much more intense and prolonged. During the Laramide Orogeny, the Colorado Plateau was shielded against heavy deformation and was simultaneously bolstered by active uplift. The plateau essentially experienced uplift, in the context of the compressive forces of orogenic activity, without the mess of excessive deformation and widespread fault activity.

After the Laramide Orogeny ended, about 40 million years ago, the Farallon plate began its final phase of subduction, taking a deep dive. This essentially allowed everything to "relax." The lithosphere of the southwestern United States had been compressed and bunched together for a long time by complex forces. After this compression (resulting from subduction) began to wind down, the lithosphere essentially relaxed and spread out. Extensional fault activity began in the Basin and Range Province, west of the Colorado Plateau, and the Colorado Plateau began to experience the second phase of uplift. The plateau gradually rose upward by isostatic uplift in response to the erosional exhumation of the sedimentary rock layers.

Apart from the mechanistic details of the changes in the crust and mantle lithosphere, it is helpful to look at the changes in terms of buoyancy. The crust is the buoyant portion of the lithosphere that makes up the continental plates. The crust has positive buoyancy, and the mantle lithosphere actually has negative buoyancy with respect to the upper parts of the asthenosphere. Uplift is therefore driven more by changes in the densities, and therefore the buoyancies, of the crust or mantle lithosphere.

The uplift of the Colorado Plateau that occurred more recently than 40 million years ago, and was especially relevant over the last 6 million years, was mostly a kind of buoyant response to erosional exhumation. Isostatic uplift of the plateau can be imagined as a bobbing upward of an inflatable raft. The raft will, for example, bob upward if a person jumps out of the raft and into the water. This analogy is not perfect but is sufficient. During the active uplift, which occurred during the low-angle subduction and the Laramide Orogeny, it is as if someone actively lifted the raft out of the water, from below, and slid another raft underneath. During the more recent phase of passive uplift, the excess weight was removed from the uplifted raft, allowing it to become more buoyant. The magnitude of isostatic uplift, in response to the removal of the dead weight of sedimentary rock layers, can be several times the thickness of the sedimentary rock that is eroded. For example, the erosion of half a mile of sedimentary rock layers might be accompanied by 1.5 miles (2.4 km) of isostatic uplift. The net increase in the elevation of the surface, above sea level, would be one mile (1.6 km).

Changes in the drainage pathways on the Colorado Plateau were also important for the actual incision process. Until about 6 million years ago, streams and drainage pathways flowed onto the Colorado Plateau from its southern and southwestern margins. Water and sediments were therefore moving toward the northeast. The tectonic events that occurred around 6 million years ago caused the direction of drainage to reverse gradually, and the Colorado River now flows southwest. The rivers and streams that flow across the northern and central parts of the Colorado Plateau have flowed in their present-day directions for between 23 and 36 million years. The path of the Colorado River, at least through the Grand Canyon, is only 6 million years old. Thus, the drainage system that dictated the direction of the Colorado River is in some ways immature.

DEPOSITION AND REMOVAL
OF MESOZOIC SEDIMENTS

A salient feature of sediments present in the Grand Canyon and other parts of the Colorado Plateau is the relative absence of sediments from the *Mesozoic era* and early *Cenozoic era*. The layers of sediments that have been exposed in the walls of the Grand Canyon were mostly deposited more than 245 million years ago. In many parts of the Grand Canyon, the sediments that were deposited during the *Permian period*, which ended 245 million years ago, extend all the way to the rim of the canyon. In some walls of the canyon, however, some thin portions of younger sediments are still present, but these sediments are only about 5 million years younger and were deposited during the *Triassic period*.

Some portions of the Colorado Plateau contain significant amounts of sediments that are younger than the Permian period, but the land around the Grand Canyon has been more heavily eroded. Some of the sedimentary basins on the Colorado Plateau still contain thick layers of sediments that were deposited within the interval of 66.4 to 1.6 million years, during the Tertiary period. These are isolated areas in which the Tertiary sediments, confined to the margins of sedimentary basins, have been preserved from erosion. The sediments that were deposited during the Mesozoic era, which occurred between 245 and 66.4 million years ago, tend to be the youngest layers that are still present near the surface. About 75 million years ago, shortly before the end of the Mesozoic era, large portions of the Colorado Plateau were still covered by another 1.7 miles (2.7 km) to 2.5 miles (4 km) of sediments. These were Mesozoic sediments that had been deposited between 240 and 75 million years ago, an interval of time that was part of the Mesozoic.

Even in the parts of the Colorado Plateau that still contain these Mesozoic sediments, the layers are not nearly as thick as the 1.7–2.5 miles that were originally present. Around the rim of the Grand Canyon, the Vermillion Cliffs contain layers of Mesozoic sediments. The Mesozoic sediments in these cliffs are younger than the sediments in the canyon walls and are separated from the canyon rim by a flat portion of the Kaibab Plateau. Thus, Mesozoic sediments are almost absent from a large portion of the Colorado Plateau that surrounds the Grand Canyon. The Grand Canyon has therefore been a major site of sediment turnover for at least the last 240 million years. In particular, the canyon has been an area of large-scale sediment erosion, which has occurred in phases and has also been accompanied by sediment delivery, for the last 75 million years.

Scientists know that the surface of the Colorado Plateau was roughly at sea level at 67 million years ago, at the end of the *Cretaceous period*, and that some combination of factors has produced the present-day elevation of 1.2 miles (2 km). This elevation refers to the elevation at the rim, or top, of the Grand Canyon, and this elevation is higher or lower at various points. Scientists know that the elevation was between 0.93 mile (1.5 km) and 1.86 miles (3 km) above sea level at the end of the Laramide Orogeny, which was about 40 million years ago and corresponded to part of the Late *Eocene epoch*. The difficulty arises in determining the relative magnitudes of the active uplift, induced by the Laramide Orogeny, and the isostatic uplift induced by the erosional exhumation of rock layers. A number of different quantitative combinations of active and passive uplift have been suggested to account for the 1.2 miles of uplift from sea level. Suffice it to say that the net uplift, above sea level, was driven by a combination of active uplift and erosion-driven isostatic uplift that was more recent.

EFFECTS OF HUMAN-MADE DAMS

Within the Grand Canyon, the Colorado River (shown in the upper color insert on page C-2) receives an input of water and sediments from about 40 *tributaries* and 490 smaller *ephemeral streams* and rivers. Some of the tributaries include the Paria River, the Little Colorado River, and Kanab Creek. The Paria River and Little Colorado River contribute sediments to the Colorado River, and these contributions are especially significant in the present day. This is because the Glen Canyon Dam, which became operational in 1963, has drastically reduced the amount of sediment that the Colorado River carries into the canyon from upstream sites. The dam is just upstream of the point at which the Colorado River enters the eastern Grand Canyon. In the portion of the river that is immediately downstream of the dam and is slightly upstream of the eastern Grand Canyon, the Colorado River is now moving roughly 1 percent of the mass of sediments that the river was moving before the creation of the dam. This reduction is not as pronounced as the river flows farther from the dam and receives sediments from its tributaries.

The regulation of the Colorado River by the Glen Canyon Dam has produced a number of interesting effects. These changes are not likely to influence the overall morphology of the Grand Canyon. It is noteworthy, however, that a regulated river can be paradoxically less stable than an unregulated one. The reduction in the sediment load has essentially abolished the seasonal variation in the temperature of the Colorado River, a variation that existed before the creation of the dam. Before the dam was built, the water temperature was close to freezing in the winter and was almost 86°F (30°C) in the summer. Remarkably, scientists noted that the Colorado River, with its decrease in turbidity and increase in heat loss, is now very similar to a glacial river with high turbidity. The Colorado River is now more similar to a glacial river, one with unusually high turbidity,

INTERACTIONS OF PLANTS, WATER, AND THE SUN

The Glen Canyon Dam produced changes in the types of plant life and other organisms that live either in the river or on the rocks that are near to the river. The dam has increased the sheer mass of biological material—which primarily consists of different forms of algae and invertebrates that are larger than bacteria—that is present in a given volume of river water. The overall diversity of these organisms has decreased, however. It is also relevant that the dam has prevented the increases in the depth of the river that used to occur, such as in response to the annual melting of snow in the Rockies and to the peaks of rainfall that occur locally at the canyon in the winter and summer. These seasonal floods used to remove some of the algae or mosses that can live on rocks near the river, and these forms of plant life are now more abundant.

Scientists have begun to explore the changes in weathering that can occur when darker or less reflective rocks are heated by the Sun. Scientists have found that the color and darkness of a rock can influence the heating of the rock by the Sun, but differences in the thermal responses of rocks to the Sun do not appear to correlate, in a predictable way, with differences in the susceptibility to types of weathering. To the extent that the wall of the north rim of the Grand Canyon has received more direct Sun, the wall might have been able to support more vegetation. When the canyon was still forming, this might have reduced erosion during floods or prevented the warming of the rock by the Sun. Either effect of vegetation could have offset any effects of the Sun on the fragility of the rock.

than it is to the variably warm, sediment-loaded river that existed before the dam was created. Sediments that are suspended in a river serve to darken the water, an effect that may increase the absorption of solar infrared radiation and heat the water.

HISTORY OF THE COLORADO RIVER

The paths of the Colorado River and some of its tributaries have changed very little over the last 1.6 million years, and the recent uplift may have contributed to this stability. The Green River, a tributary of the Colorado River, stopped flowing through some of the curves and *meanders* that the river initially flowed through. Some of the sharp curves of the Green River have been dry for 200,000 years. Many of the smaller canyons, carved by the Colorado River and its tributaries, have been more or less locked into their present-day channel systems for a million or more years. If uplift has been relatively recent, or if some factor other than uplift has caused the gradient of a river to be consistently steep, a river will sometimes follow this type of strictly defined and relatively straight drainage system. The Colorado River may eventually have time to erode away its headwaters and thereby decrease its gradient. For the time being, however, the river is following a fairly direct and efficient downhill path.

The relative absence of meanders in the central Colorado Plateau can be understood in an intuitive sense. When drops of water accumulate on the windows of a plane that is taking off, for example, the drops are pulled toward the back of the plane. The drops do not follow an S-shaped, meandering path. If the window of the plane had been scratched, the drop would probably not follow the path of the groove for any length of time. The drop would essentially cross the groove. Just as the wind velocity and force of acceleration will pull water droplets toward the back of a plane, uplift can cause a river to cut through sediments and form canyons. If the topography of the southwestern United States had been different, the Colorado River might have flowed around the margin of the Colorado Plateau or followed a longer, winding path.

It is important to remember that strictly defined channel systems can be sustained by many factors. Seasonal rainfall, as well as other climatological factors, can also favor the development of strictly defined channel systems. Even relatively shallow channels that have been incised in a desert can shuttle seasonal rainfalls away, thereby producing more incision and even intensifying the desert climate. In a similar manner, scientists noted that the steep walls of a canyon could prevent a river from deviating. By the same token, scientists found that sharp bends can sometimes be maintained during uplift. If the meanders are entrenched before the uplift begins, the rock walls might prevent the river from deviating into a more direct path. The many cycles of glacier formation and melting have also been important for the formation of the Grand Canyon. Over the last several hundred thousand years, however, the paths of the Colorado River and its tributaries have shifted—in some places, by only a few miles.

From a qualitative standpoint, the river can be compared to the immature drainage system of a young mountain range. As will be discussed in chapter 4, water will tend to flow out of a newly formed mountain range in a direction that is perpendicular to the axis, or line, along which the mountains were uplifted. Over time, the drainage network will mature and exit the mountains in lines that are parallel to the axis of uplift. The streams will first flow directly downhill, away from the mountains. Some of the streams will eventually follow switchbacks and meander out of the mountains, just as rivers on the Colorado Plateau may gradually spread out and form more meanders.

The shapes of canyons on the Colorado Plateau appear to have been influenced by the gradient of the Colorado River and its tributaries. The gradients of the Colorado River and two of its major tributaries, the San Juan River and Green River, vary across different sections of the rivers. The sections of the rivers that flow downhill at steep angles, indicating a high gradient, have produced canyons with distinctive shapes.

The bends in these rivers were found, for example, to be less numerous along sections of the rivers that flow down a high gradient. A river that follows a relatively straight line between two points is, from a general standpoint, said to have a low *sinuosity*. Rivers tend to make larger and more numerous bends on very flat land than on a steep, downhill slope. This means that canyons on the Colorado Plateau are likely to have relatively few meanders. The Colorado River and its tributaries also formed bends that were less sharp, less like hairpins and more smooth, along portions that flow down a steep gradient.

STEEP CANYON WALLS AND MEANDERS OF RIVERS

Canyon walls formed by the Colorado River and its tributaries tend to be shaped in unusual ways at the bends in the rivers. The bends in the rivers generally produce canyon walls that are asymmetrical, meaning that the wall is steeper on one side of the river than on the other. The high gradients of these rivers tends to produce a specific form of asymmetry of the canyon walls at the bends in the rivers. The wall that is on the outer side of a bend tends to have been eroded into a gentler slope than the wall on the inner side. This is known as an *ingrown meander* and is an example of an *asymmetrical meander*. If someone were facing the river and standing on the *outer wall* of a bend, the river would be entirely in front of the person. Someone standing on the outer wall of an ingrown meander would be standing on the top of a canyon wall that follows a gentle, downward slope. On the opposite side of the river, the person would be standing on the edge of the sheer cliff that is the *inner wall* of an ingrown meander.

Across the Colorado Plateau and in other areas, the degree of asymmetry changes in relation to the gradients of rivers. Rivers tend to form meanders that are strongly ingrown, or asymmetrical, on very flat ground. As the gradient of the river increases, up to a certain point, the walls become more symmetrical and tend to be vertical on both sides of a meander. This makes sense, given that a higher gradient can produce downward incision. As the gradient becomes very steep, however, the walls along a meander become less symmetrical. A very high gradient may cause the river to flow very rapidly and erode the outer edge of its channel. This bimodal relationship holds for the Colorado River and two of its tributaries, the Green River and San Juan River. Along sections of the rivers that display very low, or flat, gradients, the rivers tend to form canyons with ingrown meanders. Along sections that display gradients of medium steepness, the canyon walls tend to be vertical and symmetrical at the meanders. These are *incised meanders*. When the rivers flow down very steep gradients, through some canyons on the Colorado Plateau, the meanders again tend to be ingrown and asymmetrical.

When a river forms an ingrown meander in a canyon, the outer edge might still be steep in some places. The river might have formed incised meanders and then begun eroding the outer sides of the canyon walls at each meander. Part of the outer wall might then have collapsed and left a series of sheer cliffs and terraces. Rivers on the Colorado Plateau also form fewer ingrown meanders in rock that is more resistant. The rock is not uniformly resistant at different points in the Grand Canyon, and different meanders may display different degrees of asymmetry. The degree of symmetry of canyon walls, at meanders, tends to be more apparent in smaller or younger canyons.

RECENT INCISION, LAVA FLOWS, AND LAVA DAMS

The incision of the Grand Canyon by the Colorado River began 5 to 6 million years ago and continued until about 400,000 years ago, during the *Pleistocene epoch* of the *Quaternary period*. Scientists think that a number of factors contributed directly to the incision, and the process was sometimes rather chaotic. For example, scientists have found that fault systems in Arizona are likely to have delivered lava to the canyon and dammed the Colorado River. These lava dams may have contributed to the differences in the rates of incision at different points in the canyon. The Grand Canyon appears rather uniform in the present day, but the canyon is not simply the product of the neat and uniform plateau-wide uplift of the Colorado Plateau.

Scientists have recently estimated the different rates of incision that occurred at different parts of the Grand Canyon, and these differences highlight the dynamic qualities of river incision. Over the last 500,000–600,000 years, for example, the Colorado River produced incision at 1,312 feet (400 m) per million years [roughly 131 feet (40 m) per 100,000 years] in the eastern Grand Canyon and 230 feet (70 m) to 525 feet (160 m) per million years [roughly 23 feet (7 m) to 53 feet (16 m) per 100,000 years] in the western Grand Canyon. Scientists think the actual rate in the western portion, which is downstream of the eastern portion, was probably closer to 230 feet than 525 feet per million years. Similar differences may have been present at different times over the last 3.5 million years, and the vertical uplift along fault lines are likely to have contributed to the different rates of incision.

The Hurricane and Toroweap Fault Lines both extend from north to south and both cross the Colorado River within the Grand Canyon. The points at which fault lines intersect the Grand Canyon and Colorado River are sometimes expressed in terms of a given number of river miles, which are distances along the winding path of the Colorado River. These river miles are the distances from Lees Ferry, which is just downstream of the Glen Canyon Dam. The Toroweap Fault Line crosses the Colorado River at the so-called Lava Falls Rapid, which is at river mile 179 (km 111) of the river. This location is just upstream of the point at which Prospect Canyon feeds into the Grand Canyon. The Hurricane Fault crosses the river at mile 188 (km 117), a point that is downstream of the Toroweap Fault. Mile 188 is near the mouth of Whitmore Canyon and Whitmore *Wash,* the ephemeral stream that intermittently feeds water into the Colorado River. Both water and lava were once delivered from Whitmore Canyon into the Grand Canyon. The Hurricane Fault crosses the Colorado River near to both the remaining portions of lava that formed the Whitmore Dam, a lava dam, and the sediments that were deposited into an *alluvial fan* by water.

The fault lines also define the margins of the Uinkaret Plateau, a plateau that is part of the Colorado Plateau. *Volcanic* eruptions occurred at many different sites along the Hurricane and Toroweap Faults during the last 1.6 million years, and these eruptions produced lava flows that solidified. These deposits of lava formed the Uinkaret volcanic field, which primarily extends over the land that is in the western Grand Canyon and is north of the Colorado River. The approximate margins of the Uinkaret Plateau are apparent in the accompanying diagram, displayed earlier in the chapter. The Uinkaret Plateau is strictly defined as the land between the Toroweap Fault and the Hurricane Fault, but the Uinkaret volcanic field extends outside these margins. This is because the uplift along the two fault lines, during the Quaternary period, sectioned off a portion of the volcanic field and thereby created the Uinkaret Plateau. The points at which the two fault lines cross the Grand Canyon are only separated by nine miles (14.5 km) of the Colorado River. This short distance is apparent in the tapered wedge shape of the southernmost portion of the Uinkaret Plateau.

The Toroweap Fault separates the Uinkaret Plateau from the Kanab Plateau, and the Hurricane Fault separates the Uinkaret Plateau from the Shivwits Plateau. Upstream and to the east of the Kanab Plateau is the Kaibab Plateau, out of which the western Grand Canyon was cut. The Colorado River flows down through the Kaibab Plateau in the western Grand Canyon, flows across the Kanab Plateau, crosses the Toroweap Fault and down over the Uinkaret Plateau, crosses the Hurricane Fault at the western margin of the Uinkaret Plateau, and then flows over the Shivwits Plateau.

Both fault lines are in the western Grand Canyon and are downstream of the eastern Grand Canyon. As discussed previously, the rate of incision was once at least two times as high in the eastern Grand Canyon as in the western Grand Canyon. Thus, the rate of incision at sites upstream of the Toroweap Fault Line was more than twice as high as the rate that occurred downstream of the Hurricane Fault. In addition, the *normal fault activity* produced uplift on the upstream side of each of the two fault lines. Thus, the Colorado River flowed from the *hanging wall*, or the *upthrown block*, onto the *footwall*, or *downthrown block*, of each fault line. The faults are still displaced in this direction, and the faults can also be described as downthrown to the west. The fault-induced uplift is thought to have contributed to incision by intensifying the downward slope, or gradient, of the river. The faults also produced eruptions of basalt lava, however, and some of this lava dammed the Colorado River. These lava dams may, at times, have slowed the incision rate of the river and opposed the uplift-induced increases in the incision rate.

Scientists have found evidence of at least 13 lava dams in the western Grand Canyon, and each one of the dams is relatively near to either the Hurricane or Toroweap Fault. These lava dams may have existed, at different times, as long as 1.8 million years ago, before the Quaternary period began, and as recently as 10,000 years ago. The evidence suggests, however, that most of them were formed between 430,000 and 600,000 years ago. The dams were formed when lava flowed into the canyon, either over the canyon walls in sheets or through the tributary canyons that feed into the Grand Canyon. The lava generally flowed into the Grand Canyon from the north to the south. Some of the lava that was deposited on the Uinkaret volcanic field, which is north of the Colorado River in the western Grand Canyon, essentially spilled over into the canyon. The portions of lava that flowed directly into the canyon, in sheets that may have been similar to waterfalls, are known to have entered the canyon from its north rim.

Scientists are still not sure of the precise ways in which the lava dams influenced the incision of the canyon by the river. One group of scientists discussed the ways in which lava dams may have slowed the incision rate in the western Grand Canyon. This effect would help explain the fact that the incision rate in the canyon downstream of the Hurricane and Toroweap Faults was, at most, half of the incision rate that occurred upstream of the faults. There is also evidence that the dams broke at different times and produced catastrophic flooding of the portions of the canyon that had been downstream of the dams. Two of the 13 lava dams are known to have broken, on one or more occasions, in lava dam outbursts. Scientists also found evidence that five, and perhaps more, outbursts occurred in the canyon at different times, but some of these outbursts may have occurred at the same dam.

Some of this lava was tholeiitic *flood basalt lava*, which was low in viscosity and flowed easily into the canyon, and some was more viscous. Some of these lava flows accumulated around the fault lines as solid deposits, remained in the same location, and then were subjected to the gradual erosion and weathering that one would expect to have occurred. Some of the other lava flows first solidified in one location, as part of a terrace or dam, and were then broken up into chunks and so-called megaboulders by catastrophic flooding. These large portions of a lava flow were then carried downstream to one or more locations, and the portions that remain are known as flood deposits. Each flood deposit was first a part of a lava flow, but not all lava flows were broken up and carried, by water, to form flood deposits. Scientists have succeeded in linking some flood deposits to specific lava flows, and this process of correlation has helped scientists to piece together the times and places at which lava dams broke.

The present-day remnants of these lava flows are clustered around the fault lines, and some of the flows are still visible in the canyon walls. Scientists have assigned names to many of the so-called flood deposits that were produced by the lava flows, and the flood deposits appear as darkly colored portions of the canyon walls. Some of the lava dams that influenced the flow of the Colorado River are the Toroweap Dam, the Upper Prospect Dam, the Esplanade Dam, the Gray Ledge Dam, the Black Ledge lava dam, and the Whitmore Dam Complex. Each of the lava flows delivered a given type of lava over a specific interval of time, but not all of the lava flows actually dammed the Colorado River. Some of the lava dams consisted of lava from more than one lava flow. This means that different types of lava flowed together from different points of origin, possibly at different times, to form a dam. The Whitmore Dam Complex, for example, was formed by lava from the Whitmore Sink lava flow, lava from the Whitmore Cascade, lava from the Hyaloclastite Dam, and an unnamed lava flow. Some of this lava flowed out of Whitmore Canyon, one of the tributary canyons that feeds into the Grand Canyon and that once contained two volcanic cones.

Researchers think that any given dam was probably only in place for up to 20,000 years, and the Colorado River is known to have gradually cut through many of the dams. This gradual erosion would have delayed the incision of the canyon at the actual dam site, but the dam would also have provided basalt rock, meaning solidified lava, to be transported by the river. These fragments of basalt, carried as sediments by the river, could have contributed to the incision that took place downstream of the intact dam. The overall incision rate was, however, undeniably slower in the vicinity of the dams. If the dams accelerated the incision of the actual canyon, they probably only did so over short periods of time. It is noteworthy that the dams are relatively closely spaced, and the river may have simply flowed over one dam into the stagnant lake that had been formed by another dam. Researchers do think that the lava dams might have slowed the river and formed lakes, but scientists have not been able to identify *lacustrine* sedimentary rocks in the Grand Canyon. The river may been deeper in between lava dams, but the dams might not have slowed the river enough to create actual lake environments.

The dams may have locally increased the gradient of the river or widened portions of the canyon that were upstream of the dam. This effect could have accelerated the rate of incision at different sites, such as the section of river that was immediately downstream of the dam. If the Hoover Dam were to break, for example, one would expect an initial rush of water through the broken portion. The broken portion could also cause a long-term bottleneck in the width of the river, and this could speed up the flow of water or the rate of incision at different places.

CLIMATE IN THE PRESENT DAY

The overall climate at the Grand Canyon is semiarid, but variations in the climate also exist between different parts of the canyon. The average air temperature, over the course of the year, is lower at the rim of the canyon than at the canyon floor. This makes sense, considering that the canyon rim is up to 1.2 miles (2 km) higher than the Colorado River and canyon floor. The air temperature can generally be expected to decrease by a given amount for every 1,000 feet (305 m) of increased elevation above sea level, a rule of thumb that pilots use and that also applies to mountain ranges. Additionally, the canyon rim receives more annual precipitation and supports more plant life than the canyon floor. On the one hand, the canyon rim is subjected to the cold temperatures and added precipitation that might be associated with a mountaintop. On the other hand, the canyon rim contains more trees and plants than the lower elevations and might therefore be characterized as a less extreme environment than the canyon floor.

EARLY PREHISTORY OF NORTHWESTERN ARIZONA

The site of the present-day Grand Canyon was in a marine environment for long periods of time, and marine sediments make up significant portions of the canyon walls. Between 320 and 245 million years ago, during the *Pennsylvanian age* and the broader Permian period, the topography of the Grand Canyon and other sites in northwestern Arizona was strongly influenced by the Cordilleran Orogeny. The site of the Grand Canyon was part of the Grand Canyon Embayment, a low-lying portion of land that was roughly east of the Cordilleran *Miogeocline*. This elevated portion of land was oriented generally from south to north, tilted slightly to the northeast, and extended from southern Nevada into western and northwestern Utah. In Arizona and Utah, the land was essentially folded into an alternating pattern of basins and portions of upwarped land.

The Grand Canyon Embayment was bounded on its northern, eastern, and southeastern margins by various areas of higher elevation. The Sedona Arch was located to the southeast, the Kaibab Arch was located to the east, and the Plute-Emery Platform was located to the north. The Sedona Arch originated in central Arizona and passed through Sedona and Flagstaff. Northeast of Flagstaff, the Sedona Arch intersected at a 90-degree angle with the Kaibab Arch. The Kaibab Arch formed most of the eastern margin and some of the northeastern margin of the Grand Canyon Embayment. The Plute-Emery Platform followed the line of the Cordilleran Miogeocline and extended north, away from the Grand Canyon Embayment.

The Grand Canyon Embayment was a major site of sand dunes and was also intermittently submerged beneath the Cordilleran Seaway. The

Pakoon Limestone, a series of sedimentary layers that was first deposited in the western Grand Canyon around 286 million years ago, contains a number of notable features. Scientists know that the shoreline of the Cordilleran Seaway changed over time and sometimes covered parts of the Grand Canyon Embayment. Some of the stacking patterns and properties of sedimentary layers in the Supai Group, of which the Pakoon Limestone is part, were originally thought to have been caused by cyclic changes in the sea level. There is evidence that some of these layers of sediments, which include the ground-up coral and shells of marine life-forms, were deposited under the influences of both wind and water. Some researchers think that some of the marine matter was blown inland from the shoreline and then influenced, during the process of sedimentary rock formation, by wind.

Sediments that were deposited in an environment dominated by wind forces are known as *eolian* sediments, but eolian layers can contain fragments of marine life. A layer of marine sediments is generally assumed to have been deposited, and to have been converted into sedimentary rock, in an environment that was either underwater or subjected to tidal water. Some of the layers of the Pakoon Limestone, in the western Grand Canyon, appear to have been influenced by a wind-dominated environment but still contain fragments of marine shells or silt. These have sometimes been referred to as eolian marine sediments. Some of the patterns that distinguish between water-driven marine sediments and eolian marine sediments are evident within a given horizontal layer. In other cases, the patterns show up between multiple, adjacent layers.

Some of the marine material in the layers of eolian marine sediments, in the western Grand Canyon, is thought to have been transported across significant distances. The Cordilleran Seaway extended as far north as Canada, in a line that was parallel to the Cordilleran Miogeocline. Scientists think that the prevailing currents within the seaway, which flowed from the north to the south, may have initially carried sediments from sites that were north of the Grand Canyon Embayment. After the marine material was deposited on a beach or other dry site, the carbonate fragments may have then been blown onto dunes that were at inland sites. This is controversial, given that the eolian marine patterns could have resulted from shifts in the location of the shoreline. The marine material may have been deposited under the action of waves and then been left high and dry, such as by a localized reduction in the water level. Wind may have subsequently modified the conditions and pattern of sedimentation.

In some cases, this conclusion was based on the geographical variation in a given layering pattern of sedimentary layers. For example, one type of ground-up coral or sandstone might always be stacked above a layer that contains another type of sediment. This pattern might be very consistent in one part of a canyon wall and become less pronounced to the west and north. In the Grand Canyon, some of these geographical patterns cannot be explained in terms of changes in the currents or shoreline of the seaway.

2

The Columbia River Gorge

Northern Oregon and Southern Washington, the United States

The Columbia River Gorge is located in northern Oregon and a southern portion of Washington State. The 80-mile- (129-km-) long gorge was cut out of hardened layers of basalt lava by the Columbia River. The Columbia River is more than 1,200 miles (1,931 km) long and carries more water than any other river in North America. The gorge is located east of Portland and of the Cascade Mountains. The Columbia River originates in British Columbia, Canada, and flows, in a direction that is roughly south, through Washington. Beginning in southern Washington, the river then flows west, toward the Pacific, along the border between Washington and Oregon. The Columbia River Gorge extends along this east-west axis, upstream of Portland. As the Columbia River flows through Portland, the river is essentially at sea level. At more upstream locations, within the actual gorge, the river has cut out walls that are 4,000 feet (1,219 m) high.

The Columbia River Gorge is not located at a subtropical latitude, but the eastern parts of the gorge are outside the coastal, maritime climate zone of the Pacific Northwest. As a result, the annual precipitation decreases sharply in the parts of the gorge that are east of an imaginary line. This line has no specific name and is only apparent, on a small geographical scale, in the context of high-resolution meteorological measurements. The weather in the gorge may also be influenced by gap winds that create high winds and complex, thermal effects within the gorge.

To the east of Columbia River Gorge, the climate is that of a rainshadow desert. A rainshadow desert is also known as an *orographic desert*. The high altitudes of the cascade range serve to cool the moist air that blows in from Puget Sound and the Pacific Ocean. This cooling causes the

This picture shows the Columbia River and the sloping walls, covered by trees, of Columbia River Gorge. *(Shawna Caldwell/ShutterStock, Inc.)*

air to dump its moisture as rain or snow in the vicinity of the mountains. For example, Portland is just east of the Cascades and receives fairly abundant precipitation. Portland is therefore part of the rainshadow of the Cascades. As the dried-out air moves down from the Cascades to the Columbia Plateau, the air warms and is able to further evaporate water from the Columbia Plateau.

There is evidence that *rainshadow effects* of the Cascades may have existed for some time, but the rainshadow effects may or may not have influenced the development of the gorge. During the late *Miocene epoch*, for example, the climate in northern Washington is thought to have been fairly wet. The portions of Washington that are east of Mount Hood, for example, are part of the area that may have been wet for 5 million years or more. The exhumation of the Washington Cascades appears to have accelerated during the interval between 10 and 4.5 million years ago. The abundant rainfall may have facilitated this *erosional exhumation*. The Columbia River flows roughly south through Washington State. As the river flows alongside the Washington Cascades, the river also flows roughly south. The erosional exhumation was also accompanied by *uplift*, and a significant portion of the uplift would have taken the form of an isostatic response, the *isostatic uplift* that is a form of *passive uplift*, to erosional exhumation. This uplift is likely to have increased the gradient of the Columbia River, at least along the portions of the river that are upstream, and north, of the gorge. The precipitation in northern Washington might have actually contributed to the *incision* of the gorge, given that uplift was occurring. Apart from the amounts of precipitation, however, the uplift in Washington would have increased the overall *gradient* of the river.

That said, the orographic desertification of the Columbia Plateau would have also been developing within the last 10 million years. The Snake River, for example, feeds into the Columbia River from the east. It is not clear if the climate around the eastern *tributaries* of the Columbia River had any impact on the formation of the gorge. Similarly, it is not clear that the gorge has been maintained, and spared the erosive effects of weathering, as a result of the gap winds in the gorge or the low precipitation on the Columbia Plateau.

The incision of the Columbia River Gorge occurred between 1 and 2 million years ago. This incision is thought to have been driven by the uplift that has occurred in the Cascades. Researchers have generally attributed the incision of the gorge to uplift in the Cascades and land in northern Oregon, but uplift also occurred in the Washington Cascades. This uplift in Washington may have contributed to the incision of the gorge. After an initial phase of exhumation had ended, the process of erosional exhumation began to accelerate about 10 million years ago. Between 10 and 4.5 million years ago, the Washington Cascades were subjected to significant uplift. This uplift was temporally associated with an accelerated phase of erosional exhumation, a process that began 10 million years ago. This would suggest that the uplift was partially isostatic. However, some of the lava of the Columbia River Basalt Group has been deformed by uplift. In the vicinity of Mount Rainier, some parts of the Columbia River Basalt have been upwarped, uplifted and "tilted" by more than .93 mile (1.5 km). The uplifted portions have been uplifted with respect to the other sections of the same members and *lava flows*. This indicates that some of the upwarping occurred after 17.5 million years ago, when the lava of the Columbia River Basalt Group was first deposited.

ORIGIN OF THE COLUMBIA PLATEAU

The site of Columbia River Gorge was originally within part of a *backarc basin*. The land beneath Washington and Oregon was part of the *backarc zone* of the Cascade Arc. The Juan de Fuca plate, which is beneath the Pacific Ocean off the coast of the Pacific Northwest, has been undergoing *subduction* beneath the North American plate. The subduction is occurring along a line, extending roughly from north to south, off the coasts of Washington and Oregon. The Juan de Fuca plate is now a fairly small plate and is much longer, along a north-south axis, than it is wide. The plate extends from just north of Vancouver Island to about the uppermost part of northern California. The plate only extends beneath the ocean for an average of, roughly, 124 miles (200 km). In the near-shore areas of the Pacific Northwest, this *subduction zone* is known as the Cascadia Subduction Zone. The Pacific plate is on the seaward side of the Juan de Fuca plate.

For the sake of discussion, it is helpful to refer to this depression of the continental *crust*, the backarc zone that was filled in to become the Columbia Plateau, as the Columbia Backarc Basin. After the backarc basin was covered by four miles (6.4 km) or more of *flood basalt lava*, the Columbia Plateau was formed. The Columbia River Basin is the area of land that drains into the Columbia River. The margins of the Columbia River Basin are not the same as the margins of the Columbia Plateau (the "filled-in" portion of the Columbia Backarc Basin). In the vicinity of the gorge, the margins agree in a loose and general sense. But the Columbia Plateau does not extend into Canada. The Columbia River Basin does. The Columbia River originates in Columbia Lake, in British Columbia, Canada, and its drainage basin exists around the entire length of the river. Researchers have noted the potential for confusion in this context, given that the term *Columbia Basin* is generally applied very loosely. At the western, most downstream, end of the gorge, the Columbia Backarc Basin ends and blends into the Portland Basin. The Portland Basin is a small basin that was produced by tectonic activity, largely consisting of extensional fault activity. The part of the Cascadia Backarc Zone that surrounds the Columbia River Gorge and overlaps with the Columbia Plateau will, for the sake of simplicity, be regarded as the Columbia Backarc Basin.

In the diagram on page 34, the land within the Columbia Plateau is shaded. The Columbia River originates north of the Columbia Plateau, flows roughly south across part of the plateau, veers west, and then continues west through Columbia River Gorge.

It is helpful to note that the lava of the Columbia River Basalt Group was not confined to a small, neatly defined backarc basin. The lava flowed out over a large area. The Columbia Plateau is the present-day remnant of the parts of the lava that accumulated in especially thick layers, within the backarc zone, and that was subsequently uplifted.

The subduction process off the shores of Washington and Oregon has been occurring for the last 40 million years. After the backarc zone and Columbia Backarc Basin were first formed, the backarc zone was initially subjected to a phase of *compressional fault activity*. Subsequently, the Columbia Plateau area has primarily experienced extensional fault activity. This is analogous to the Basin and Range extension that began to occur

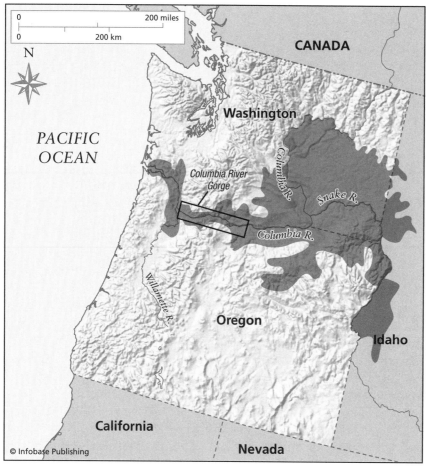

This diagram shows the margins of the Columbia Plateau (shaded zone) and the length of Columbia River Gorge (rectangular box).

in more southern states after the Laramide Orogeny. The gradual extension began in and around the Columbia Backarc Basin during the *Eocene epoch*, between 57.8 and 36.6 million years ago, and continued until after the first flood basalt eruption.

Extensional faulting in Oregon was probably not directly responsible for the flood basalt eruptions, but the Yellowstone *hot spot* may have contributed to the eruptions of the Columbia River Basalt Group. The Yellowstone hot spot appeared in northern Nevada between 16 and 17 million years ago, which is about the time that the flood basalt eruptions began. The hot spot may have been created by a *mantle plume*, but this is controversial. The hot spot may have interacted with the existing extensional faults, but this is also controversial. Before the Columbia River Basalt Group eruptions began, and before the Yellowstone hot spot emerged, the Pacific Northwest had already been affected by a different kind of *volcanic activity*. Since the Eocene epoch, which spanned the interval of 57.8 to 36.6 million years ago, two overall types of lava have been deposited in Oregon. The more abundant of the two is the flood basalt lava that forms the bulk of the Columbia Plateau. The eruptions that deposited this type of lava occurred over a much shorter period of time than the eruptions of the other, more viscous type of so-called calc-alkalic lava. This more viscous and alkaline form of lava was deposited both before and after the flood basalt eruptions occurred. Thus, the emergence of the Yellowstone hot spot coincided with the delivery of a new form of lava that had not previously been erupted in Oregon and Washington.

Another relevant aspect of the region is the relatively thin crust. The crust and *mantle lithosphere* beneath the Columbia River Gorge are relatively thin and are just west of the so-called *craton* margin. The craton margin is the outermost margin of the craton. The thicker continental crust of the craton begins beneath Idaho and extends east, beneath the central portions of the North American plate. This thinning of the crust may have set the stage for volcanic eruptions. The thin crust and mantle lithosphere may also have been favorable for extensional fault activity. The role of extensional fault activity in the basalt eruptions is, however, relatively unclear.

The Columbia Plateau is therefore a *volcanic plateau*, but its geological history has some characteristics in common with the histories of sedimentary plateaus. The deposition of these volcanic flood basalts in an existing depression of land, such as the backarc basin, is analogous to the deposition of marine *sediments* in such a basin. First, the basalt lava filled in the Columbia Backarc Basin and surrounding backarc zone. The lava itself was thick enough to increase the elevation and create the Columbia Plateau, and the erosional exhumation of some of the lava appears to have further contributed to uplift of the plateau.

SCABLANDS AND CATACLYSMIC FLOODING

Some portions of Columbia River Gorge were submerged and modified by cataclysmic flooding, but these floods did not really contribute to the incision of the gorge. During the last ice age, or last glacial maximum, much of Montana was covered by a lake that is known as Lake Missoula. The glacial lake was made up of glacial meltwater, and its water was contained by glacial ice dams. As the glaciers melted, large volumes of water flooded the drainage basin of the Columbia River. At least 25 of these cataclysmic floods have occurred within the last 19,000 years. The floods transported large boulders and rocks through the area, and these rocks produced denting and cracking in some parts of the ground. However, researchers recently found that only some, out of the many individual floods, actually produced any real erosive work. In the context of erosion, work refers to the movement of sedimentary rock, across a net distance,

The water in Multnomah Falls, located in the Columbia River Gorge in Oregon, falls more than 600 feet. (*Natalia Bratslavsky/ShutterStock, Inc.*)

in response to an applied force. To a significant extent, many of these cataclysmic floods just created a mess.

In the context of canyon formation, this finding highlights the true forcefulness of isostatic uplift and other forms of uplift. Essentially, canyon formation requires more than the forceful delivery of rocks and water. The rocks might create dents and cracks, but the dents might rapidly be filled in with *alluvial sediments*. Canyon formation requires the consistent application of some set of nonequilibrium conditions. If a flood lasts two months or even two years, the river is likely to rapidly restore the river-sediment system to an equilibrium state. The flood might spin a lot of rocks around and move sediments a short distance, but this is not necessarily work. The work of canyon formation, from the standpoint of physical science, requires both the application of force and the movement of rocks across a net distance. A flood may do work on individual rocks and not perform work, in the form of *fluvial incision* or mechanical erosion, on any segment of the canyon. A canyon or gorge can be flooded with tremendously large amounts of water and rocks, and the rocks may not produce a net change in the depth of the canyon.

Some erosion was produced by boulders and other rocks. The fast-moving water caused rocks to be spun around, drilling giant potholes into portions of the Columbia River Basalt. Some of the dents can still be seen in a flattened, lowland channel that runs parallel to the Columbia River. In this scablands area, which includes some *hillslopes* that slope down into the gorge, some large boulders are still scattered across the rugged landscape. During the floods, some of the extra water was diverted through a kind of overflow channel. This channel is now dry, primarily because the main channel of the gorge can adequately transport the water of the Columbia River. The dents would have been produced in both the main channel and the overflow channel, but the river has not usually been flowing through the overflow channel. Because the overflow channel has been dry and has not been smoothed by fluvial processes, the overflow channel still contains more of the flood-induced dents and potholes.

SITES AND CHARACTERISTICS OF THE ERUPTIONS

The eruptions of the Columbia River Basalt Group began 17.5 million years ago and occurred along *linear vent systems*. The present-day remnants of these linear vent systems are *dikes*. The dikes often appear as V-shaped or I-shaped intrusions of basalt lava into a cliff face. A vent is a site at which lava erupts or flows out of the ground. A linear vent is associated with a *fissure*, which is a linear crack in the layers of preexisting rock that are near to the surface. In Oregon, Washington, and Idaho, the lengths of the linear vents range from a couple of dozen kilometers to a few hundred kilometers. The dikes tend to be at one end of the linear vent.

Many of the present-day dikes are localized around the point at which Washington, Oregon, and Idaho intersect. For example, the Joseph Creek Dike and Limekiln Rapids Dike were located in southeastern Washington. Interestingly, the Joseph Creek Dike was part of a linear vent system that extended into northern Oregon. The Pruitt Draw Dike, in the western portion of Idaho, was part of another vent system that delivered lava of the Columbia River Basalt Group. This dike was located west of the Salmon River and east of the Snake River.

The individual lava flows, each of which deposited a portion of the Columbia River Basalt Group, tended to be very brief and voluminous. Individual lava flows of the Grande Ronde Basalt contained, in some cases, more than 240–600 cubic miles (1,000–2,500 km³) of lava. In some cases, an individual lava flow is thought to have delivered this lava over the course of a few weeks or months. An individual lava flow, of the Grande Ronde Basalt eruptions, would sometimes cover land that was 186 miles (300 km) from the dike. Some flows of the Grande Ronde Basalt eruptions delivered and deposited lava at points that were 466 miles (750 km) from the vent sites, linear vents that were sometimes very long. The difference between the ranges of 466 miles and 186 miles may, in some cases, be attributed to the differences in the lengths of the linear vents.

Very large amounts of lava were delivered and deposited as part of the Grande Ronde Basalt Formation. The eruptions of the Grande Ronde Basalt occurred between about 17 and 15.6 million years ago. The amount of lava that was delivered by the Grande Ronde Basalt eruptions was very large, comprising 67–85 percent of the lava of the Columbia River Basalt Group. It is important to note that these eruptions generally occurred intermittently. The Grand Ronde Basalt lava was delivered by about 120 lava flows. Each lava flow was a single eruption event.

Roughly 75 percent of the Columbia River Basalt lava erupted from the vents that were associated with dikes of the Chief Joseph Dike Swarm. This *dike swarm* consists of about 20,000 dikes. Many of these dikes are in northeastern Oregon, but some are also in western Idaho and southeastern Washington. Another dike swarm is the Monument Dike Swarm, which is in north-central Oregon and is just west of the Chief Joseph Dike Swarm. The dike-fissure-vents in both groups are generally oriented along northwest-southeast axes, with the lines tilted more toward the north-south axis than the west-east axis. As discussed in the sidebar on page 39, researchers often apply these terms in ways that are potentially confusing. The dike swarms are mapped out as collections of lines, but

LINEAR VENTS AND FOCAL POINTS OF ERUPTION

Researchers recently analyzed the Maxwell Lake Dike and gained insight into the flood basalt eruptions. This dike is in northeastern Oregon and is part of the Chief Joseph Dike Swarm. Researchers think that the lava initially erupted from many points along the so-called dike-fissure-vent system. Along some of the narrow parts of the fissure-vent system, the lava is thought to have melted the rock and solidified. After the fissure-vent became solidified and crusted over at many points, the lava probably erupted from only a few points along the fissure. The terminology is applied somewhat loosely and is potentially confusing. The vent is the site at which lava flows out of the fissure, but fissures are sometimes referred to as linear vents. Given that the vent sites tended to shift and move along the fissure, it is helpful to discuss the eruptions in terms of fissure-vent systems. The dike is the present-day, solid remnant of the magma intrusion that occurred along the fissure-vent system.

the dikes may only appear in rock walls in a few sites. The dikes are the present-day remnant of part of a linear vent-fissure system. Researchers can map out a vent-fissure system by analyzing the chemical compositions of visible dikes and connecting the dots, so to speak.

There is evidence that the individual lava flows may have required 1.8–2.2 years to solidify in a meaningful way. For example, the Ginkgo flow, discussed below, is thought to have formed an outer *vesicular crust* after about two years. This crust was between about 33 feet (10 m) and 98 feet (30 m) thick, and the relevant portion of the Ginkgo flow was evidently between 295 feet (90 m) and 492 feet (150 m). Thus, the crust was only a fraction of the thickness of the entire flow. Some lava may have been able to move beneath the newly solidified crust. This lava did not solidify in the same manner as the outer crust, however.

EARLY VERSIONS OF COLUMBIA RIVER GORGE

The present-day walls of Columbia River Gorge are thought to have been incised between 1 and 2 million years ago, but earlier forms of the gorge have existed for at least 14 million years. These early versions of the gorge were simply canyons that had been incised along different paths. These paths were channels that were incised by the Columbia River. In general, these alternate paths were formed when the Columbia River was diverted from its previous path. These diversions occurred when the early versions of Columbia River Gorge became blocked by lava deposits. In other cases, the lava flows did not immediately solidify into lava deposits. For example, some of the early versions of Columbia River Gorge became, temporarily, rivers of freely flowing lava.

Perhaps the earliest diversion of the Columbia River, by the Columbia River Basalt Group eruptions, was produced between 15.6 and 15.3 million years ago. During this interval, the Ginkgo flow deposited lava over portions of the present-day site of Columbia River Gorge. The lava flow also produced an *intracanyon flow* within the portion of the Willamette River valley that is upstream of Portland. The flow also extended across the parts of Columbia River, and two of its tributaries, that flow across southern Washington. Additionally, the Ginkgo flow covered the parts of the channel of the Columbia River that are between Portland and the Pacific Ocean. The Ginkgo flow was among the most voluminous of the individual flow events that were part of the Columbia River Basalt Group eruptions. In the central parts of the Columbia Plateau, between 98 feet (30 m) and 230 feet (70 m) of basalt, from the Ginkgo flow, generally remain. Along some parts of the Willamette River valley, between 295 feet (90 m) and 492 feet (150 m) are evident. The Ginkgo flow was one of four flow units of the Frenchman Springs Member, which itself was part of the Grande Ronde Basalt Formation.

TURBULENT FLOW, LAMINAR FLOW, AND INTRACANYON FLOWS

The viscosities and speeds of lava flows can vary, even in relation to the landscape the lava flows move across. Lava displays different flow characteristics, and these characteristics change as the velocity of the flow increases. When lava of the Columbia River Basalt Group was flowing over relatively flat land, it was moving like a *sheet flow*. When a lava flow is traveling through a canyon, the lava tends to flow more rapidly and is regarded as a *pipe flow*. The parts of the Ginkgo flow that were traveling through canyons were moving like pipe flows. The parts that spread out across flat land were moving like sheet flows.

The more important distinction is between laminar flow and turbulent flow. A pipe flow can display either laminar or turbulent flow characteristics, and a sheet flow can also be categorized as laminar or turbulent. Given that a canyon or channel will confine the boundaries of a lava flow, the canyon will tend to speed up the lava. Thus, a sheet flow could flow into a narrow canyon and become a pipe flow. The term *laminar* essentially means "layered." In laminar flow, the lava might spread out like molasses or like a kind of expanding, layered "blob." To display characteristics of turbulent flow, lava has to be moving faster than a given critical velocity. A turbulent lava flow is frothing and circulating around, and this produces tremendous heat loss. In laminar flow, a thin crust tends to form around the pipe-shaped or sheet-shaped portions of moving lava. This crust tends to be formed and reformed dynamically, and the crust serves as an insulator that prevents heat loss. Thus, the words *sheet* and *pipe* refer to the shapes of the crustal shells that exist around the moving lava. The words also refer to the different mathematical models used to describe, from a mathematical or hydrological standpoint, the flow characteristics of the lava.

Researchers originally thought the Ginkgo flow would have had to display turbulent flow characteristics. The evidence now suggests that the Ginkgo flow was a fast-moving, laminar flow. This allowed it to travel large distances in a relatively short time. If the flow had been moving faster, the turbulent behavior might have accelerated heat loss too much. This rapid heat loss could have caused the lava to solidify too rapidly, thereby limiting the distance the lava could flow across. Given the maximum flow velocity of 18 miles per hour (29 km/hr) to 22 miles per hour (36 km/hr), the Gingko flow is thought to have traveled a bit slower than the critical velocity. Even though the Ginkgo flow was not turbulent, its lava was fluid enough to travel through the narrow walls of a canyon.

Portions of the Columbia River would have been diverted as a result of the Ginkgo flow, but the path of the new channel is not clear. It is also not clear that the Columbia River actually incised a new channel, or canyon, along its new path.

One of the earliest versions of Columbia River Gorge existed at least 14 million years ago. This was a canyon that had been cut, in part, out of the Skamania lava flows. The Skamania lava flows were delivered to the area during the Eocene epoch, the *Oligocene epoch,* and the early portions of the Miocene epoch. Thus, the Skamania lava was delivered to the area before the lava of the Columbia River Basalt Group was delivered. Portions of the Skamania lava still exist on Crown Point, a peninsula that points west and is on the southern side of the Columbia River. (Crown Point can be seen in the lower color insert on page C-2.)

The path of the Columbia River through this early gorge was diverted by the delivery, into the gorge, of the lava of the Priest Rapids Member. The Priest Rapids Member was deposited between 13.5 and 14 million years ago, during the middle portion of the Miocene epoch. The Priest Rapids Member was not the first portion of lava that was delivered as part of the Columbia River Basalt Group. Nonetheless, it is deposited above the Skamania lava in some parts of the walls of Columbia River Gorge. It is helpful to remember that the Columbia River had incised a channel out of the Skamania lava. Researchers know that the early layers of lava in the Columbia River Basalt Group had begun to be deposited at least 15.8 million years ago, which is at least 1.8–2.3 million years before the Priest Rapids Member was deposited. Some of these portions of lava were deposited in different parts of the early gorge, but these were eroded away from some parts of the gorge. At Crown Point, for example, the Columbia River had incised down into the Skamania lava.

The delivery of the Priest Rapids Member caused the Columbia River to be diverted south, a diversion that ultimately served to incise the Priest Rapids Channel. This channel extended southwest in a long, curved line. The curved path then flattened and turned slightly northwest. The Priest Rapids Channel joined the present-day path of the Columbia River, and the channel of Columbia River Gorge, at Crown Point. The chemical composition of the lava in the Priest Rapids Member is known as a Rosalia-type composition. The major intracanyon flow of the Priest Rapids Member lava, which may have been erupted in more than one flow, is sometimes referred to as the Rosalia flow. The intracanyon flow of the Priest Rapids Member is also referred to as the Rosalia Priest Rapids flow. There is no Rosalia formation or Rosalia member, however. The Rosalia flow moved through the previously formed gorge, and this diverted the Columbia River into the path that became the Priest Rapids Channel.

The Priest Rapids Member was the last type of lava to be delivered as part of the eruptions of the Wanapum Basalt, which is one subdivision of the Columbia River Basalt Group. The Wanapum Basalt was the lava that was erupted and delivered across the area. The basalt then solidified into layers of the Wanapum Basalt Formation. For the sake of discussion, it will be helpful to refer to the various subdivisions in these types of strict terms. The Columbia River Basalt Group has been divided into subgroups. Each subgroup has been subdivided into formations. Each formation has been subdivided into members. The major subgroup that is relevant to the history of Columbia River Gorge is the Yakima Basalt Subgroup. This subgroup includes essentially all of the formations and members that were deposited between 15.8 and 6 million years ago. The earliest formation that was deposited as part of the Yakima Basalt Subgroup was the Grand Ronde Basalt Formation. The members of this formation were deposited, in general, between 15.8 and 14 million years ago. The layers of the Wanapum Basalt Formation were deposited between 13.5 and 14.5 million years ago. Thus, there was temporal overlap between the eruptions that deposited the Grande Ronde Basalt Formation and the Wanapum Basalt Formation. The Priest Rapids Member was the last type of lava to be deposited as part of the Wanapum Basalt Formation. The timing of its delivery and deposition was closer to 13.5 million years ago than 14.5 million years ago.

THE BRIDAL VEIL CHANNEL

The next major version of Columbia River Gorge was the Bridal Veil Channel, which existed between about 12 and 2 million years ago. Researchers think that the Bridal Veil Channel developed after debris filled in the Priest Rapids Channel. During an interval of time before 12 million years ago, lakes and pools began to transport very large amounts of debris from the Priest Rapids Member lava. This lava was transported into the Priest Rapids Channel by streams and the like. This is thought to have produced *aggradation* or perhaps damming of the Priest Rapids Channel. This, along with new flood basalt eruptions, ultimately caused the Columbia River to be diverted slightly north. The northward diversion led to the incision of the Bridal Veil Channel, which was south of the present-day gorge and north of the Priest Rapids Channel. This Bridal Veil Channel is sometimes called the Pomona Channel. Lava of the Pomona Member was delivered into the Bridal Veil Channel as an intracanyon flow. It is important to note, however, that the eruptions of the Pomona Member did not cause the Bridal Veil Channel to be created. Eruptions began to deposit the Pomona Member about 12 million years ago. The Pomona Member is one member of the Saddle Mountains Basalt Formation.

In various parts of the walls of Columbia River Gorge, the lava of the Pomona Member is between 19.7 feet (6 m) and 400 feet (122 m) thick. The lava of Pomona Member is noticeably visible in the walls of the gorge that are near the town of Bridal Veil, Oregon. The Bridal Veil

Channel was at least 801 feet (244 m) thick and 1.5 miles (2.4 km) wide in some places, but researchers are not sure of the initial thickness of the Pomona Member. The evidence does, however, indicate that the flows of the Pomona Member did not completely fill in the Bridal Veil Channel. As a result, the Pomona Member did not cause the river to be diverted from the Bridal Veil Channel. The Pomona Member could not have been deposited after 10.5 million years ago. The Pomona Member was therefore deposited for at most 1.5 million years. The actual interval of time, during which flows of the Pomona Member occurred, was probably shorter than 1.5 million years. Erosional *unconformities* exist above the Pomona Member in different places. In some places, the layers of the Troutdale Formation are above the layers of the Pomona Member and are separated from the Pomona Member by an unconformity.

The gravels of the Troutdale Formation are thought to have been delivered into the Bridal Veil Channel between 9.6 million and 2 million years ago. The Troutdale Formation is not technically part of the Columbia River Basalt Group, even though the Lower Member (the earlier member) of the Troutdale Formation was deposited, at about 9.6 million years ago, before the eruptions of the Columbia River Basalt Group had ended. The Troutdale Formation consists of gravel, lava debris, and lacustrine sediments that were transported by fluvial mechanisms. The age of the Lower Member of the Troutdale Formation is not certain, but some of it is 9.6 million years old. Some of the Troutdale Formation may be almost 12 million years old, but the Troutdale Formation is thought to have been deposited after the Pomona Member.

The upper member of the Troutdale Formation began to be deposited between about 5.3 and 3.6 million years ago, an interval that is part of the early *Pliocene epoch*. This deposition continued until 2 million years ago. The Troutdale Formation is more than 1,099 feet (335 m) thick in some parts of the walls of Columbia River Gorge. The Troutdale Formation was generally found on the Oregon side of the gorge and was not really found on the Washington side. This, together with other lines of evidence, indicate that the present-day gorge was not incised until after the most recently deposited layers of the Troutdale Formation were deposited. This indicates that the Bridal Veil Channel existed until at least 2 million years ago. Some time in the last 2 million years, the Bridal Veil Channel filled in completely and diverted the river north. There, the river incised the present-day gorge.

JOINTS, COLUMNS, AND LAYERING PATTERNS IN LAVA

The division of a given formation into members is based on the timing of deposition, of the chemical composition of the lava that solidified into a member, and the structural composition of the solidified basalt that presently exists. Researchers consider, for example, the percent compositions of silicon dioxide (silica), magnesium oxide, aluminum oxide, and other minerals that exist in each lava member. In some cases, the members have not been deposited in a clearly defined sequence of layers.

Many of the different patterns and textures of the layers of lava—patterns and textures that are evident in the walls of Columbia River Gorge—were created by different actions of water. For example, shallow lakes were formed around the early gorges. Some of the layers of the Priest Rapids Member were modified, primarily after but also during their solidification, by the *lacustrine* environment to which they were subjected. In other cases, fluvial erosion modified the lava by unknown mechanisms. The modifications only occur in some sections of the Priest Rapids Member. For example, the lake might have existed above 20 feet (6.1 m) of the lava in the Priest Rapids Member for a given interval of time. The lake might have then dried up and been covered by another 50 feet (15.2 m) of the Priest Rapids Member. The lacustrine modifications would still have been preserved beneath the 50 feet. Subsequently, a stream might have incised 70 feet (21.3 m) down. All of the 50 feet of newly deposited, cooling lava might have been subjected to the "fluvial modification," but the 20 feet (6.1 m) of lacustrine layers would still have retained their lacustrine signature. The entire area might then have been covered over by lava. When the Columbia River finally incised the present-day gorge, the layering pattern would still have been apparent in the walls. The walls could be expected to contain 50 feet of fluvially cooled basalt over 20 feet of lacustrine-cooled basalt, rather than 70 feet of fluvially cooled basalt. If lava is cooled by the lacustrine conditions of a lake, then one pattern will be produced in the solid basalt. If the solid, lacustrine pattern is later eroded by fluvial modifications, some or most of the lacustrine "cooling signature" will probably still be apparent and will not be "erased" by the fluvial modifications.

Many of the multilayered patterns in the walls of the gorge are the result of differences in the conditions that existed during the cooling of the lava. These can be thought of as "cooling patterns." The cooling pattern is produced by the water environment that exists during the cooling of the lava. After this pattern is established, the solid pattern of the basalt may be further modified by rivers or lakes. Many of the fluvially modified sections of the Priest Rapids Member, discussed above, were produced after the lava had cooled. Often, however, the cooling pattern is more apparent than the subsequent, erosional modifications.

In the walls of Columbia River Gorge, many of the individual lava flows have solidified into three overall sections. These sections contain various patterns of *columnar jointing*. These are vertically oriented *col-*

umns that appear in the walls. The uppermost and thickest section is the *entablature*, which often contains a pattern of slender and fanlike columns. The fanlike columns, also known as *fanning columns*, tend to be oriented more or less vertically but also tend to be swirled and curved slightly. The uppermost portion of the entablature is the vesicular top, which is the same thing as the *vesicular crust*. The vesicular crust is the crust that was discussed above, in the case of the Gingko flow. The crust solidifies first, into thick and vertically oriented *pipes*. The pipes contain circular vesicles, or vesicle-shaped dots. Thus, the vesicular crust of a lava flow is the part that solidified first. As the underlying portions solidified and cooled, different patterns of columns were formed at different layers. Thus, cooling lava does not behave like cooling water. A crust of ice will form on the surface of water, as the water freezes into ice cubes. The ice will ultimately be more or less uniform and homogeneous throughout the ice cube. The same homogeneity does not occur as a lava flow cools.

Below the entablature is the set of columnar patterns that comprise the *colonnade*. The *Pillow Palagonite Complex* comprises the columnar patterns that are below the colonnade. The columns and joints of this complex are thought to be formed when a lava flow enters an existing pool of water. The lava moves into the lake, and then some layers are covered by standing water. The Pillow Palagonite Complex pattern is ultimately produced by the existence of lacustrine conditions, meaning standing water, above the cooling lava. In some parts of the Pillow Palagonite Complex sections, layers of *interbasaltic sediments* also exist. These are thought to have been produced when sediment-laden water flowed over portions of lava that had partially cooled.

The joints and columns in the colonnade and entablature are thought to have been formed by the vertical motion of water, both up and down the cooling lava flow. When the cooling process has not been occurring for very long, water mainly moves down through the lava. This top-down motion makes sense, given that liquid water would become steam in the hotter, deeper layers of the flow. The water percolates down and creates joints. Some of these more significant joints are known as *master joints*. The very slender and fanlike columns in the entablature are thought to be formed later. After the lava flow has cooled substantially, water can be carried upward by convection. Water is thought to enter the lower layers of the solidifying flow and be carried upward, by convection. The upward motion often occurs along master joints, and the water may move in a curved path. The fanlike patterns are, subjectively at least, reminiscent of the shape of a rising plume of steam.

3 ✧✧✧✧✧✧✧✧✧✧✧✧✧✧✧✧✧✧✧✧✧✧✧

The Three Gorges of the Yangtze River

Hubei Province and Sichuan Province, Southern China

The Three Gorges of the Yangtze (Yangzi, or Chang) River, also known as the Yangtze Gorges or simply the Gorges, are located in the central portion of southern China. The Three Gorges are Wu Gorge, Qutang Gorge, and Xiling Gorge. The Three Gorges extend along about 124 miles (200 km) of the path of the Yangtze River, which itself is approximately 3,915 miles (6,300 km) long. In the most upstream portions of the Three Gorges, such as near the *karst* platforms of the Wushan Hominid Site, the walls extend at least about 1,969 feet (600 m) to 2,297 feet (700 m) above the surface of the Yangtze River. Along other parts of the Three Gorges, the terraced walls extend only 656 feet (200 m) above the surface of the Yangtze River. (The upper color insert on page C-3 depicts a section where the walls are exceptionally steep.)

The walls of the Three Gorges consist of layers of limestone, an example of a carbonate-based *sedimentary rock*, and other types of sedimentary rock. Researchers estimate that up to 36 percent of the surface of China is covered by relatively significant portions of carbonate-based rock layers.

The recent history of the area around the Gorges shows some similarities to the recent histories of other canyons, but the terrain around the Gorges has been shaped by an extraordinarily complex set of *tectonic* events. The formation of the Gorges was most directly driven by local and regional *uplift*, which increased the downward *incision* by the Yangtze River. In conjunction with this uplift, the climate became more arid and therefore helped to limit the erosion of the walls by weathering. Apart from these similarities, the Gorges have been cut out of very mountainous terrain. Scientists are still attempting to understand the tectonic processes that shaped this variegated, ancient terrain.

The Yangtze River is sometimes referred to as the Changjiang River. The word *Changjiang*, which appears in much of the scientific literature about the Yangtze, is the phonetic expression of the Chinese name for the river. The Jiang portion of the phonetic name refers to the word *river*.

The long-term history of the Gorges contains both broad similarities to the histories of other canyons and some unique geological events. Many unusual and complicated geological forces helped to shape the land around the Gorges and contribute to their formation.

GEOLOGICAL HISTORY OF THE AREA

The present-day topography of China has been viewed as an amalgamation of three overall regions. The first region is the Tibetan Plateau, which covers much of western China. The second region covers central and northwestern China and consists of several plateaus, such as the Inner Mongolia, Ordos, and Loess Plateaus. The third region is the eastern, coastal portion of China. Along a west-east axis, the elevations tend to be highest on the Tibetan Plateau and in the rest of western China. The Yangtze River originates on the Tibetan Plateau, flows roughly southeast into south-central China, changes direction and flows northeast, and then flows, to the east, across central China. The Three Gorges were cut out of the thick layers of sedimentary rock that accumulated, in central China, between the Middle Triassic age and the late *Cretaceous period*.

In each of the three geological regions of China, the *lithosphere* tends to be thickest below land that is highest above sea level. The elevation of the land on the Tibetan Plateau averages between 2.5 miles (4 km) and 3.4 miles (5.5 km) above sea level and is higher than the land in the other two regions. The lithosphere beneath the Tibetan Plateau tends to be slightly more than 37.3 miles (60 km) thick. The geological region in central China averages 3,281–6,562 feet (1,000–2,000 m) above sea level, and the lithosphere beneath it is between 25 miles (40 km) and 31 miles (50 km) thick. Both the elevations and the lithosphere become progressively and substantially thinner in eastern China. The elevation in eastern China averages about 656 feet (200 m) above sea level and sits atop lithosphere that is only about 15.5–18.6 miles (25–30 km) thick.

The Yangtze incised the Three Gorges out of the relatively mountainous landscape that is downstream from the Sichuan Basin and upstream of the Jianghan Basin. The Sichuan Basin is at lower elevations than the Tibetan Plateau, but the landscape of the Sichuan Basin is still rugged enough to prevent the Yangtze from really fanning out and reaching its full width. The Three Gorges are just upstream of the the *alluvial* network of

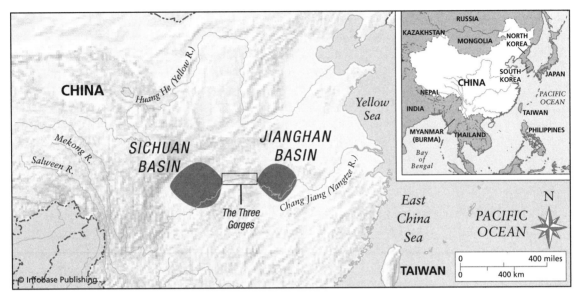

This diagram shows the margins of the Sichuan Basin, a rectangular outline of the Three Gorges, and the margins of the Jianghan Basin.

the Yangtze, a widening network of channels that begins in the western portion of the Jianghan Basin. In the context of this fanning out of the Yangtze and other rivers, the low elevations of eastern China have been viewed as a kind of vast floodplain.

In the above diagram, part of the Yangtze River is shown to flow northeast through the southern portion of the Sichuan Basin. After flowing out of the Sichuan Basin, the river flows through the Three Gorges. After the river exits Xiling Gorge and the Three Gorges Dam site, the river flows through the southern portion of the Jianghan Basin.

Both the Sichuan Basin and the Jianghan Basin were initially formed as *foreland basins*, and both were formed as a result of the Qinling-Dabie Orogeny. The Sichuan and Jianghan Basins both came into being during the early portions of the Upper Triassic age of the *Triassic period*, an age that spans the interval between 230 and 208 million years ago. The Jianghan Basin was first formed about 230 million years ago, a date that corresponds to the early portion of the Upper Triassic age.

The overall event that formed the Sichuan and Jianghan Basins, as well as the Three Gorges area that exists between the basins, was the collision between the South China Block and the North China Block. The South China Block is also known as the Yangtze Block. As the Qinling-Dabie Orogeny was forming the Sichuan Basin, a segment of land separated the Sichuan Basin from the North China Block. The Sichuan Basin was formed on the South China Block, but the northern margin of the Sichuan Basin was somewhat south of the actual collision zone between the South and North China Blocks. A band of mountains and high elevations was formed, a segment that extended along an east-west axis, north of the Sichuan Basin. This band consisted of the East and West Qinling Zones, and these were parts of the northern edge of the South China Block.

In the vicinity of the Jianghan Basin, to the east of the Sichuan Basin, another wedge of land was compressed and sutured between the South and north China Blocks. This portion of lithosphere, known as the Qinling-Dabieshan *plate* or Qinling-Dabieshan Zone, was compressed and metamorphosed extensively. As a result, only a tiny wedge of the plate remains. The land is in eastern China and has been thoroughly joined, or sutured, to the North and South China Blocks. The word *shan* refers, essentially, to mountains. *Dabieshan* and *Daba Shan* can be roughly translated as "mountains of the Dabie."

The precise nature and origin of the Qinling-Dabieshan plate is still an area of controversy. China was formed by the conglomeration of numerous lithospheric blocks, which some researchers have referred to as "microcontinents." For the sake of discussion, the Qinling-Dabieshan plate will be referred to as the Qinling-Dabieshan Zone. Researchers have also referred to this zone as the northern Dabie Complex. This zone was subjected to extraordinarily powerful and chaotic tectonic forces. Some of the zone may have been formed as a result of the Qinling-Dabie Orogeny. In other words, deformations and normal faulting resulted from the *subduction* process and enlarged the Qinling-Dabieshan Zone. Subsequently, the ultra-high-pressure *metamorphism* may have enlarged the zone.

This complex tectonic history is evident in the ages of gneisses in the so-called northern Dabie Complex. (The northern Dabie Complex is another name for the Qinling-Dabieshan Zone.) One group of researchers found that some of the gneisses were 1.9–2.0 billion years old, some were 750 or roughly 770 million years old, and others were 113–117 and 125–127- million years old. As discussed below, the 750- and roughly 770-million-year-old gneisses were probably formed, such as during metamorphism, in the context of the breakup of Rodinia. The 113–117- and 125–127-million-year-old foliated gneisses, which are gneisses that were subjected to one type of metamorphism, were probably formed during the post–Qinling-Dabie orogenic metamorphism. These younger gneisses were, however, not modified by the ultra-high-pressure metamorphism that occurred after the Qinling-Dabie Orogeny. Researchers concluded that the northern Dabie Complex was part of the Yangtze Craton (the South China Block) and that portions of rock in the complex were subjected to metamorphism after the Qinling-Dabie Orogeny. The northern Dabie Complex can, nonetheless, still be viewed as a distinct zone. The complex is distinct because it was not subjected to the ultra-high-pressure form of metamorphism that affected other nearby portions of rock.

For the sake of discussion, it is helpful to consider the overall picture. The Qinling-Dabieshan Zone is north of the Jianghan Basin and is somewhat, but not entirely, analogous to the East and West Qinling Zones that are north of the Sichuan Basin.

DEVELOPMENT OF THE SICHUAN AND JIANGHAN BASINS

The tectonic events that occurred after the Qinling-Dabie Orogeny were extremely complex. The eastern margin of the Sichuan Basin was subjected to *transpressional faulting*, and much of the South China Block was gradually rotated. The site of the present-day Three Gorges was formed at the intersection of the Daba Shan Fold-Thrust Belt, which was formed as the northeastern margin of the Sichuan Basin, and the East Sichuan Fold-Thrust Belt, which was formed as the southeastern margin of the Sichuan Basin. The East Sichuan Belt extends from southwest to northeast and meets the Daba Shan Belt, which extends along a slight northwest-southeast axis. The Yangtze enters the Three Gorges in the vicinity of this intersection zone. Some *fault* lines have also been formed, more recently than the Triassic period, along the axes of these *orogenic* belts. The faults may have been reactivated along the suture zones, and the path of the Yangtze has been influenced by these *fault systems*.

During the late portion of the Paleozoic era, the South China Block was separated from the Qinling-Dabieshan Zone by the Mianlue Ocean. The Jianghan Basin did not exist at this time, but the present-day basin would have been on the northern portion, either part of the coast or submerged, of the South China Block. This relatively small ocean or seaway was formed as a result of *rifting* that had occurred earlier. Beginning about 240 million years ago, the South China Block began to undergo subduction beneath the North China Block. The Qinling-Dabieshan Zone was situated, as a zone of deformation and faulting, between the North and South China Blocks. This closed the ocean and also produced *orogenic uplift*, on the northern edge of the nascent Jianghan Basin. As the Jianghan Basin came into being, about 230 million years ago, the orogenic uplift delivered *sediments* to the basin from the north. The process of subduction, of the South China Block beneath the North China Block and the Qinling-Dabieshan Zone, gradually morphed into a suturing process. The suturing process continued until the early portion of the Cretaceous period, which began 144 million years ago.

The Jianghan Basin was originally formed out of part of the Middle Yangtze Foreland Basin, which extended from west to east. This basin was formed, beginning about 240 million years ago, to the south of the Mianlue Suture Line. The Qinling-Dabieshan plate has also been sutured to the North China Block. The Qinling-Dabieshan Zone is a relatively thin wedge of lithosphere that extends, along a slight northwest-southeast axis, across central China. In the vicinity of the Jianghan Basin, this wedge of lithosphere is north of the Yangtze Block and south of the North China Block. Northwestern China and other, smaller blocks of lithosphere, in northwestern China and elsewhere, were sutured together to form present-day China. In this book, the tectonic histories of these smaller lithospheric blocks will not be discussed.

The Jianghan Basin was originally formed as a foreland basin but has since been influenced by extensional faulting and rifting. The Jianghan Basin has been depressed downward in response to extensional *fault activity* and a failed rifting event. Given that rifting and extension allowed sedimentary rocks to accumulate in the Jianghan Basin, the basin is sometimes classified as a "rift basin." At a minimum, the sediments that accumulated during rifting can be viewed as "rift basin sediments." The rifting and extension simply allowed different layers of sediments to accumulate above the older layers of sedimentary rocks. The older layers, some of which have been eroded away from portions of the Jianghan Basin, were delivered before the extension began.

During the time that the Jianghan Basin was a foreland basin, numerous layers of sediments were deposited. These sediments, which are now sedimentary rocks, were deposited between about 230 and 154 million years ago.

As early as 200 million years ago, some extensional fault activity began to occur within the Jianghan Basin and the Qinling-Dabieshan Zone that was north of the basin. Thus, there was some overlap between the earliest extension and the end of the convergent deformations of the Qinling-Dabie Orogeny. The early, overall axis of extension was located along the suture zone between the Qinling-Dabieshan plate and the North China Block. This served to produce *fault-associated uplift*, which was accompanied by extension on a north-south axis, to the north of the Jianghan Basin.

Beginning about 154 million years ago, the Qinling-Dabieshan Zone began to be subjected to major uplift and *erosional exhumation*. This band of lithosphere was compressed between two plates for a long period of time. Between 154 and 96 million years ago, this zone of lithosphere was subjected to remarkably powerful metamorphism. This ultra-high-pressure metamorphism was accompanied by pronounced uplift and erosional exhumation. Between 154 and 96 million years ago, approximately 62 miles of rock layers were removed, by erosional exhumation, from the Qinling-Dabieshan Zone. Part of the uplift appears to have been *isostatic uplift*. The rest may have been driven by a kind of extensional "response" to the erosional exhumation. As the weight of the 62 miles of rock was shifted to the north and south, by erosion, the shift in weight may have facilitated extension along a north-south axis. Suppose, for example, that

20 people are standing at the back, or stern, of a small boat. If all 20 people suddenly moved from the stern to the bow, the boat would shift from being "stern-heavy" to "bow-heavy." The people would not just weigh down on the bow, however. The shift in weight would tend to push the boat forward, horizontally and across the water. A similar process can sometimes drive rifting or extension.

LAYERS OF JURASSIC AND TRIASSIC ROCKS

The Three Gorges have been cut out of the rock layers and mountains that exist between the Sichuan and Jianghan Basins. They have been cut out of land that can be viewed as a mountain belt. Some of the eastern portions of the Three Gorges have been cut out of a kind of dividing line between a sedimentary basin and a mountain range. The land around the Three Gorges also received inputs of sediments from the north, much as a sedimentary basin would.

Just downstream of the Sichuan Basin, the most upstream portions of the Three Gorges are near the Daba and Wu Mountains. The Daba Mountains extend along a line, oriented slightly from the northwest to the southeast, that is roughly parallel to the Yangtze River. The Daba Mountains are part of the present-day manifestation of the Daba Shan Fold-Thrust Belt. The Daba Mountains extend along the northeastern margin of the Sichuan Basin. Along this portion of the Gorges, the Yangtze is flowing east. Along this stretch, which is downstream of the point at which the Wu River feeds into the Yangtze River, the Daba Mountains are north of the Yangtze River. To the north of the Daba Mountains, the Qinling Mountains stretch along a west-east axis. The Qinling and Daba Mountains are only some of the present-day landforms that were formed as a result of the Qinling-Dabie Orogeny. Another short distance downstream of the Sichuan Basin, the Yangtze passes through the Wu Mountains. These mountains extend from north to south and exist on both sides of the river.

From a qualitative standpoint, the Three Gorges can be seen as having been cut out of the zone at which two or more sedimentary basins intersect. The most upstream portions of the Gorges have been cut out of the extreme northeastern margin of the Sichuan Basin. As the Yangtze approaches the margin of the Jianghan Basin, the river passes through the edge of the Zigui Basin. This is a low-lying portion of land that is adjacent to, and mostly west of, the Huangling Anticline, which is immediately adjacent to the site of the Three Gorges Dam; the dam itself is upstream of the Jianghan Basin.

The youngest sedimentary rocks in the walls of the gorges are, for the most part, Jurassic layers that are more than 135–144 million years old. Many of the rocks in the lower portions of the walls are more than 438 mil-

This picture helps put the width of the Yangtze, shown here flowing through the Three Gorges section of the river, into perspective. *(Taolmor/ShutterStock, Inc.)*

lion years old. In the eastern portions of the Three Gorges, downstream of Badong and upstream of Xiangxi, the Yangtze River passes through thick layers of rocks from the Jurassic period. These are the solidified rocks that were formed by the deposition of sediments in the Zigui Basin, which is west and upstream of the Huangling Anticline. The Zigui Basin has also been referred to as the Zigui Syncline. The Zigui Basin is really like the syncline that "accompanies" the adjacent Huangling Anticline.

In this portion of the Zigui Basin, the walls of the gorge contain about 656 feet (200 m) of the rock layers that comprise the Hsiangchi Formation. The layers of sedimentary rock in the Hsiangchi Formation contain the fossils and pollen fragments of 72 or more species of ferns and plants. The layers of the Hsiangchi Formation were deposited during the Lower Jurassic Age of the Jurassic period, during the interval between 203 and 175 million years ago. The layers of the Hsiangchi Formation were deposited above the layers of the Shazhenxi Formation, which were deposited during the later portions of the Triassic period. The Hsiangchi and Shazhenxi Formations are subdivisions of the Hsiangchi Group. The walls of the gorge, in the Zigui Basin, also contain layers of rock that were formed during the Middle and Upper Triassic ages. These layers were deposited, above the Hsiangchi Formation, between 175 and 135 million years ago.

In parts of the Zigui Basin, up to 9,187 feet (2,800 m) of sediments were deposited during the Middle Jurassic age. The walls of the Gorges are not 9,187 feet, however. In the Jianghan Basin and parts of the Zigui Basin, these layers from the Middle Jurassic age include the Shaximiao Formation and the Qianfuyan Formation. The layers of the Qianfuyan Formation were deposited below the layers of the Shaximiao Formation.

The walls on either side of the Three Gorges Dam are composed of the Huangling granite that exists at the center of the Huangling Dome. The Huangling Dome may not be perfectly equivalent to, or overlap perfectly with, the Huangling Anticline. The Yangtze flows through, essentially, the geographical center of the Huangling Dome. The Huangling Anticline is sometimes discussed as being north of the Three Gorges Dam site. The sedimentary rocks that were above the center of the Huangling Dome have been excavated or eroded, much as the center of an ice cream scoop could be scooped out by a spoon. Now, the high elevation of the "mountain," or anticline, is north of the center of the original dome. Another dome, the Shennongjia Dome, is present near the Huangling Dome.

The Huangling granite also forms the base of the dam site. Some of this granite, which forms the walls of the dam site in Xiling Gorge, is 819 million years old. As discussed below, this time frame corresponds to the arrival of a *mantle plume*. The formation of the granite may have occurred in the context of this mantle plume, which is thought to have broken up the supercontinent of Rodinia. Some of the rocks that are very old, rocks that are visible in the walls of the gorges in the vicinity of the Huangling Anticline, form layers of the Nantuo Formation and Liantuo Formation. Near the Three Gorges, the 819-million-year-old rocks are immediately below the roughly 748-million-year-old layers of the Liantuo Formation. An unconformity exists between the Liantuo Formation and the underlying rocks that are about 819 million years old. A disconformity exists above the Liantuo Formation and below the Doushantuo Formation, which is above the Liantuo Formation. Rodinia was breaking up between 820 and 748–750 million years ago, and this was accompanied by complex processes. A mantle plume probably produced granite intrusions in some places, but the events were quite complex and chaotic.

If any layers of sediments were deposited during the Jurassic period on the parts of the Huangling Dome that the Yangtze flows through, they have been largely eroded. The Yangtze River cut through the area in and around the Huangling Dome in the last 1.18–2.2 million years. The erosional patterns around the Three Gorges are very intricate, given that the area is, more or less, the beginnings of a mountain range. A more detailed discussion, from a geographical and geomorphological standpoint, of the erosional patterns around the Gorges would be excessively complex and potentially confusing.

BROADER CONTEXT OF THE DOMING AND VOLCANIC ACTIVITY

During the time that Rodinia began to break up, both southern China and a broader region were subjected to so-called *anorogenic uplift*. Beginning around 840 million years ago, a mantle plume began to cause vast portions of the continental lithosphere to be pushed upward in a dome-like shape. This doming of the region is thought to have been caused, as discussed below, by the arrival of a mantle plume. Scientists think that this plume also caused the Neoproterozoic volcanic activity and rifting in southern China.

In portions of the Gorges, visible layers of both volcanic and granite rocks are thought to have once been deposited, a long time ago, as a result of a mantle plume. Between 840 and 828 million years ago, researchers think this mantle plume had still not broken through the *lower mantle* but nevertheless began producing dome-shaped deformations of the crust. This "doming" occurred along two sides of the plume, much as water from a hose would splash out in two directions as it hit, for example, a concrete wall. The plume then broke into the *mantle lithosphere* and the crust and, between 825 million and 819 million years ago, caused so-called granite intrusions to be pushed into the lithosphere. Scientists first thought that these granite intrusions, which are apparent in portions of the Gorges and the surrounding region, were folded or pushed upward by more run-of-the-mill orogenic processes.

Researchers think that the arrival of this mantle plume eventually led to a more widespread *upwelling* of the mantle, a so-called superswell, that caused Rodinia to break up. In the breakup of Rodinia, south China separated from Australia and Laurentia. As the mantle plume broke through from the more liquidlike lower mantle into the more viscous upper mantle, the mantle began producing uplift and extensional rifting of several portions of Rodinia. A group of researchers has estimated that the mantle plume beneath southern China may have been up to 3,728 miles (6,000 km) in diameter, and large portions of the rocks of the continental plate were melted by the heat of the plume. Thus, the plume changed large portions of the topography by a number of mechanisms.

In the vicinity of the Gorges, the first of two periods of volcanic eruptions began at around the same time that the mantle plume arrived and the rifting began. The first period of volcanism occurred between 830 and 795 million years ago. During this interval, the volcanic activity was most intense at the 820-million-year time point. The rifting also began at almost exactly the same time point. As discussed above, the mantle plume was also breaking through parts of the mantle lithosphere at this time.

A second period of volcanic eruptions occurred between 780 and 745 million years ago, and rifting continued throughout this period. Scientists think the 15-million-year "hiatus," or break, in the volcanic activity may have been the result of the moving of a single superplume from one place to another, but no one is absolutely certain of the reason.

Several different types of *lava* were deposited during this volcanic activity, and scientists have had difficulty distinguishing between different eruptions. The layers of lava that are visible in the walls of the Three Gorges were not always deposited in neat, distinct layers. Scientists think that different types of lava may have been remelted and mixed together at times, and this can complicate the process of dating the lava. Some of the layers of lava are flood basalts, which are freely flowing and highly liquefied forms of lava. Unlike the walls of the Columbia River Gorge, which are of mostly *flood basalt lava*, the walls of the Three Gorges reveal that flood basalt eruptions only occurred intermittently and on a smaller scale.

Although much of the rock in the Three Gorges is limestone, some portions of the Gorges expose rocks that are on the order of 3 billion years old. These are gneissic rocks and are the oldest rocks that are known to be part of the Yangtze Craton (part of the South China Block). In the vicinities of the towns of Shennong and Huangling, portions of 2.9-billion-year-old gneissic and 2.9–3.3-billion-year-old paragneissic rocks are exposed.

Other layers of rock exposed in the walls of the Gorges are very old marine and glacial sediments, which provide a record of the movement of the Yangtze Craton over the last billion years. The area of land that is occupied by the Gorges was at tropical or subtropical latitudes during one or more ice ages, and this helps to explain the exposed layers of marine sediments and fossils. At first glance, scientists noted that the sediment layers were consistent with *lacustrine* sediments, which would have been deposited at the bottom of a stagnant lake or inland body of water. It is now apparent, however, that thick layers of sediments were deposited when the Three Gorges region was a tidal, marine environment. In the walls of the Gorges, for example, researchers have found geological evidence that thick "microbial mats" covered the region around 500 million years ago.

Some of these marine sediments, which are now sedimentary rock layers, are comparable to the marine sediments found in portions of Australia (see chapter 5). More specifically, there is evidence that some of the same species of small marine organisms were present in both the Three Gorges region and Australia. Some of the layers of sedimentary rock that comprise the Doushantuo Formation, specifically, are visible in the Three Gorges. The layers of this formation are similar to the sedimentary rocks that comprise the Peritataka Formation, found in Australia. This is not surprising, given that, between the interval of at least 748 million years ago until 400 million years ago, both Australia and parts of the South China Block were at equatorial or subtropical latitudes.

INCISION OF THE THREE GORGES

The Yangtze began cutting out the Three Gorges between 1.8 and 1.16 million years ago, a process which has occurred in distinct stages but has still been fairly consistent. The walls of the Three Gorges are roughly V-shaped cliffs and were cut by the Yangtze during periods of tectonic uplift. In the area in and around the Gorges, however, there are multiple layers of older and more gently sloped portions of the river valley. Some of the highest landforms that surround the Gorges appear as mountains. Some of the highest elevations around the Three Gorges were shaped by fluvial erosion and the deposition of alluvial sediments. Some of the alluvial sediments on these high elevations were deposited during the middle and late portions of the *Tertiary period*. At this time, the overall drainage network of the Yangtze did not exist. Thus, the highest elevations around the Three Gorges cannot be regarded as being part of the Yangtze River valley.

In and around the Gorges, these high elevations can be divided into two layers of rolling highlands and flattened plateaus. These flattened layers, which were formed during the middle and late portions of the Tertiary period, surround the Three Gorges and slope downward to the Yangtze Valley. These planation surfaces were formed when there was relatively little tectonic uplift. The elevations of the planation surfaces are also above the elevations of the highest points in the Three Gorges.

The highest elevations of the walls of the Three Gorges are about 1,969 feet (600 m) to 2,297 feet (700 m) above the bottom of the Yangtze River channel. Above the upper portions of the actual gorge walls are the erosional surfaces and the planation surfaces.

Various *karst* platforms and erosional surfaces exist between about 2,625 feet (800 m) and 3,937 feet (1,200 m) above the floor of the river channel. Some of the karst platforms are lower, at about 2,297 feet and are at the highest points on the actual walls of the gorges.

The lower of the two planation surfaces varies between 3,937 feet and 4,922 feet (1,500 m) above the floor of the Yangtze. These are mountains that are set back from the Gorges. The lower planation surface was formed between 3.6 and 3.4 million years ago.

The upper planation surface, known as the Exi surface, was formed during the middle or late portions of the Tertiary period, which spanned the interval between 23.7 and 66.4 million years ago. This is essentially the time frame, which was probably closer to 23.7 million years ago than 66.4 million years ago, at which drainage pathways deposited the sediments. The upper planation surfaces are between 5,906 feet (1,800 m) and 6,562 feet (2,000 m) above the floor of the Yangtze River. The planation surfaces could be seen from a low-flying airplane but might not be apparent from a lower vantage point.

TERRACES AND CLIFFS IN THE WALLS OF THE GORGES

In portions of the Three Gorges and the surrounding Yangtze Valley, the Yangtze has carved out seven well-defined terraces. These alluvial terraces sometimes take the place of the V-shaped cliffs in some stretches of the Gorges. The terraces can also be found upstream and downstream of the Gorges. The steepest cliffs in the Gorges were cut out of resistant rocks that are not easily weakened or eroded by weathering. In contrast,

The Yangtze River flows through the Three Gorges, with the walls displaying a V-shaped channel profile. *(Taolmor/ ShutterStock, Inc.)*

the terraces consist of less *resistant* rock that was eroded in stages and also underwent periodic rock slides. Thus, the seven terraces were cut by the Yangtze during the same time period as the steepest portions of the Gorges.

The steeper portions of the seven terracelike structures are V-shaped and are as steep as the continuous, V-shaped cliffs. The steeper slopes were formed when tectonic uplift was significant and caused the Yangtze to cut downward rapidly. The portions of the terraces that are more sloping and are U-shaped were formed when the tectonic uplift was less pronounced. The steepest cliffs are composed of resistant rock and were not eroded during these "low-uplift" intervals of time. Thus, the steepest cliffs were still cut out by seven phases of uplift but do not have distinct, U-shaped portions of rock.

At the top of the V-shaped walls of the Gorges, in some parts, caves and flat portions of land exist. Some of the layers of rocks and sediments on these flat portions of land, which are not really parts of the incised walls of the Gorges, were deposited between 1.8 and 2.01 or 2.37 million years ago. Thus, the actual V-shaped walls were incised after these layers were deposited by, for example, rivers or streams.

THE TIBETAN PLATEAU AND THE PATH OF THE YANGTZE RIVER

There is evidence that the exhumation and uplift of the Tibetan Plateau played a major role in guiding the path of the Yangtze River. The crust of the eastern portion of the Tibetan Plateau, which is up-drainage of the Sichuan Basin, was thickened in response to the formation of the Himalayas. The Tibetan Plateau cooled gradually, between 100 and about 20 million years ago, and then cooled more rapidly. As the plateau began to cool more quickly, at about 13 million years ago, canyons and gorges began to be incised out of the plateau. During the interval between 13 and 9 million years ago, these gorges and canyons were carved by rivers, out of the eastern margin of the Tibetan Plateau. A similar phase of incision occurred in parts of the Sichuan Basin, between 12 and 5 million years ago. Essentially, the incision process was the erosional exhumation of the Tibetan Plateau. As a result of this erosion and incision, the Tibetan Plateau was subjected to significant isostatic uplift. Portions of the Sichuan Basin were also subjected to this isostatic uplift, a response to exhumation. The incision and uplift that occurred in the Sichuan Basin, between 12 and 5 million years ago, preceded the incision of the Three Gorges.

The isostatic uplift of the Tibetan Plateau and parts of the Sichuan Basin that are upstream of the Three Gorges is thought to have helped intensify the East Asian monsoonal pattern. This seasonal rainfall

CRUSTAL THICKENING, LITHOSPHERIC THICKENING, AND UPLIFT OF PLATEAUS

The thickening of the eastern, and southeastern, portion of the Tibetan Plateau is thought to have resulted from the injection, or transfer, of crustal material from the west and also the north. This explanation is partially based on data about the ages of crustal material at different depths, beneath the surface of the southeastern Tibetan Plateau. More generally, however, there is the absence of evidence of recently created folds and deformations of the rocks in the southeastern plateau. The crust can be thickened by orogenic processes that fold and deform the rock layers, much as the front end of a car can be crumpled upward after a fender-bending accident. The southeastern Tibetan Plateau is not perfectly flat, but the surface irregularities were not created recently enough, and were not extensive enough, to account for the relatively recent uplift.

This uplift by crustal thickening, in the absence of crustal shortening by crumpling, may also have contributed to the uplift of the Colorado Plateau. This aspect of the Colorado Plateau is discussed in chapters 1 and 7. Moreover, researchers noted the similarities between the geological histories of the Colorado Plateau and the eastern Tibetan Plateau.

Interestingly, scientists noted that the Eastern expansion of the Tibetan Plateau, expansion that elevated the eastern/southeastern plateau, may have produced important climate changes. Researchers suggested that the high elevations in the eastern plateau may have intensified both the extent and seasonality of the precipitation in the Sichuan Basin. The increase in rainfall was suggested to have been partially the result of an *orographic* effect of the plateau. This effect, which would have increased the delivery of sediment-laden water to the Sichuan Basin, is thought to have contributed to incision on the Tibetan Plateau and in the Sichuan Basin. This rainfall is also thought to have become more seasonal. The East Asian and Indian monsoonal patterns began to intensify about 8.5 million years ago, shortly after some of the uplift occurred.

Part of this effect can be viewed as an eastward shift of the rainshadow. In the present day, the annual rainfall varies inversely with elevation on the Tibetan Plateau. This means that the highest elevations receive the least rainfall, and rainfall decreases as elevation increases. It is not clear if the Three Gorges are being influenced by any supposed *rainshadow effect* of the plateau, at least in the present day. When the eastern Tibetan Plateau was receiving more rain, however, the water is thought to have contributed to the incision, east of the plateau, of canyons and gorges.

pattern began to become well established about 8.5 million years ago, partially in response to the erosional exhumation and uplift of the Tibetan Plateau.

CHANGING THE DIRECTION OF THE MIDDLE YANGTZE

The Yangtze River also reversed direction during the interval between 30 and 10 million years ago, corresponding to the late *Oligocene epoch* and the first half of the *Miocene epoch*. This event is thought to have been driven by activity along the eastern margin of the Sichuan Basin, along the Yalong Belt and perhaps the Longmen Shan Belt. The reversal of the path of the Yangtze occurred in the vicinity of the so-called first bend, at which the river shifts from a southeast to northeast direction of flow. The portion of the Yangtze that extends downstream from the first bend to the end of the Three Gorges is known as the Middle Yangtze. The shift in direction helped set the stage for the incision of the Three Gorges, which began about 1.8 million years ago.

The Three Gorges may have been preserved by the existence of the East Asian monsoonal system, but the Sichuan and Jianghan Basins are not part of a semiarid climate. The climate in the headwaters of the Yangtze River, on the Tibetan Plateau, is, however, arid or semiarid. This may have somehow helped to preserve the Gorges, since the time of their incision. The terraces on the Three Gorges are generally rich in vegetation, a factor that could help prevent landslides. The rock layers may also be resistant enough to limit erosion by rainwater or the like.

RECENT HISTORY OF CLIMATE CHANGES

The climate in the Three Gorges area appears to have become more arid around the beginning of the *Quaternary period*, and this may have helped limit erosion of the developing Gorges. The climate in central China was very hot and humid in the late *Neogene age*, which corresponds to the interval of 5.3 to 1.6 million years ago. During this interval of time, the Yangtze drainage basin received 43.3 inches (1,100 mm) of rain per year. This heat and moisture was favorable for processes of chemical weathering and, hence, unfavorable for canyon formation and preservation. If a given layer of rock has a low content of calcium carbonate, for example, scientists can conclude that more of the mineral, as in limestone, was dissolved and washed away by moving water.

Over the last 1.6 million years, as the Three Gorges were actually being incised by the Yangtze, the climate changed in ways that were favorable to canyon formation. Beginning at about 1.6 million years ago, from the beginning to the middle of the Quaternary period, the climate gradually became cooler and more arid. The effects of weathering are known to have decreased during this period. The climate in central China has been influenced for a long time by the path and intensity of the so-called East Asian summer monsoon, a wind pattern that brings increases in summer rainfall to certain areas. This highly seasonal pattern of rainfall may, as discussed in the sidebar on page 62, have been favorable to the formation and preservation of the Gorges.

EFFECTS OF VEGETATION

Seasonal rainfall and drainage may also influence canyon formation by interacting with plants and vegetation on the walls of a canyon. Although

SEASONAL RAINFALL, RIVER CHANNELS, AND DESERT FORMATION

One factor that may limit erosion of newly formed canyon walls is an increase in the seasonality of rainfall and the drainage of rainwater by a river. Scientists have noted that a trend toward more seasonal patterns of rainfall can favor incision by a river. More interestingly, researchers have hypothesized that the presence of incised channels and steep-walled river valleys can actually contribute to seasonality of rainfall patterns. In the context of the increasingly arid climate of modern-day Israel, for example, scientists have suggested that this sort of interplay is promoting the "desertification" of Israel.

Although Israel is on the western coast of a large body of seawater and is geographically more analogous to a subtropical desert, as is discussed in chapter 8, other canyons that are in semiarid regions appear to have been formed or maintained as the climate became more seasonal. This seasonality can, generally speaking, allow gorges and canyons to be maintained during periods of humid weather and fairly high annual rainfall.

Thus, an increase in the seasonality of precipitation can allow a canyon to be minimally eroded in a climate that is not a true desert. Essentially, the presence of sharply defined channels and gullies can efficiently shuttle water and sediments away. If the channels were not present, the river would expand outward, or laterally, as in a floodplain. As the river slowly drained the floodplain, the river valley or would-be-canyon walls would tend to become sloped and eroded down. The rainfall in the Three Gorges area is seasonal and is influenced by a monsoonal system, but it is not clear that this monsoonal pattern has contributed to the incision or preservation of the gorges.

the climate in the area of the Gorges has often been humid, thick vegetation can actually help to limit weathering. Vegetation on the walls of a canyon can buffer the erosive effects of water and sediments, but sediments and water can also gradually wash or wear away the vegetation on steep cliffs. Thus, a humid and tropical climate can sometimes be a neutral force in canyon formation. A canyon might not be able to develop easily in a subtropical climate, but vegetation might also prevent millions of years of sedimentary rocks from being washed away.

Although the steepest cliffs of the Three Gorges are often bare of vegetation, the foliage can be remarkably dense on very steep portions of the Three Gorges. The vegetation was much more dense at the times that the climate was more hot and humid, especially during the roughly 5-million-year interval before the Gorges were formed. This vegetation may have buffered the effects of rainfall on the lateral erosion, the planing or side-to-side erosion, on the banks of the Yangtze.

KARST FORMATIONS AND THE THREE GORGES RESERVOIR

The construction of the Three Gorges Dam began as early as 1993, and the completed dam will provide numerous beneficial effects. The dam is 1.43 miles (2.3 km) long, 276 feet (84 m) wide, and 607 feet (185 m) high. The movement of water through the dam will provide very large amounts of hydroelectrical power, and this electricity will help to modernize the conditions under which people, in the vicinity of the dam, live and work. The dam will help workers to prevent future floods, particularly floods that have been destructive to the flat land, downstream of the dam, that surrounds the Yangtze River delta. The dam will also allow water to be transferred to sites at which the demand for water, for irrigation or other purposes, is not being met. Additionally, larger ships will be able to transport their cargos from the ocean to cities as far upstream as Chongquing. The locks at the dam site are already able to provide transport for some ships. The reservoir will be filled to the final depth, as discussed in the subsequent section, by 2009.

Karsts and karstlike caves are fairly abundant in the walls of the Three Gorges, and engineers have to consider the potential for karsts to weaken the walls of the Gorges. Some of the karst caverns are in the lower parts of the walls of the Gorges, but most karst features have been eroded from relatively high sections of the walls.

Most of the public discussion of the Three Gorges Dam project has been centered around the structural stability of the dam itself and the environmental consequences of landslides. Sediments will also accumulate upstream of the dam site. Researchers are concerned that the dam will not be able to regulate the transport of these sediments through the dam site. Farmland and homes have been moved to some of the steep *hillslopes* that are between the gorges, such as on the lower planation surface. Agricultural developments on these slopes may trigger landslides or deliver massive amounts of sediments into the reservoir. That said, researchers have mapped out the portions of land that are most vulnerable to landslides. Engineers have also used complex mathematics to model the volumes and structural stability of karst formations in the vicinity of the Gorges.

From a structural standpoint, karst formations, in the walls of a gorge, can be analogous to holes or *fissures* in a concrete wall. Significant numbers of karst formations exist in the upper portions of the walls of the Three Gorges, and these formations may be eroded or submerged as the Three Gorges Reservoir causes the Yangtze to rise. The karst formations in the upper portions of the walls may, for example, be submerged along the more downstream portions of the Gorges. Along these portions, the walls are not especially high.

GEOLOGICAL EFFECTS OF THE RESERVOIR

When the Three Gorges Reservoir has filled completely, in 2009, between 1 million and 1.9 million people will have to vacate the land that is near the Yangtze River. The reservoir will be about 574 feet (175 m) deep and will extend along 373 miles (600 km) of the Yangtze and its tributaries. Researchers estimate that the weight of the water will ultimately cause localized, crustal subsidence of 1.59–1.90 inches (40.1–48.3 mm). This means that the entire crust beneath the reservoir will be pushed downward by up to 1.90 inches. This crustal subsidence will be maximal at the points that are just upstream of the dam site.

The mass of the water will produce a localized gravity anomaly and may also modify the tilt of the Earth. The network of satellites that comprise the Global Positioning System—satellites that would provide positional data to someone standing on the Three Gorges Dam—will have to be adjusted to compensate for these changes. The potential for the reservoir to modify the tilt of the Earth is remarkable. Researchers have, for example, been concerned, in the context of predicting the extent of crustal subsidence, that only the changes in "Newtonian" gravity are being taken into account.

The weight of water may very well trigger some relatively small earthquakes, and the earthquakes may trigger landslides. The dam has been designed to withstand an earthquake of 7.0 on the Richter scale. The earthquakes that have occurred in the area, at least in recent decades, have all been less than or equal to magnitude 6.0. Nonetheless, researchers are concerned that larger earthquakes might occur. Dams have been known to survive major earthquakes with nothing more than cracks, but earthquakes in the Three Gorges area could trigger landslides.

Peonera Canyon

Aragón Province, Northeastern Spain

Peonera Canyon is in northern Spain, at the southern edge of the Spanish Pyrenees. The canyon was formed by the Alcanadre River, a *tributary* of the Ebro River, which flows south and drains a portion of the Pyrenees. The Alcanadre River and several other rivers follow roughly parallel courses, and some of these rivers have carved out a variety of unusual canyons. Peonera Canyon and its neighboring canyons were cut out of layers of *sediments* that built up in a portion of the External Sierras. These are relatively young thrust belts that are immediately north of the Ebro Basin, a depression of land that is adjacent to the Pyrenees. The *incision* of the walls of the canyon probably began to occur, based on the earliest estimates, about 5 or 6 million years ago. This corresponds to the late *Miocene epoch* and the early *Pliocene epoch*. The incision appears to have been driven by the opening of the Ebro Basin to the Mediterranean, by climate changes and by a relatively recent phase of erosion in the southern Pyrenees.

In this portion of Spain, several geological events are likely to have contributed to canyon formation. Peonera Canyon was cut out of *sedimentary rocks* that accumulated along the upstream margin of a *foreland basin*. The Ebro Basin, a foreland basin, is a portion of rock that was pushed downward as the Pyrenees were being raised upward by *plate* convergence. The rivers that drained the Pyrenees then deposited sediments in the Ebro Basin. After the formation of the Pyrenees, which are still a relatively young mountain range, the *uplift* of the Ebro Basin helped the rivers to rapidly cut downward and form canyons.

In the map on page 66, Peonera Canyon is shown to be located on the northern margin of the Ebro Foreland Basin. Some of the *Eocene*-age rock layers still exist, in bands that extend from east to west, to the north of the margin of the Ebro Basin. Peonera Canyon is located in this landscape, a terrain that is part mountain range and part sedimentary basin. Layers of sedimentary rocks have been eroded and deformed, in a chaotic

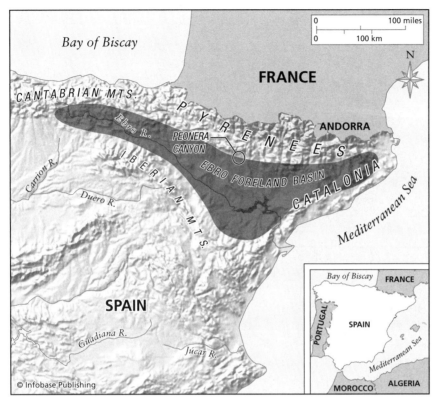

This map shows the margins of the Ebro Foreland Basin and Peonera Canyon, located on the northern margin of the basin.

manner, in and among the small mountains of the Sierra de Guara and External Sierras. Some of the sedimentary rocks that are south of the External Sierras and Sierra de Guara were deposited as alluvial fan sediments. This terrain extends along a thin band that follows the northern margin of the Ebro Basin.

The Ebro Basin was subsequently closed off from the Atlantic Ocean and the Mediterranean Sea, and this prevented the movement of water and sediments out of the basin. *Tectonic* events caused the Ebro Basin to become an endoreic basin, meaning that the drainage of the basin was cut off from the ocean. Rivers continued to deliver water and sediments into the basin, but no water or sediments were carried by rivers from the basin to the ocean. This type of basin can generally only exist in an arid or semiarid climate. During the time that the Ebro Basin was closed off, however, the climate may not have been consistently arid.

The proximity of the Alcanadre River and its neighboring rivers to the main drainage divide of the Pyrenees is also likely to have helped canyons form. This divide, an imaginary line that extends from across the Pyrenees, is a line of high elevation that determines the paths of drainage from the mountains. This is analogous to the Continental Divide in the United States. On the western side of the Continental Divide, rivers flow west to the Pacific. On the eastern side of the Divide, rivers either flow to the east or roughly to the south. A drainage divide does not necessarily follow a simple line. The drainage divide may wind around. The drainage divide in the southern Pyrenees is not really oriented along a line that is parallel to the east-west thrust fronts, in part because the Pyrenees were formed along two major thrust axes. This is not especially relevant, however. It is only relevant that the canyon is downstream of a nearby mountain range, which has provided an input of sediment-laden water, and upstream of lower elevations, which serve as an outlet and allow sediments to be flushed downstream.

As the Alcanadre flows downward, out of the mountains, it first flows southward and then follows a southeasterly course. It joins the Ebro River after following this southeasterly course for a short distance. The Ebro River then flows, along a path that is roughly southeast, into the Mediterranean.

Peonera Canyon and the Ebro Basin are at the northern edge of a region that now has a semiarid climate, and this helped to minimize weathering of the canyon. The Atlantic, southern Mediterranean, and southeastern Mediterranean coasts of Spain are widely recognized as being coastal areas that are low in rainfall. However, the climate around Peonera Canyon is also semiarid or arid. Portions of the central Ebro Basin receive less than 12–14 inches (30–36 cm) of rain per year, making the climate not much wetter than some desertlike climates. Some factors that contribute to this climate are the jet stream, which limits precipitation in the winter months, and a *rainshadow*, or *orographic*, effect of the Iberian Mountain range, which occupies the southern edge of the Ebro Basin. Some aspects of the weather also interfere with the growth of plants and trees, and the sparse vegetation prevents the ground from holding moisture.

Peonera Canyon is one of more than 80 canyons in the Sierra and Canyons de Guara Natural Park, a destination for climbers and "extreme tourists." People with climbing experience have visited Peonera Canyon and other canyons in this park on canyoneering, or canyoning, trips. Many of the canyons in the region are very narrow and difficult to access, even for those with the requisite climbing equipment.

EARLY HISTORY OF NORTHEASTERN SPAIN

One of the earliest events in the history of northern Spain was the Variscan *orogenic* cycle, resulting from the collision between Laurentia and Gondwana. Some of the mountains that were formed during this collision are still apparent in northern and northwestern Spain.

After this collision and mountain-building period, rifting and other extensional processes began to occur along the northern portion of the Iberian Peninsula. During the late *Permian period* and early *Triassic period*, around 245 million years ago, a period of *rifting* created rift-associated basins in the land that is now northeastern Spain. Next, during the *Mesozoic era*, crustal extension and rifting formed the Basque-Cantabrian Basin and resulted in the formation of the north Atlantic Ocean and Bay of Biscay.

FORMATION OF THE PYRENEAN RANGE AND EBRO BASIN

The Iberian plate, of which Spain is now a part, was pushed into and under the European plate at about 66 million years ago. The South Pyrenean Thrust Belt is the band that is north of the Ebro Basin and south of the *Axial Zone*. The Pyrenees were formed along an axis that generally extends from west to east, but the mountains were actually formed along two axes. One axis extends in a direction that is slightly northwest to southeast, and the other axis extends from the southwest to the northeast. The two axes intersect and intermingle with each another in the vicinity of the eastern Ebro Basin. This corresponds to the southernmost limit of the arc-shaped Axial Zone. The arclike, or arcuate, shape of the axial zone is reflected in the bowlike shape of the northern margin of the Ebro Basin. The approximate margins of the Ebro Foreland Basin, which is shaped like a flattened triangle, are apparent in the diagram on page 66.

The Alcanadre River, which flows through Peonera Canyon, originates in land that is south of the Axial Zone and flows south to join the Ebro River. To the west of the Alcanadre River are the External Sierras, or the Sierra Exteriores. The Sierra Marginales are to the east of the Alcanadre River. Both of these ranges extend, essentially, from east to west and are located to the north of the northern margin of the Ebro Basin. These Sierras—the word translates to mean "mountains"—are the portions of land on which the thickest layers of sedimentary rock still remain. They are like a cross between a mountain and a plateau. In some parts of the Ebro Basin, during the time that the basin was endoreic, up to 16,405 feet (5,000 m) of sediments were originally present. In other parts, only about 1,969 feet (600 m) of sediments accumulated.

Before the Alcanadre River flows out of the south-central Pyrenees and enters the Ebro Basin, the river flows between two *anticlines*. These are mountains in the southern portion of the Pyrenees. The Balces Anticline is to the east of the Alcanadre River, and the Arangol Anticline is west of the Alcanadre River. The Boltana Thrust Sheet is northeast of the Balces Anticline, and the Barbastro Thrust Sheet is located to the east of the Balces Anticline. These thrust sheets are both east of the Alcanadre River.

The actual formation of the South Pyrenean Thrust Belt began about 55 million years ago and continued until 25 million years ago, which corresponds to part of the *Oligocene epoch*. The initial phase of the orogenic process was especially rapid and occurred between 55 and 47 million years ago. The erosion, or denudation, of the southern Pyrenees began about 40 million years ago and is still continuing, at least to some extent. The denudation was most intense—and was responsible for the most significant net delivery of sediments into the Ebro Basin—between 40 million years ago and about 25 million years ago. The process of denudation of a mountain range, a process that has also been referred to as excavation, is essentially equivalent to *erosional exhumation*. For complex reasons that have to do with the thickness of the *crust* beneath mountain ranges, the erosional exhumation of a mountain range is not always accompanied by *isostatic uplift*. For the sake of discussion, however, it is only necessary to note that the exhumation of the Pyrenees provided a source of sediment-laden water.

Other orogenic basins were formed, together with the Ebro Basin, along the southern portion of the Pyrenees. This overall group of basins, of which the Ebro Basin is one, is known as the South Pyrenean Basin.

Between 60 and about 13.5 million years ago, many of the rivers that drained into the Ebro Basin did not also drain into the Mediterranean. This allowed sediments to accumulate at the floors of inland lakes. A river that ends at an inland lake or other inland point is known as an endoreic, or endorheic, river. Similarly, the Ebro Basin did not provide a drainage outlet to the Mediterranean for many millions of years and was therefore considered to be an endoreic basin. As such, the Ebro Basin was covered by a very large lake for long periods of time. The Ebro Basin was essentially a fairly flat, triangularly shaped bowl that accumulated drainage water and was bounded by mountains on three sides. Rivers carried sediments from the mountains, and these sediments accumulated on the bottoms of the lakes in the basin.

When the lakes in the Ebro Basin began to "break through" the coastal mountain range and drain into the Mediterranean, these *lacustrine* sediments were up to 1.2 miles (2 km) thick. This drainage into the Mediterranean occurred during the middle and late portions of the Miocene epoch, between 13.5 and 5.3 million years ago. When the water in these lakes began to drain, many of the lakes ceased to exist. The Ebro Basin ceased to be an endoreic basin at this point, and the Ebro River also ceased to be an endoreic river. The Ebro and other rivers simply flowed over the dry lake beds, which had accumulated layers of sedimentary rock. The lacustrine sediments had been converted, by pressure and other forces, into sedimentary rocks.

RELATIVE ELEVATION OF THE EBRO BASIN

Although the Ebro Basin is at lower elevations than the Pyrenees, portions of the basin are still fairly high above sea level. The Ebro Basin is also bounded by mountains on two of its borders. Orogenic processes created the basin, thereby allowing the basin to accumulate sediments from rivers that drained the mountain ranges.

It is, again, important to note that the Ebro Basin is essentially a basin that is underneath a kind of plateau. The Ebro Basin began as a foreland basin that accumulated sedimentary rocks and became a sedimentary basin. Most of the canyons in this book have been cut out of very thick sediments that are layered above an orogenic basin, a forearc basin, or a backarc basin. Roughly 6,300 feet (1,920 m) of sediments have accumulated, in many parts of the basin, to create a quasi-plateau. The Ebro Basin is not commonly viewed as a plateau, but it is helpful to think of the basin in the context of familiar terms. The layers of sedimentary rock sit atop the depression of rock that determined the original margins of the Ebro Foreland Basin. Multiple rivers then incised through the sedimentary rock layers that had built up in the basin.

RIVER FLOW AND THE VALENCIA TROUGH

Another factor that may have contributed to the downward incision of rivers was the presence of the low-lying Valencia Trough, into which the Ebro River drains and which is now submerged by the Mediterranean. The Valencia Trough was formed as a result of extensional *fault activity*, which occurred after the Pyrenean and Iberian Ranges had stopped forming.

At about 24.7 million years ago, during the late Oligocene epoch, the formation of the Pyrenees was ending and the offshore, extensional fault activity was beginning. The extensional process that created the Valencia Trough occurred during the period of 23.5 and 8 million years ago. This extension occurred along the same axis, a line extending from the southwest to northeast, that the uplift in the Catalan Coastal Range occurred along. There appear to have been some interactions between the two processes. The southeastern portion of the Ebro Basin was subjected to some uplift by this process, but the roughly 3,281 feet (1,000 m) of uplift was mainly confined to the Catalan Coastal Range. This served to keep the southwestern margin of the Ebro Basin closed off from the Mediterranean.

The effects of this offshore extension in the Mediterranean were complex. The extension appears to have contributed to the incisional potency of the Ebro River and its tributaries, after the Ebro Basin was opened to the Mediterranean. This augmentation of incision would have been driven by the deepening of the Valencia Trough, a deepening process that served to increase the relative elevation of the Ebro Basin. Before the basin opened to the Mediterranean, the extension appears to have facilitated the drainage of rivers into the lake that covered parts of the Ebro Basin. This extra input of sediment-laden water would not have occurred along the northern margin of the Ebro Basin, but the northern margin of the basin was still influenced by the coastal uplift. The uplift of the Catalan Coastal Range would have allowed the lake, covering parts of the Ebro Basin, to remain deep for a longer time interval. This could have helped to ensure lacustrine sediment deposition along the northern margin of the Ebro Basin.

FLEXURAL UPLIFT AND INTERMONTANE BASINS

Flexural uplift is a process by which a fairly flat portion of rock is lifted or pushed upward, thereby allowing the rock to be distorted but not folded or broken. Geologists sometimes model this uplift, using mathematics, by treating the portion of rock as if it was two-dimensional. The rock below the Ebro Basin, for example, moved as if it were a flat piece of paper that could be rounded or distorted. Instead of crumpling, like a piece of paper, or cracking, like a piece of stale bread, the rock beneath the Ebro basin flexed upward. The uplift is thought to have been partially driven by the isostatic rebounding effect, which is isostatic uplift. This is a type of passive uplift that results from erosional exhumation, which is the erosion of sediments from a large, relatively uniform portion of land. Flexural uplift, in an intermontane basin, also may have an active component to it. Any active component, however, would probably not have been comparable to the active uplift to which the Colorado Plateau was subjected.

As this uplift occurred, the Ebro Basin was still much lower than the Pyrenees but was being raised above the Valencia Trough. During this interval of time, the Ebro Basin was still accumulating *alluvial sediments,* was lower than the Pyrenean and Iberian Ranges, and was being lifted higher above the Valencia Trough. When the extensional activity began forming the Valencia Trough, which is oriented roughly north-south, the Ebro Basin was roughly triangular-shaped. The Ebro Basin was therefore an orogenic, intermontane—or intermountain—basin that was and is between two mountain ranges. The two mountain ranges helped, to a large extent, to "lock in" the two longest sides of the wedge-shaped Ebro Basin.

For a long time, the compressive forces that were lifting the Iberian and Pyrenean Ranges were driving the downward *subsidence* of the Ebro Basin. Rather than being compacted in on itself, the Ebro Basin was accumulating sediments from two input sources. For a time, the Ebro Basin underwent subsidence. Researchers sometimes refer to flexural subsidence in the context of an intermontane basin. As with flexural uplift, the subsidence can be largely passive. The flexing of the rock layers occurs because of the unique effects of the two mountain ranges, on either side of the basin, on isostatic responses beneath the basin. Instead of bobbing straight up or sinking straight down, the rocks beneath the Ebro Basin flexed.

As the Pyrenean and Iberian Ranges stopped forming, fault activity helped to raised the elevations of the Coastal Catalan Range. However, extensional fault activity also occurred in the vicinity of the Valencia Trough. This extension served to deepen the trough and may have helped to intensify the erosional exhumation, of the sedimentary rocks in the Ebro Basin, the uplift of the basin, and the incision of gorges in the External Sierras.

INTERACTIONS OF CLIMATE CHANGES AND TECTONIC FORCES

The Ebro Basin was covered by a lake for about 25 million years, during the time that the basin was endoreic. The climate in northeastern Spain was arid between 33.7 and 28.5 million years ago, during the early portion of the Oligocene epoch, and this climate is thought to have helped the lake develop. The rivers from the mountain ranges supplied the input of water to the closed-off Ebro Basin, and the arid climate helped ensure that the lake level did not rise too high. Periodic rises in the water levels in the lake are thought to have ultimately opened the Ebro Basin to the Mediterranean. The climate became wetter during the Miocene epoch. The climate is known to have been quite wet at 9.4 million years ago, and this is thought to have contributed to lake level rises. The preservation of an endoreic lake in the Ebro Basin helped to set the stage for canyon formation. Many of the sedimentary rock layers that exist in the Ebro Basin and the External Sierras were deposited under these lacustrine conditions.

The climate of the Ebro Basin and northeastern Spain has been somewhat inconsistent over the last 20,000 years. Even since the last period of glaciation, the so-called last glacial maximum, the humidity level has increased and decreased across several cycles. Shortly after the end of the last glacial maximum, between 18,000 and 15,000 years ago, the climate of northeastern Spain was warm and humid. Between 14,600 and 12,400 years ago, there is evidence that the climate became cooler and drier and showed more seasonal patterns of precipitation. Beginning at 12,230 years ago, the climate is thought to have again become cool and humid.

Scientists have used a number of techniques to piece together the climatological history around northeastern Spain, and an overall picture has only emerged from multiple snapshots. One approach that scientists use to monitor climate changes is to drill into a dry lake bed with a hollow drillbit and extract a cylindrical core of sedimentary layers. Scientists can then separate the rock from small portions of organic pollen and other plant fossils. By analyzing the age of the pollen fragments or the minerals surrounding them, scientists can draw conclusions about the types and amounts of vegetation that were present. Geologists can also analyze the fossilized imprints of trees or plants.

ALLUVIAL FANS, IMMATURE DRAINAGE, AND DENUDATION OF THE PYRENEES

The present-day paths of the Alcanadre and its neighboring rivers appear to have been dictated by the Pyrenean Orogeny. These rivers drain the Pyrenees and, generally, enter the Ebro Basin from the north. As the rivers enter the Ebro Basin, the rivers tend to flow over very old *alluvial fans*. Some of the canyons in the area have been cut out of the sedimentary rocks that form these old alluvial fans. Two of these alluvial fans were formed during the Miocene epoch and are oriented in a roughly north-south direction, meaning that the rivers entered the Ebro basin at a 90-degree angle. This is known as a *transverse drainage* path because the rivers flowed in a direction that was perpendicular to the higher elevations of the Pyrenees. The present-day tributaries of the Ebro River, of which the Alcanadre River is an example, still follow this overall, transverse pattern of drainage as they enter the Ebro Basin.

This is telling, given that a transverse drainage pattern is usually only found in a river that is young or is flowing out of a young, recently formed mountain range. The Pyrenees are not still forming. From the standpoint of the drainage pathways that feed into the Ebro Basin, the maturation process may have interacted with the opening of the drainage pathway to the Mediterranean. Scientists estimate that the denudation rate of the south-central Pyrenees began to occur at a low level between 40 and 35 million years ago. The rate of denudation is thought to have been maximal between 35 and 30 million years ago. Between 20 and 15 million years ago, the rate of denudation leveled off and followed a relatively slow, steady rate. The Ebro Basin became opened to the Mediterranean between 13 or 13.5 and 8.5 million years ago, and this may have interrupted the drainage-maturation process in the south-central Pyrenees.

Just as the erosion of sediments from the Pyrenees was stabilizing, the *gradients* of the Ebro River and its tributaries sharply increased. As discussed in chapter 1 and in other chapters, an increase in the gradient of a river will tend to limit the development of *meanders*. Instead of spreading out, forming a diffuse network of channels, and following the axial "grain" of the Ebro River and its valley, the Alcanadre River and its neighbors became entrenched.

Even if the Ebro River had not opened to the Mediterranean, it is conceivable that the tributaries of the Ebro River might still have retained their transverse drainage pattern. The notion of this type of maturation process, the shift from a transverse to an *axial drainage* pattern, is somewhat subjective, because no one knows what length of time would normally be required for the maturation process to occur. The arcuate shape of the Pyrenees also means that its drainage divide is asymmetrical. The Ebro Basin appears to have received a higher load of sediments, delivered as part of the erosion of the Pyrenees, than did the foreland basins on the northern side of the Pyrenees. This is unusual because the Ebro Basin and its neighboring basins are part of a pro-foreland basin. The retro-foreland basin was formed on the northern side of the Pyrenees. Normally, the retro-foreland basin would be expected to have received more sediments from the eroding Pyrenees. For complex reasons, this evidently did not occur.

Researchers think that the unusually large amount of uplift caused the rivers to retain their immature drainage pattern. If there had not been the isostatic uplift of the Ebro Basin, most or all of its tributaries, along with the rivers nearby, might have developed more strongly axial drainage patterns. A river following an axial pathway would begin flowing east, parallel to the high elevations of the Pyrenees, "immediately" upon entering the Ebro Basin.

There is, in fact, evidence that there was a recent phase of accelerated erosion of the Pyrenees, a so-called re-excavation of the southern portion of the Pyrenean Axial Zone. The "second wind" of erosion of the Pyrenees may have slightly lagged behind the opening of the Ebro Basin to the Mediterranean. As discussed above, the initial phase of the erosion of the southern Pyrenees had become stable between 20 and 10 million years ago. During this time, portions of the southern Pyrenean Axial Zone, north of Peonera Canyon, were buried by lacustrine sediments and alluvial fan sediments. Beginning about 5 or 6 million years ago, during the late Miocene to early Pliocene epochs, the erosional excavation, or erosional exhumation, of the Pyrenees accelerated again. This is thought to have been driven, in part, by extensional activity in the vicinity of the Valencia Trough.

Researchers also think a drop in sea level may have contributed to the recent phase of erosion of the southern Pyrenees. It is not entirely clear, however, that this drop in sea level contributed strongly to the incision by the Ebro River and its tributaries, incision that would have been driven by an acceleration in the erosion of the Pyrenees. More specifically, the duration of the sea level drop is unclear. A desiccation crisis, also known as the Messinian desiccation crisis, occurred in the Mediterranean during the Late Miocene. There is evidence that the sea level of the Mediterranean may have decreased by 1,640 feet (500 m) during the interval of 6.14 to 5.26 million years ago, which corresponds to part of the Late Miocene and to the first 40,000 years of the Pliocene. Other evidence suggests that the sea level drop may have lasted a much shorter time. To the extent that the decrease in sea level was relevant to the Ebro Basin, the flow of the Ebro River delta would be expected to have been accelerated. The effect would have been, essentially, to increase the effective gradient of the river.

GEOTHERMAL ACTIVITY AND THERMAL SPRINGS

In addition to the Alcanadre River that flows through Peonera Canyon (shown in the lower color insert on page C-3), there is reason to think that subsurface water was also involved in the incision of the canyon. Peonera Canyon has been regarded as a slot canyon, which is a narrow canyon with nearly vertical walls. Peonera Canyon and other slot canyons might be viewed as a cave-canyon hybrids or *karstlike* canyons. The *geothermal activity* around Peonera Canyon, which is located in the Aragón region of Spain, may have indirectly participated in the actions of subsurface water.

The movement of large volumes of water through the *thermal springs* in the Aragón region, of which Peonera Canyon is part, is driven by focal points of geothermal heat. These geothermal foci are the result of a broader, regional geothermal gradient. The layers of sedimentary rocks in this region have, for example, been modified to

SLOT CANYONS OR KARSTLIKE CANYONS?

Scientists have not conducted very much research on the actual mechanisms by which slot canyons form. In some cases, the walls of a slot canyon are thought to have been formed by a kind of pure incision. The walls of a canyon will tend to be smoothed and widened by *hillslope* erosion, also known as hillslope denudation. A canyon that has been subjected to hillslope denudation might develop walls that gradually slope into the stream. If two U's are turned upside down and placed side by side, the line between the two U's would approximate this sort of "concave-down" shape of the walls between channels. To visualize this, it is helpful to imagine that the lines of a tree branch have been drawn, close together with a dense network of fanned out branches, on a landscape. If the channels themselves are the tree branches, the land between two channels is the upside-down U of the hillslope.

As a channel network becomes denuded, or eroded, the channels become less sharply defined. Hillslope denudation often creates a diffuse channel network, in which the channels have been merged and morphed into one another by erosion. Thus, researchers sometimes refer to hillslope denudation as a process that leads to hillslope diffusion. The diffusion refers to the diffuse, branched-out quality of the tree branches. The smoothed-down hillslopes between channels have sometimes been referred to as analogous to melting ice cream. According to some researchers, a channel that is incised in the absence of hillslope diffusion is a slot canyon. This definition probably does not adequately describe the processes by which Peonera Canyon was formed. Many of the rock formations in Peonera Canyon are karstlike. The presence of these karstlike features suggests that subsurface water, in the form of springs or aquifers, was involved in their formation.

Evaporite karst formations also are known to exist in portions of the Ebro River valley. In some areas, sinkholes also exist. Various karst formations, formed by subsurface water, may have formed and then influenced the paths along which the tributaries of the Ebro River flow.

form *geothermal formations*. A geothermal formation is a collection of sedimentary rock layers that has been altered, on a mineralogical level, by hydrothermal activity.

GEOTHERMAL ACTIVITY, SLOT CANYONS, AND GUARA LIMESTONE

The walls of the canyons in the Sierra de Guara Range are largely composed of limestone layers, many of which were deposited during the Eocene epoch. Peonera Canyon is located in the Sierra and Canyons de Guara National Park, which is within the Aragón region of northeastern Spain. The name of the park can be translated as "Mountains and Canyons of the Guara." The word *Guara* may have been chosen as a reference to the limestone layers of the Guara Formation, also known as the Guara Limestone or Alveoline Limestone. The Sierra de Guara are part of the band of mountains that are generally known as the External Sierras. The External Sierras were formed, late in the Pyrenean Orogeny, as part of the Guarga Thrust Front. This produced about 1,641 feet (500 m) of uplift during the middle and late portions of the Oligocene epoch. The Pyrenean Orogeny ended about 24.7 million years ago, a time that corresponds to the Late Oligocene.

There is evidence that some fault activity occurred in the External Sierras during the early Miocene epoch, which began at 23.7 million years ago. For the most part, however, the layers of sedimentary rocks in the External Sierras have not been significantly warped or deformed over the last 24.7 million years. Nonetheless, the area around Peonera Canyon contains numerous *synclines* and anticlines. Even though these have been buried by lacustrine sediments, they can help to guide the flow of water in thermal springs.

The area around Peonera Canyon contains numerous small, subterranean springs that have modified the layers of sedimentary rocks. Across northeastern Spain, the most powerful springs have been found to the north and south of Peonera Canyon and the Ebro River Basin. At least two geothermal formations are likely to exist in the Sierra de Guara region, of which Peonera Canyon is a part. Scientists refer to these formations as either GF7 and GF8, with the GF an abbreviation for geothermal formation, or FG7 and FG8. The FG also serves as an abbreviation for geothermal formation.

The GF7 and GF8 layers are most likely to exist, or to have once existed, in the walls of canyons in the Sierra de Guara. The collections of layers that comprise GF7 and GF8 are essentially all less than 66.4 million years old. The *Tertiary period* began 66.4 million years ago, and the layers of Tertiary rocks were modified to form GF7 and GF8. The GF8 layers consist of sandstone, clay, and rock that were formed from mixtures of conglomerated debris. These layers were deposited during the Miocene epoch and Oligocene epoch of the Tertiary period, corresponding to the interval between 36.6 and 5.3 million years. Some of these layers of Miocene and Oligocene rocks were modified by the actions of hydrothermal water to form GF8 layers. The layers of GF7 are older than the GF8 layers. The GF7 layers were originally deposited during the *Paleogene epoch* and Eocene epoch, which are the first two intervals within the Tertiary period. The layers of modified rock in the GF7 are mainly limestone and closely related, carbonate-containing rocks.

It is important to note the distinction between the deposition and geothermal modification of these rock layers. The groupings of layers into numbered sets of geothermal formations (GF7, GF8, etc.) is not based on the time at which thermal spring water eroded the rocks. The geothermal gradient in Spain is, essentially, the result of the relatively recent orogenic activity in the Pyrenean and Iberian Ranges. For the sake of discussion, the geothermal gradients can be attributed to the ongoing cooling of the crust and rocks beneath the mountain ranges. The geothermal heat is localized into focal points that are scattered around Spain. The conductive heating of rocks in these focal points has modified the existing rocks at different times. Thus, the GF7 layers may refer to modified layers of sedimentary rocks that are of Eocene ages. The layers of the Guara Formation, for example, were deposited during the Eocene epoch. Some of the layers of the Guara Formation have been modified by hydrothermal forces, but the modification did not necessarily occur during the Eocene. It is clear, however, that the geothermal modifications occurred at different times between the time of formation of the rocks, during the Eocene, and the present day.

The walls of Peonera Canyon may contain layers of the Guara Formation or other rock layers. The layers of the Guara Formation vary between 82 feet (25 m) and 820 feet (250 m) in the External Sierras. The layers of the Guara Formation are beneath the layers of the Arguís and Campodarbe Formations and above the layers of the Tremp Formation. Some of the layers of the Tremp Formation were deposited during the *Cretaceous period* and exist above other Cretaceous rock layers, including the Adraen and Bona Formations. The oldest rocks in the External Sierras are layers of the Pont de Suert Formation, deposited during the Triassic period.

The Ebro Basin is generally regarded as a *Tertiary* basin, which means that Tertiary rock layers are abundant and are often the uppermost layers. Thus, the Ebro Basin can be a Tertiary basin and still contain older layers of sedimentary rocks, layers that are typically stacked beneath the Tertiary layers. The layers of the GF5 and GF6 exist in some parts of the Ebro Basin, and these are hydrothermally modified layers of, respectively, *Jurassic* and Cretaceous rock layers. The GF5 and GF6 layers primarily consist of limestone and other carbonate-rich rocks.

DETAILS OF GEOTHERMAL FORMATIONS

When layers of limestone or another sedimentary rock are more permeable than the surrounding layers, the water of a thermal spring may flow through the permeable layer. In the Pyrenean and Iberian Mountains, the geothermal heat is provided by granite intrusions that are still hot. These granite intrusions transfer geothermal energy to subsurface groundwater by conduction.

Different layers of sedimentary rocks will have different permeabilities. Different zones within a granite intrusion will, similarly, be more permeable than other zones. Subsurface water, in an aquifer or spring, will flow through fractures in granite or through the most permeable layers of limestone. Even in the absence of a spring or geothermal heat source, almost all portions of granite contain some zones that are more permeable than others. If water is flowing through granite that contains permeable zones and is conducting heat, the water will be heated. An important point is that the granite, not the limestone, is the rock that is capable of conducting and transferring its heat. Based on drilling data from the Aragón region, for example, scientists know that the temperatures of the groundwater, in thermal springs, are higher at deeper depths. This temperature difference ultimately drives the movement of water, from deeper depths toward the surface, in the thermal springs. As an ice cube melts in a cup of hot coffee, for example, the movement of hot water into the cold ice crystals will tend to move the ice cube slightly. The heat transfer is a spontaneous process that ultimately serves to equalize the temperatures of the melted ice and coffee. The movement of water in a thermal spring is ultimately driven by this sort of hydrothermal convection. The path that the springwater takes is determined by differences in the permeabilities and layering patterns of the rocks. The moving water will often also enlarge the fractures or permeable portions of rocks, for example, dissolving calcium carbonate out of limestone.

In the Aragón region of Spain, many of the thermal springs flow into the Ebro Basin along north-south axes. The major geothermal sources tend to be in the Pyrenean or Iberian Mountains, and the thermal springwater tends to flow between layers of sedimentary and metamorphic rocks. The springs tend to follow paths that are similar to roller coasters, rising and falling in association with the buried anticlines and synclines. The anticlines and synclines were simply formed by orogenic activity, which has folded and deformed the rocks that are at the surface and below the surface.

In the following diagram, thermal springwater can be seen to flow away from granite rocks and up through sedimentary rock layers. The water flows along buried anticlines and synclines, and the flow is not meant to represent the path to any one, specific spring. The Balneario

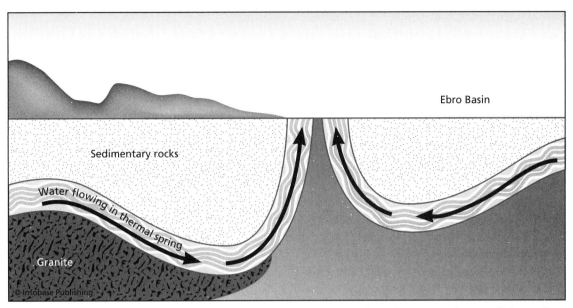

In the Sierra de Guara region, the water in the thermal springs tends to flow upward, toward the surface, along arc-shaped paths.

de Panticosa, Puyarruego, Baaeos de Benasque, Asso Veral, and Tiermas Springs are generally either north, northeast, or northwest of Peonera Canyon. The focal point, the site of localized heat flow and heat transfer, of each spring is potentially up-drainage of Peonera Canyon, assuming that springwater tends to move in an overall direction that is south and away from the Pyrenees. The Tiermas Spring is an especially powerful heat source. The Nueno and Alquezar Springs are also near to Peonera Canyon but may be downstream or "down-spring" from the canyon. As the thermal springs flow toward the surface, the springwater may have produced erosion and guided the path of the Alcanadre River.

It is noteworthy that a geothermal heat point can send heated springwater across a distance. The heated springwater can flow away from the focal point of geothermal, conductive heat and then impart its heat to other layers of rocks. This can produce indirect modification, by geothermal modification, of the rocks that are somewhat distant from the focal point of geothermal heat. The original focal point of heat transfer is some intrusive body of granite. Heated water may travel away from the original granite intrusion and heat other granite. This secondary heat transfer could then influence the paths of other springs in the area. By the time the water moves out of the granite and into limestone, or other sedimentary rock layers, the water may be distant from the primary site of heat transfer. The solubility of mineral substances, such as the calcium carbonate in limestone, can be influenced by the temperature of the water. The amount of evaporation of water is also dependent on temperature. As a thermal spring enlarges a fracture in limestone, the widening of the corridor may influence the direction or speed of the flowing water. If a larger volume of water can flow through a cold, limestone corridor, the water may lose heat more rapidly. This heat loss may, in turn, alter the processes of hydrothermal convection.

POTENTIAL INTERACTIONS BETWEEN RIVERS AND THERMAL SPRINGS

Some of the thermal springs that flow through the Pyrenees transport very large amounts of water, such as a few thousand liters of water per second, and the water temperatures can be very high. The Ojos de Pontil spring, which is fairly near to the point at which the Alcanadre joins the Ebro River, has a water temperature of 73.8°F (23.2°C) and transports water at a flow rate of 66 gallons (250 L) per second. The mean air temperature tends to be about 55.4°F (13°C) in this portion of the Pyrenees.

The high flow rate can also serve to hide the apparent strength of the geothermal energy sources. High volumes of water are being moved rapidly through these thermal springs, and this tends to draw heat away from the rocks. The rocks can be transferring a lot of heat and still remain relatively cool, given that the water is drawing heat away from the rocks. Researchers noted this paradoxical aspect of heat transfer in the context of springs by themselves. The process may also be relevant to the interactions of rivers with thermal springs. The flow rate of springwater may be more relevant to canyon formation than a geothermal heat source per se.

Some of the unusual rock formations in Peonera Canyon also hint at the involvement of underground springs in the formation of the canyon. In some parts of Peonera Canyon, the river flows through what is essentially a rock tunnel. Moreover, the rocks on the partial "ceiling" of the tunnel are sloped downward in an almost spherical arc. The shape of this type of rock formation is strongly reminiscent of the paths that numerous springs follow in the Aragón region. Many of the springs rise to the surface along this type of arclike path. The spring will flow horizontally, for example, and then flow to the surface along a steep arc. In many cases, the flow will be almost vertical as the water nears the surface.

Researchers noted that many of the paths of the springs interact in consistent ways with deformations and layering patterns in the rocks. Most of the springs appear to follow a nearly vertical path to the surface, and this arcuate path is sometimes guided by the rising slope of an anticline. In the portions of the mountains that have been covered over by layers of Tertiary sediments, such as in the boundary between the Ebro

The Alcanadre River flows through lower Peonera Canyon, with the shape of the rock ceiling reminiscent of the upward, arc-shaped, spherical/circular paths of thermal springs in the area. *(Guara-Canyoning)*

Basin and the Pyrenees, the horizontal layers of rock can help the thermal springwater to retain its heat. Thus, the springs tend to consistently ascend to the surface in this sort of half–U shaped, ascending arc. Even though the properties of the rocks tend to favor flow that occurs between layers of rock, the springs can cut upward through portions of horizontally deposited sedimentary rock. This occurs, for example, in the Arnedillo Spring and the Fitero Spring. These springs occur along the southwestern margin of the Ebro Basin, along the line at which the Iberian Mountains meet the basin.

It is important to recognize that other processes may have driven the tunnel-like and cavelike formations in Peonera Canyon. Clearly, some of the walls were formed by fluvial incision. It is nonetheless helpful to consider the mechanisms by which thermal springs could influence the formation of underground structures. The upper portions of the walls of

Peonera Canyon are, for example, narrower than the lower portions in some places. Moreover, the shapes of parts of the walls and rock tunnels in the canyon are similar to the formations that exist in karst terrains. It is conceivable that glaciers, for example, also participated in the formation of these cavernous underground sections of the canyon.

Windjana Gorge

The Napier Range,
Northwestern Australia

Windjana (pronounced WIND-juh-nuh) Gorge is located near the northwestern coast of Australia, in the state of Western Australia. The walls of the gorge are composed of layers of limestone and related sedimentary rocks. These rocks are mostly limestone and were originally deposited as marine sediments more than 360 million years ago, during the latter portions of the *Devonian period*. The walls of the gorge are technically part of the Napier Range, a band of limestone that accumulated over an older belt of fold-thrust mountains. The older rocks are not really high enough to be mountains by themselves and are buried under deep layers of the limestone that makes up the Napier Range. The Napier Range can be regarded as the layered remnants of the carbonate sediments of numerous reefs. The limestone layers of this range appear to have also been uplifted by *fault-associated uplift*.

Windjana Gorge was formed by the Lennard River, which is now an *ephemeral stream*. Various *karst formations* exist in the Napier Range, out of which Windjana Gorge was incised. These karst formations indicate that groundwater has helped shape the topography. Windjana Cave, for example, is just upstream of Windjana Gorge and is an example of a karstlike formation. In the vicinity of the Chedda Cliffs that are near Windjana Gorge, researchers have reported the existence of sinkholes that are roughly 3.3 feet (1 m) deep. There are also remnants of very old karst formations that are visible, or just beneath the rock faces, in parts of the Napier Range and Windjana Gorge. The climate is very dry, and the erosive activities of water have essentially moved underground. The formation of the actual gorge was clearly produced by some *fluvial incision*. It is not as clear, however, that this *incision* resulted from clearly defined intervals of *uplift*.

The timing of incision of Windjana Gorge, or of any other gorge in the Napier Range, is not immediately apparent. At 49 inches (124 cm) below the surface of Carpenter's Gap, a rock structure in Windjana Gorge National Park, the *sedimentary rock* layers are about 49,000 years old. The significance of this is not entirely clear. One implication is that the gorge could have been incised relatively recently, given that numerous

A karstlike rock cavern has been carved out of a wall in Windjana Gorge, providing a kind of horizontal time line, with vertically oriented layers, of growing and shifting reefs. *(Australian Picture Library)*

wet intervals have occurred. The northwestern Australia summer mon-soonal system is evidently at least 14,000 years old and has, between that date and the present day, been delivering summer rain, between November and April, to Windjana Gorge. That said, water-driven weathering does progress rather slowly. The absolute age of an "active" *tufa* deposit in the Napier Range has been established as being about 2,160 years old. The age of the tufa deposit simply allows one to say that the air was very dry and that some surface water was moving things around, at that time and at a given point in the wall or mountain cliff.

Looking at an extreme range of dates, it is possible to say that the gorge was probably not incised more than several million years ago. Rather, the gorge, like other canyons, was probably incised within the last few million years or so. However, the gorge may have been incised much more recently, such as within the last 1–3 million years or later. Numerous playa lakes—those that are maintained by glacier-induced changes in the locations of rainfall—have existed, within the last million years, in northwestern Australia. Importantly, surface landforms do not tend to survive in pristine form for intervals on the order of 350 million years. The reef terraces in and around Windjana Gorge were formed 350 million years ago, but the reef was enormous and vast. These present-day reef terraces are only likely to be apparent from an airplane.

In spite of the unanswered questions about the incision of the gorge, the history of the region surrounding the gorge bears many similarities to the histories of other canyon-rich regions. The gorge, like other canyons, is downstream from a mountain range, upstream of a sedimentary *basin*, and is located next to the margin of the sedimentary basin.

When more water was flowing in the Lennard River and the region surrounding it, such as during the melting of the *Permian* glaciers, its proximity to the low-lying Canning Basin allowed the Windjana Gorge region to accumulate *sediments*. As the glacial sediments gradually hardened and were subjected to erosion, the gorge was still higher than the basin and lower than neighboring areas.

In the vicinity of the gorge, the present-day path of the Lennard River (shown in the lower color insert on page C-4) roughly follows the north-northeastern border of the Canning Basin and the reefs that existed on it. The Napier Range, together with other parallel formations, define this border. In Windjana Gorge, the Lennard River crosses through the Napier Range. The Canning Basin, a diamond-shaped portion of land that has accumulated sediments, is an extensional basin. Intermittent periods of extensional activity along *fault* lines have produced and reshaped the Canning Basin over the last 550 million years. The fault lines that produced this extension are mainly parallel to, south of, and near the Napier Range. The most inland margin of the basin is defined by a small number of fault lines that extend from north to south and are perpendicular to the Napier Range. For a long time, the Canning Basin has been lower than the Napier Range and King Leopold Mobile Belt, an *orogenic* belt that produced a mountain range.

The Napier Range defines part of the border of the Canning Basin with the Kimberley Region, or Kimberley Block, an especially old portion of Australia. The King Leopold Mobile Belt (KLMB), also known as the King Leopold Orogenic Belt, is located within the Kimberley Region and is just north of the Napier Range. Again, both of these areas of high elevations are generally northeast of the Canning Basin. The southwestern margin of the Kimberley Block, which is essentially equivalent to the northeastern margin of the Canning Basin, was shaped by orogenic events that occurred 1.8 billion years ago. A bow-shaped pair of mountain ranges, known collectively as the Kimberley Arc, were formed around this time. The southwestern arm of the Kimberley Arc is the KLMB. The KLMB consists of granite that was folded and deformed into small mountains. Some of this 1.8-billion-year-old granite is buried under the limestone of the Napier Range, which is south of and parallel to the KLMB.

In the adjacent diagram, the Kimberley Block is labeled as the Kimberley Plateau. The region has also been referred to as the Kimberley Basin. These names essentially refer to the different forces and conditions that have, at different times, characterized the region. The region is very old and has been quite tectonically stable, particularly in comparison to the Canning Basin. Basalt and sedimentary rocks have accumulated and been eroded from the Kimberley region at different times, and the elevations are now relatively high and uniform. The Napier Range extends along the northern margin of the Canning Basin, through Windjana Gorge, and blends into the Oscar Range. The Oscar Range was formed as part of the Devonian Reef environments. The Canning Basin fault systems are generally parallel to the northern margin of the Canning Basin, are spaced fairly evenly, and are perpendicular to the coastline.

The orogenic activity and metamorphism along the King Leopold Mobile Belt ultimately helped to define the northeastern margin of the Canning Basin, but the overall shape of the Canning Basin was formed more recently. Beginning about 550 million years ago, extensional *fault activity* and *volcanic activity*, in central Australia, helped to shape the topography of the Canning Basin and establish the directions of some early drainage pathways.

The uplift of the Amadeus Basin, during the late *Ordovician period*, was one event that was associated with the formation and development of the Canning Basin. Before this uplift, the Amadeus Basin and much of central Australia was submerged beneath an intracontinental seaway. This seaway, known as the Larapintine Seaway, extended from east to west and essentially separated Australia into northern and southern "islands" of land. At this time, the Canning Basin was submerged and

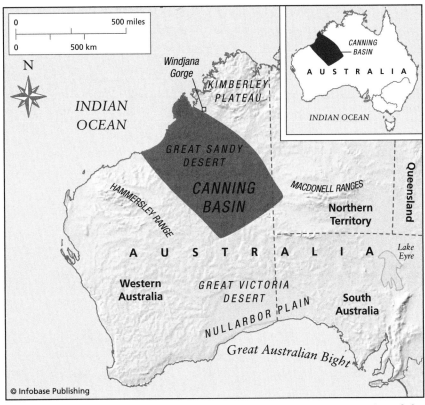

This map shows the location of Windjana Gorge, the approximate margins of the Canning Basin, and the Kimberley Region that is north of the Canning Basin.

was just the western mouth of the Larapintine Seaway. The uplift of the Amadeus Basin, in central Australia, caused the Larapintine Seaway to be closed. This created an eastern margin for the Canning Basin. The uplift therefore closed the Canning Basin from the eastern portion of Australia, causing the Canning Basin to essentially become a large inlet of the ocean. During the Emsian age of the Devonian period, between 394 and 387 million years ago, uplift in central Australia helped to allow water and dissolved sediments to be delivered, from the east, into the Canning Basin.

The closing of the Larapintine Seaway, together with climate change, set the stage for the development of the Devonian Reef in the Canning Basin. Before the Larapintine Seaway was closed, the Canning Basin was more analogous to a very wide river or ocean than a sedimentary basin.

Around the same interval of time, extensional forces began to elevate the land to the northeast of the Canning Basin. These extensional events occurred along *fault systems* that were roughly parallel to the eastern arm of the Kimberley Arc, which is the Halls Creek Orogenic Belt.

FAULT SYSTEMS AND UPLIFT IN THE CANNING BASIN

Around 240 million years ago, fault systems were reactivated along an axis that is parallel to this arm of the Kimberley Arc. The Canning Basin had formed during the Ordovician period, but this fault reactivation allowed more sediments to accumulate in the Canning Basin. During these Permian and *Triassic* extensional events, sediments were deposited at the bottoms of rivers and lakes. These alluvial and *lacustrine* sediments are still present today in different areas of the Canning Basin.

In the northeastern portion of the Canning Basin, just southwest of and parallel to the Napier Range, these Permian sediments cover the Devonian Reef sediments. On the Lennard Shelf, a band of sediments that extends along the northeastern Canning Basin, up to 1.2 miles (2 km) of Devonian sediments are covered by much thinner layers of these younger, Permian sediments.

Geological measurements taken from oil wells in the onshore Canning Basin have revealed that uplift occurred, on a fairly large scale, during a number of intervals over the last 230 million years. Uplift, such as of *fault blocks* in the Canning Basin, may have participated in more subtle ways in the formation of Windjana Gorge. This is because some of the uplift that has occurred, in the vicinity of Windjana Gorge and in the long term, has occurred as a result of fault activity. During some of these intervals, however, more than 1.55 miles (2.5 km) of sedimentary rocks were pushed upward by fault activity. These intervals of fault-associated uplift are likely to have occurred too long ago to significantly influence the incision of Windjana Gorge, but fault activity has also occurred, in the Canning Basin, during more recent intervals of time. Relatively recent fault activity could conceivably have influenced the gradient of the Lennard River or other drainage channels.

DEVONIAN FOSSILS AND A MASS-EXTINCTION EVENT

Some scientists have referred to this reef as the Devonian Great Barrier Reef, and the Canning Basin contains fossilized remains of the organisms that inhabited the reef. Some of the fossilized structures in the walls of Windjana Gorge have been smoothed or "polished" by the Lennard River and preserved by the desertlike climate. Some of the sedimentary rock layers in the gorge contain complex, microscopic structures that provide a fossilized record of diverse microbolites. Microbolites are formed when bacteria or algae secrete calcium carbonate. When the organism dies, calcium carbonate, in a shell or other shape, is left behind as a sedimentary deposit.

Researchers have studied these fossils to understand the ways that microbes, in algae mats, evolved and responded to environmental cataclysms. A mass-extinction event occurred during the Devonian period, during the boundary between the Frasnian age and the Famennian age. Scientists are still not sure of the most important cause or causes of the event. Some scientists originally suggested that a meteor impact was responsible, but researchers have primarily attributed the extinction to global temperature reductions and reductions in the overall sea level. The reef did recover from the event, but the post-extinction reef supported a much less diverse range of organisms than the pre-extinction reef. The layers of sediments that were deposited before, during, and after the extinction event have been very well preserved at Windjana Gorge and adjacent gorges, which include Geike Gorge.

In the walls of Windjana Gorge, very intricate structures of fossilized limestone have been preserved by the arid climate and stable geological conditions. Some of the microbes that populated the Devonian reef built filamentous layers of mesh, a netlike structure that held the reef together and is still apparent in fossils. In other cases, microbes existed in clotlike clusters that accumulated in stacks of hollow chambers.

These fossils have been used to study the ways that microbolites evolved and interacted with environmental changes, such as a shift to a low-oxygen environment. By studying fossil evidence at Windjana Gorge and nearby sites, for example, geologists have largely ruled out anoxia, meaning a lack of oxygen, as a cause of the extinction event. Rather, the evidence suggests that a decrease in the global sea level produced the widespread extinctions and loss of biological diversity in the reefs.

TERRACED STRUCTURES AND CYCLES OF UPLIFT

Sea-level changes were, in fact, already occurring when the Devonian reef was still present. These fluctuations were probably unrelated to the global sea-level reduction and mass extinction, but these localized changes in the "shoreline" of the reef produced changes in sediment deposition (shown in the upper color insert on page C-5). In some portions of Windjana Gorge, layers of different types of sediments are thought to have deposited during cycles of *tectonic activity*. It is important to emphasize that these terraced structures, which are large-scale structures that can sometimes only be seen from an airplane, were made by seawater and not river water. Although some of the same repeating patterns of limestone can be seen in the walls of the gorge that were cut by the Lennard River, some of the original reef-associated terraces are still intact.

The relevant effect of any tectonic activity was to interact with the changes in the water level and the dimensions of the reef. Various types of reefs existed in northwestern Australia during the Devonian period.

These included barrier reefs, fringing reefs, and patch reefs. In general, the reefs at the site of Windjana Gorge were shaped like barrier reefs during the Frasnian age and more like fringing or platform reefs during the Famennian age. After the extinction event, Famennian reefs were flatter and grew less robustly.

The different types of reefs can be understood in terms of their similar overall geometries. The most active part of a reef is an elevated band of organisms, which are either above the ocean surface or slightly below the surface. A barrier reef, for example, is like a band of carbonate layers—formed by bacteria and algae and other reef-building organisms—that is separated from the shoreline by a lagoon. A barrier reef may arc away from the shore and then arc back inland, forming an enclosed lagoon. The reef itself appears, from above, like a hill or levee that is under shallow water or above the surface. The high points of this "wall" of a barrier reef, points that are above the water level, are the reef crest. Between the shoreline and the reef crest is the lagoon, closed off from much of the ocean wave activity by the reef crest. The reef expands itself, in the vicinity of the crest, from side to side, along the shoreline, and also in a seaward direction. The expansion occurs as the organisms produce calcium carbonate shells and other structures.

In large reefs, such as the Frasnian Reef Complex that is revealed in Windjana Gorge, the crest is less like a hill and more like a mound or raised, miniature plateau. In this case, the reef crest is referred to as the reef flat. The seaward edge of the reef flat is the reef margin. For the sake of discussion, the Frasnian and Famennian reef flats and reef margins can be thought of as being analogous to a reef crest. The backreef zone, or backreef platform, is on the inland side of the crest and is beneath the water of the lagoon. On the seaward side of the crest are the forereef and, farther offshore, the forereef slope. The highest parts of the slope are sometimes referred to, such as in the walls of Windjana Gorge, as the marginal slope or proximal forereef slope. It is helpful to simply consider the reef crest, backreef platform, and forereef slope. In the diagram on page 91, the basic components of a barrier reef are apparent. A fringing reef would essentially appear as a barrier reef with a minimal backreef zone and no real lagoon.

A barrier reef, in the context of the terminology, can be analogized to a volcanic arc. A volcanic arc has a backarc basin, analogous to the backreef platform, and a forearc basin, analogous to the forereef slope. The important point is that the older reef structures, the structures of the Frasnian reef, are in eastern Windjana Gorge. The younger, post-extinction reef, the Famennian reef, is in western Windjana Gorge. The walls of the gorge are mostly oriented along an east-west axis, and the walls cut through two reefs.

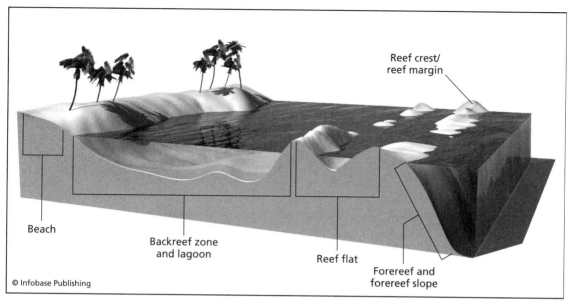

This diagram shows the backreef zone, the reef flat and crest, and the forereef zone of a fringing reef or barrier reef.

There are geographical variations in the different forereef and back-reef structures, and these are potentially confusing. In eastern Windjana Gorge, the Lennard River flows from east to west through the Frasnian backreef platform. Here, the walls of Windjana Gorge consist mainly of the layers of sedimentary rock that are known as the Pillara Limestone. The Pillara Limestone is the remnant of the Frasnian backreef plat-form. The river then continues, flowing west, through the Frasnian reef "crest," which consists of the reef flat and reef margin. Next, the river flows through the forereef and forereef slope of the Frasnian reef. As the extinction occurred, the reef gradually shifted west and slightly south-west, away from the Devonian shoreline. In central Windjana Gorge, the sedimentary rock layers of the forereef and forereef marginal slope are in the walls of the gorge and are known as the Napier Formation.

In the adjacent diagram, a representative portion of the wall of Wind-jana Gorge is shown. The layers of the Napier Formation represent shifts in the position of the Frasnian forereef and forereef slope over time. The Pillara Formation includes the Frasnian reef margin, or reef crest, and parts of the reef flat and backreef zone. In many parts of the gorge, the river has cut through curves and inlets that existed in the reef compo-nents at different times. As a result, the orientations of the reef struc-tures are not always as apparent in the walls.

In western Windjana Gorge, the Lennard River finally flows through part of the post-extinction Famennian reef crest, the reef flat and reef

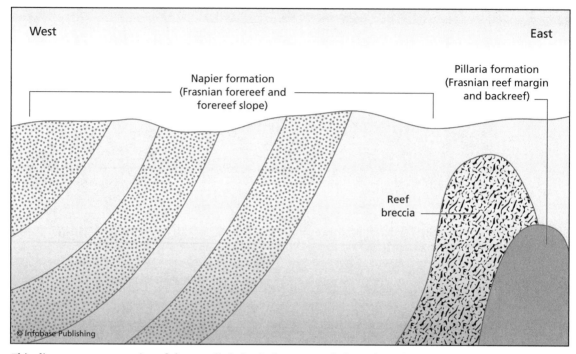

This diagram, representative of the so-called classic face or south face of Windjana Gorge, shows the transition from the layers of the Frasnian backreef and reef margin to the Frasnian forereef layers.

margin, and the Famennian forereef. The layers of the Famennian reef margin, analogous to a reef crest, are known as the Windjana Limestone.

The seaward shift in the location of the reef crest was a response to localized reductions and to cyclic fluctuations in the sea level. It is important to note that the mass extinction was probably not the result of a reduction in sea level. Either fault-associated uplift or orogenic uplift appears to have contributed, by uplifting the shoreline and deepening the offshore ocean bottom, to some of the changes in the sea level. The change in the position of the reef appears to have been driven by changes in sea level, partially resulting from tectonic forces. The mass extinction did change the size, extent, and diversity of the organisms that existed in the post-extinction Famennian reef.

In parts of the Canning Basin, the Famennian rock layers are relatively flat and are above the older Frasnian layers. In Windjana Gorge, however, the overall time line of Frasnian to Famennian is revealed along a roughly east-west progression. Along the curved line, an erosional boundary, between the Frasnian and Famennian carbonate layers in the gorge, the Famennian layers are generally above the Frasnian layers. To a large extent, however, the depositional time line moves horizontally and from east to west, rather than vertically and from low to high, in the walls of the gorge.

VERTICAL LAYERS AND TECTONICALLY DRIVEN UPLIFT

In some parts of Windjana Gorge, either incised by the Lennard River or preserved in terraces separated from the river, other types of vertical layering patterns exist. These layering patterns indicate that the water levels changed, and interacted with the reef, across both short-term and long-term cycles. Thus, there were cycles within cycles of changes in the water levels and in reef growth. Reefs tend to grow most actively in water that is not too deep, given that shallow water allows organisms to receive more sunlight than deep water does. In Windjana Gorge, the longer-term cycles are evident in portions of limestone that are between 65.6 feet (20 m) and 98.4 feet (30 m) thick. Most of the longer-term cycles contain between four and six of the smaller, and shorter-term, cycles. Almost every one of the large-scale and small-scale patterns of sediments contains a limestone cap, which indicates that the water suddenly became deeper. In the walls of the gorge, the cycles are evident in these layering patterns. On the western and eastern ends of the Napier Range, actual large-scale terraces, like steps, are visible from an airplane or other aerial perspective. Some of the cyclic changes in the sea level were probably driven by localized uplift along fault lines in the Canning Basin. The shoreline and the land that was inland of the reef was, essentially, uplifted with respect to the deeper, more seaward fault blocks. There is also some evidence that sea-level changes occurred during the Devonian period on a global scale.

CALCITE AND ARAGONITE IN OCEANIC CARBONATE FACTORIES

During the interval between about 420 and 370 million years ago, large portions of the Earth were covered by shallow water reef communities. These so-called Siluro-Devonian reefs were more extensive during this interval than at any other time in the last 545 million years. The major factor that drove the expansion of these reefs, which produced calcium-carbonate sediments and thereby acted as "carbonate factories," was the high content of dissolved carbon dioxide (CO_2) in the oceans.

Between 376 and 350 million years ago, especially during the so-called Frasnian-Famennian boundary (F/F boundary) at 371 million years ago, the CO_2 content in the oceans decreased significantly. This was partially the result of cooling of the oceans and partially the result of the growth of terrestrial plants. In part because of plant growth, the concentration of dissolved oxygen increased as the CO_2 content decreased. During the first half of the Paleozoic era, the concentration of CO_2 in the atmosphere was between 14 and 24 times the present-day concentration. When the CO_2 concentration increased significantly in the atmosphere, more of this CO_2 was driven into the oceans as dissolved gas. This climate, which was extremely hot and CO_2-rich, allowed the Siluro-Devonian reefs to peak, but it also set the stage for the destruction of the reefs. As the growing rain forests used more CO_2 and produced more oxygen, for example, CO_2 was drawn out of the water.

This decrease in the content of dissolved CO_2 was favorable to those marine organisms that produced aragonite skeletons and shells. The organisms that had been flourishing on reefs and producing calcite skeletons were less able to survive in the low-CO_2 oceans. Some scientists refer to the early Paleozoic, and pre-Devonian, oceans as having been in "calcite mode." During the F/F boundary and the Famennian age overall, the so-called calcite oceans shifted to the "aragonite oceans." The aragonite ocean environment, which emerged about 370 million years ago, has persisted into the present day.

PRESENT-DAY CLIMATE

Windjana Gorge is located at subtropical latitude, is in a semiarid climate, and receives most of its rainfall during the Australian summer. The gorge is between 17 and 18 degrees south of the equator and is just north of Australia's Great Sandy Desert, which is part of a large, arid region in Western Australia. The area around the gorge receives between 19.7 inches (50 cm) and 23.6 inches (60 cm) of rain per year, but 90 percent of the rain falls between November and April. These months correspond to the Australian summer. During the rainy season in the Kimberley Region, just north of Windjana Gorge, single rainfalls have been found to drop more than six inches (15.2 cm) of rain. The precipitation is therefore low and rigidly seasonal, with essentially no rain falling for six, or more, consecutive months out of the year.

The air in the region around the gorge is both dry and hot, with a daily high temperature of about 87.8°F (31°C) in the winter and 102.2°F (39°C) in the summer. Even during the rainy summers, the hot and dry air allows ground-level water to evaporate extremely rapidly. Partially as a result of this rapid evaporation, water that accumulates in the channels and creeks tends to flow vigorously and then quickly turn into pools and puddles. As discussed in the sidebar, the presence of so-called *tufa dams* along the sides of channels and creeks is another factor that limits erosion and weathering.

INTERACTIONS OF VEGETATION WITH DRAINAGE PATHWAYS

In Windjana Gorge and other semiarid regions, the re-precipitation of dissolved calcium carbonate can also be promoted by plants and microorganisms. Plants can also interact with recently deposited calcium carbonate to increase the turbidity of a stream or gully, an effect that further

TUFA DAMS, WEATHERING, AND SEASONAL RAINFALL

The area around Windjana Gorge has both highly defined drainage channels, as one would expect to see in a semiarid region with seasonal rainfall, and some interesting structures associated with the channels. When a big rainfall dissolves and carries away some of the limestone of the Napier Range, the dry air and the plants that line the channels and creeks absorb much of the water. As a result, the calcium carbonate in the water precipitates out and forms dams, also known as tufa dams, along the banks of the channels.

These calcium carbonate structures tend to become well-developed and solid structures, especially during the dry season, and can act as a sponge during subsequent rainfalls. These tufa dams contain clumps and small spheres of calcium carbonate that shore up plant growth on the banks of channels and also allow water to be stored, as it trickles downward beneath the surface, after a rainfall. The warm air causes evaporation, which concentrates and causes the precipitation of dissolved calcium carbonate. Warm air also warms the pools of standing water that accumulate after a rain, and this increase in water temperature further promotes the precipitation of calcium carbonate out of solution. Tufa dams therefore help maintain channel structures, and channels provide the carbonate-rich water that maintains tufa dams.

increases calcium-carbonate deposition. Seasonal rainfall around the gorge tends to flow very rapidly and vigorously into strictly defined channels, and some plants on the banks of the channels are able to accelerate the precipitation of the carbonate anion (CO_3^{2-}) from the rainwater as the solid chemical $CaCO_3$ (calcium carbonate). Plants may accomplish this by extracting dissolved carbon dioxide (CO_2) gas from the water, much as the warming of standing water decreases dissolved CO_2 and causes CO_3^{2-} to precipitate. Interestingly, researchers have found that an increase in the turbidity of a stream causes the release, or degassing, of carbon dioxide from the water.

Plants can accelerate calcium-carbonate deposition by both active mechanisms, such as the extraction of carbon dioxide for photosynthesis, and passive mechanisms, such as by increasing the turbidity of a stream. The presence of plant structures and the rough tufa formations both increase the extent of frothing and turbidity of the moving water, thereby causing calcium carbonate to precipitate around mosses or algae or other plants. Thus, the calcium-carbonate structures support plant growth along channels and gullies, and the plants can help maintain the structures.

VEGETATION, SEASONAL DRAINAGE, AND THE LENNARD RIVER

The Lennard River is, perhaps not surprisingly, an ephemeral river, also known as an *ephemeral stream*, and carries no water for much of the year. In between rainfalls, during the rainy season, and also during the dry season, small pools and puddles of water do remain in the river-bed. Additionally, water is able to percolate and accumulate near the surface of the limestone in and around the gorge. As a result of this surface water and near-surface water, some portions of land retain permanent supplies of water throughout the year and can support small trees or bushes. Ephemeral grasses, which only appear during the rainy season, and desert grasses can be found on land that is less able to retain moisture.

The Lennard River receives water from a number of major *tributaries*, and the Lennard itself is a tributary of the Meda River. A few dozen miles west of Windjana Gorge, the Lennard River essentially turns into the Meda River. In this vicinity, the May River and Hawkstone Creek converge as tributaries to form the Meda River. The Lennard River can therefore either be regarded as the northwestern portion of the Meda River or the largest tributary of the Meda River.

The Meda River empties into the Indian Ocean and into a number of inland sites. The Meda River could be seen as being partially an endoreic river, which is a river that empties into an inland site. These branches of the Meda either empty into tidal pools and floodplains or gradually appear to dry out. The Windjana Gorge National Park is approximately 90 miles from King Sound, an inlet of the Indian Ocean that defines part of the northwestern coast of Australia.

SEASONAL RAINFALL AND GULLY HEADCUT RETREAT

A highly seasonal pattern of rainfall that occurs in a semiarid climate, such as at Windjana Gorge, can cause a gully to expand and deepen in the upstream direction. When a large rainfall occurs during the rainy season, water that is entering a gully or channel may form small waterfalls at one or more heads, or water-entry points, in a winding gully. With this kind of waterfall, the bank that the water falls over will tend to erode itself "backward" and expand the newly incised channel. Water does not often enter the winding path of a gully at one end of the path. Rather, water tends to flow from the higher elevations of the plateau and hit the path of the gully from the side, at the multiple points that are the heads of the gully.

Because these heads tend to enlarge, as a result of headcut retreat, they tend to occur at the bends in the gully. Thus, the flash-flood conditions that occur during a rainfall will produce incision and also intensify the bends in the gully. This can produce the kinds of S-shaped bends that one would find in a river, but the bends in the gully are not produced by water flowing in the gully. Instead, the bends in the gully are expanded by water entering the gully from one side. The vertical incision from the water that is rapidly flowing in the gully produces small cliffs and waterfalls at the head. The cliff that is at the head of every gully creates the waterfall and is known as a headcut, or vertical headcut. The waterfall at each headcut causes the backward erosion, or retreat, of the headcut. This headcut retreat first lengthens the gully and then expands the gully from side to side. This process can also occur on a large scale, such as in the formation of the canyon that is downstream of Niagara Falls.

Small clusters of fairly dense vegetation can be found in some of the gullies around the Napier Range, a limestone range that surrounds the gorge and through which the Lennard River passes. These clusters have been referred to as vine thicket and are like small portions of rain forest, in the sense that they contain a diverse range of plants. To the extent that a gully can provide shelter from extremes of weather and support many more types of plants than the surrounding landscape can, a portion of vine thicket is a kind of self-contained ecosystem.

6

Monterey Canyon

Monterey Bay, Central California, the United States

Monterey Canyon is a *submarine canyon* that has been cut out of the *continental shelf* at the bottom of Monterey Bay, in California. Monterey Canyon consists of a submarine channel that extends 56 miles (90 km) into the Pacific Ocean. When scientists consider the added length of the valley that surrounds the Monterey Fan, a submarine *alluvial fan* that extends seaward from the western margin of Monterey Canyon, the canyon and valley are 292 miles (470 km) long. The walls of the canyon are roughly 1.1 miles (1.7 km) high in some places, and the canyon is up to 7.5 miles (12 km) wide. The floor of the canyon begins at a depth of 32.8 feet (10 m), just offshore from Moss Landing Harbor, and ends in water that is 9,843 feet (3,000 m), or 1.9 miles (3 km), deep. This means that a submersible perched on the rim of the canyon could be a mile above the canyon floor and conceivably be up to 4,265 feet (1,300 m) below the ocean surface.

The Salinas River and Pájaro River empty into Monterey Bay and provide *sediments* to the underwater head of the canyon. The head of the canyon, which is near the shoreline, receives sediments from these rivers and also from an ocean current that runs parallel to the shoreline. This is directed from north to south and is known as a longshore current, which is produced as waves hit the shoreline at an angle. The longshore current that is relevant to Monterey Canyon is produced as waves intersect the California coast, in the vicinity of the coastal Santa Cruz mountains, along a northwest-southeast line. Longshore currents essentially follow the shoreline of Monterey Bay in an arc-shaped path, with an overall movement to the southeast. This direction then essentially reverses at the head of the canyon, at which sands and sediments derived from cliff erosion are directed into the canyon.

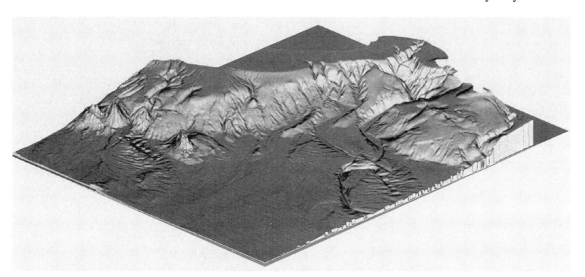

This shaded relief image shows the channel of Monterey Canyon, winding seaward from the upper right end to the foreground of the diagram. *(Steve Matula/National Oceanic & Atmospheric Administration)*

The *incision* of the canyon occurred primarily within the last 10 million years. Some researchers argue that incision began, on some level, as long as 20 or 30 million years ago. Other intervals of incision have occurred within the last 1.6 million years, during the *Quaternary period*. The *continental shelf* beneath Monterey Bay is part of the Salinian structural block, also known as the Salinian Block province or simply the Salinian Block, and *uplift* of this portion of land has driven some of the incision. The first 2.5 miles (4 km) of the canyon, a distance that extends from the shore to the sea, is contained within the Salinian structural block. The eastern margin of the Salinian Block is defined by the San Andreas Fault System, which is to the east of Monterey Canyon. The western margin of the Salinian Block is defined by the Palo Colorado–San Gregorio Fault Zone. This *fault* zone also represents the dividing line between the Salinian Block, which extends away from the coast, and the eastern margin of the San Simeon Block, which begins in the ocean and extends seaward.

These two blocks comprise the transform boundary that is craton-ward, which in this case refers to the direction to the inland and east, with respect to the active *continental margin* of the *continental plate*. The topography of the canyon has been influenced by the activities of the various fault systems that exist in Monterey Bay and that are inland of Monterey Bay. The terrestrial faults that are near the coast of California have, for example, influenced the drainage pathways of rivers that deliver sediments to Monterey Canyon.

Monterey Canyon is one of the relatively few submarine canyons that extends across most of the continental shelf. In the case of a submarine canyon that receives land-derived, or terrigenous, sediments from a river, the head of the submarine canyon will typically not extend into the continental shelf. For example, the Columbia River empties sediments into the Pacific Ocean at a point that is 87 miles (140 km) south of the head of the undersea Quinault Canyon. Quinault Canyon also does not extend into the shelf, off the coast of Washington, to a significant degree. It is therefore clear that a river can empty into the ocean at a point that is separated from an undersea canyon by miles of coastline and miles of shelf.

In the diagram below, submarine canyons are shown as having been incised out of the continental shelf and part of the *continental slope*. In the specific case of the Monterey Fan, much of the fan actually extends across the continental slope. In contrast to the general case that is depicted in the diagram, the Monterey Fan begins landward of the continental rise.

FEATURES OF MONTEREY BAY

A number of aspects of Monterey Bay (shown in the lower color insert on page C-5) are important for the maintenance of Monterey Canyon. The continental shelf beneath Monterey Bay extends a fairly large distance out into the ocean. This helps to maintain the longshore current that directs sediments into the bay from the north. The shape of the bay is also thought to be important for maintaining Monterey Canyon. The head of

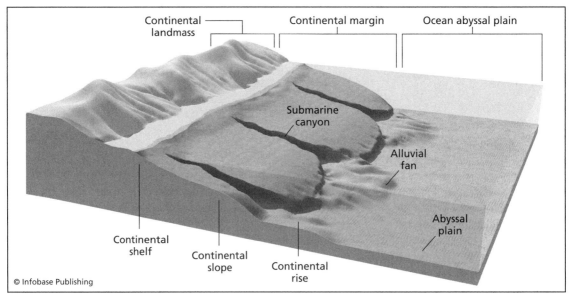

This diagram shows submarine canyons, incised out of the continental shelf and continental slope, and multiple submarine fans.

Monterey Canyon receives sediments from three major directions and a series of smaller inputs, and Monterey Bay is surrounded on its three sides by mountains.

The different sources of sediments provide a diverse range of sedimentary materials to various parts of the head of Monterey Canyon. The different types of sediments mix together and help to remodel the head of the canyon. The Salinas River empties into the bay from the south, the Pájaro River flows into the bay from the east, and the longshore current is directed into the bay from the north. Smaller longshore currents also exist, however, and these currents may direct sediments into the canyon head from the south. Other currents may also direct sediments into the canyon at smaller channels in the canyon walls, channels that exist at points that are distant from the head. The sediments delivered by longshore currents ultimately mix with the sediments that are delivered from dry land by the rivers. The rivers provide sediments that tend to be heavy and that consist of bedrock or heavy minerals, and the longshore currents provide other types of sediments.

THE MONTEREY FAN AND ALLUVIAL CHANNELS

The sediments that are carried through Monterey Canyon form a very large undersea alluvial fan, a *submarine fan* known as the Monterey Fan, on the ocean floor. Researchers have mapped out at least three distinct channels, referred to as submarine fan channels, of the Monterey Fan. Parts of the central fan channel are loosely defined by the shapes of the canyon walls, but the other channels are roughly parallel to the central channel and occur on either side of the main axis of the canyon. The central fan channel of the Monterey Fan is referred to as an axial channel. This simply means that the sediments are deposited along a line that is roughly parallel to the lines that are formed by the walls of the canyon. The other fan channels are also roughly parallel to both the axis of the canyon and that of the central fan channel. These other fan channels are not, however, as clearly parallel to the canyon walls as the central channel is. Only the central fan channel is actually contained within parts of the seafloor that are defined by the canyon walls. The central channel then exits the canyon, and the sediments are deposited over a fairly vast, fanned-out area.

The overall shape of the Monterey Fan is reminiscent of alluvial fans that are formed on land. On land, alluvial fans are often formed as rivers flow out of a mountain range and onto a broad, flat valley. The water and suspended sediments are not confined to a channel system, and the flat valley may abruptly decrease the gradient of the river. This decrease in gradient will slow down the river and cause it to fan out. Both of these changes can promote the deposition of sediments. In an arid environment, the water may evaporate and leave sediments behind. The water is also likely to be flowing too slowly to prevent sediments from settling, under the force of gravity, to the floor of the alluvial valley.

The lobes of deposited sediments that comprise the Monterey Fan are distinctly spread and stretched out. The fan channels both accumulate sediments, such as sand and mud, and transport sediments to the outer reaches of the fan. As a result, the most spread-out portions of the Monterey Fan appear to be separated, by a considerable distance, from the most seaward end of Monterey Canyon. As discussed above in the case of Quinault Canyon, which is separated from the mouth of the Columbia River by the continental shelf, the transport of sediments is often not entirely coupled, geographically, to the deposition or erosive action of the sediments on the ocean floor. (The word *coupled* is not meant to be a technical term in this context.)

If this geographical disconnect were to occur on land, one might see a river flow over a cliff and then require an unusually large amount of time to reach the ground. Instead of falling straight down, the waterfall might arc out through the air. The sediments in the river might still be able to drive the incision of a canyon or settle into an alluvial fan, but the canyon or fan might be oddly stretched out or separated from the cliff. The sediments of the Monterey Fan form a broad fan but are more localized, to channels, at sites that are closer to the coastline. Detached lobes also exist near the main lobes of Monterey Fan. The lobes are disconnected from the main fan channels. The detached lobes are not thought to have ever been main lobes. They are more like sections of Monterey Fan that have accumulated sand and sediments as spillover. There is evidence that small, poorly defined channels may have allowed these sediments to be deposited beside one of the main lobes. Some of the detached lobes are analogous to the muddy water that builds up on a floodplain near a river. A pool might exist after every big rainfall and still be mostly separated from the river, for example by a small hill.

The Monterey Fan is not the only site at which sediments can accumulate. Scientists think that the floor of upper Monterey Canyon, the portion that is relatively close to shore and that is no deeper than 4,922 feet (1,500 m), has recently been undergoing a net accumulation of sediments. This process of deposition is similar to the accumulation of *alluvial sediments* at the bottom of a stream. It is noteworthy that the deposition is occurring in the parts of Monterey Canyon that are at higher elevations than many of the other, "down-current" sites. Given this relatively localized character, the deposition of sediments has produced a kind of undersea *aggradation*. Even in terrestrial rivers, however, aggradation is not really equivalent to alluvial sediment deposition per se. Aggradation refers to sediment deposition that occurs at a relatively discrete site, usually a site that receives abundant inputs of water and sediments, and that causes a localized increase in the gradient of the river. Sediment deposition in the form of aggradation may locally decrease the height of the walls of a terrestrial canyon, but this aggradation may increase incision at points that are downhill with respect to the aggradation site. In a submarine canyon, however, the localized deposition of sediments will not necessarily, or predictably, produce downstream incision. The deposition may eventually be removed by a seasonal flushing event, as discussed below, or by some other submarine phenomenon.

STRUCTURAL FEATURES OF THE CANYON AND SUBMARINE FAN

The shapes of the channels of the Monterey Fan have also been influenced by the topography of the ocean floor. The paths of the canyon walls and the central fan channel follow *meanders* that are similar to meanders formed by rivers on land. For example, the fault lines of the Monterey Bay Fault Zone have directed some of the meanders in upper Monterey Canyon. This is the portion of the canyon that extends from the head to the points at which the water is deeper than 4,922 feet (1,500 m). The shape of a meander can be influenced by the *resistance* of rocks and by other factors, including *tectonic* events. The flow of sediments can be directed by rocks and tectonic events, but the underwater currents and sediments can also "push back" and trigger massive erosion events. Researchers think, for example, that some of the hardened layers of *sedimentary rock* were made more fragile by *fault activity*. The fragile areas were then preferentially eroded into meanders by moving sediments.

FAULT SYSTEMS AND TOPOGRAPHY OF MONTEREY CANYON

The fault systems in the vicinity of Monterey Canyon appear to have influenced more aspects of the canyon than the shapes of its meanders. Monterey Canyon is, as noted above, located within a transform *plate* boundary. This portion of the North American plate is near the *subduction zone*, between the North American and Pacific plates, but is not the actual continental margin. The fault activity that typically occurs at a transform boundary is strike-slip motion, in which one portion of rock moves horizontally with respect to the rock on the other side of the fault. Folding and thrusting of the land can also create mountains along a transform boundary. The San Andreas fault system is part of the transform boundary in central California, and this well-known fault system clearly exhibits predominantly strike-slip, side-to-side motion. The transform boundary includes both the onshore and offshore portions of central California. Monterey Canyon is located near the Monterey Bay Fault Zone and the Palo Colorado–San Gregorio Fault System, and both fault systems are offshore. Several dozen earthquakes of approximately magnitude 2.0, a magnitude on the Richter scale that is considered a very weak quake, have occurred in the Monterey Bay area since 1967.

Monterey Canyon and the valley of the Monterey Fan extend through several distinct fault lines, and some of these lines are parts of the larger fault systems. The uppermost portion of the canyon passes through the Monterey Bay Fault Zone, the most inland of the offshore fault systems. This fault system contains several fault lines that intersect Monterey Canyon and are thought to have influenced the shape of the canyon. The Monterey Bay Fault Zone is essentially confined to the margins of Monterey Bay. This fault system contains two small fault lines, the Navy Fault and Seaside Fault, that appear to have influenced the meanders and shape of Monterey Canyon.

The Seaside Fault crosses through three morphological features of Monterey Canyon. The first of these features is the Seaside Fault constriction, a site that is adjacent to the Monterey Meander. The channel of Monterey Canyon becomes narrow along this curve. North of this constriction is a debris field that was the site of past landslides and other mass wasting events. The activity along the Seaside Fault is thought to have contributed heavily to these landslides. The Seaside Fault also intersects the point at which Soquel Canyon, a *tributary* canyon, feeds into Monterey Canyon from the northeast. Thus, the activity along the Seaside Fault Line is likely to have contributed to meander formation, large-scale sediment landslides into Monterey Canyon, and the point at which the canyon is joined by a tributary canyon.

The Navy Fault intersects Monterey Canyon at the Navy Slump, also known as the Navy Fault Slump. This slump is a topographical feature of the canyon and a site of sediment input to Monterey Canyon. The Navy Fault is parallel to and roughly west of the Seaside Fault.

Just outside Monterey Bay, Monterey Canyon first passes through the Palo Colorado–San Gregorio Fault Zone and then passes through the Ascension Fault. Ascension Canyon is among five submarine canyons that exist in the Monterey Bay area and that are smaller than Monterey Canyon. Scientists have also been able to measure the effects of individual earthquakes on sediment transport within the canyon.

The fault systems and fault-associated *volcanic* domes exert important effects on both the topography of Monterey Canyon and the marine life of Monterey Bay. Scientists working at the Monterey Bay Aquarium Research Institute have used two remote-operated vehicles (ROVs), which are unmanned submarines, to study Monterey Bay and Monterey Canyon. Between the years of 1989 and 2005, scientists sent the two ROVs on at least 2,400 dives in Monterey Bay and sites that are just outside the bay. The data collected on these dives have helped scientists understand submarine canyons, undersea fault systems, and the marine life-forms that interact with these geological systems. In 1998, for example, scientists discovered a cold fluid vent on the north wall of Monterey Canyon. This vent was not a *hydrothermal* vent but was nonetheless able to support a community of tubeworms at 7,579 feet (2,310 m) below the surface. Scientists also found that the Davidson Seamount, an underwater volcano in the Monterey Bay area, supports a rich community of corals.

INTERACTIONS OF FAULTS, SEDIMENTS, AND MARINE LIFE

The fluid vent that was discovered in 1998 is regarded as a cold seep, a site at which fluid is delivered into a canyon. A cold seep is a type of fluid seep. The term *seepage* describes the influx of water, such as from a spring or aquifer, into a terrestrial canyon or submarine canyon. Chaco Canyon contains numerous seeps, as will be discussed in chapter 9. The seep that was discovered in 1998 is located on the Tubeworm Slump, a sloping structure that is part of the so-called Smooth Ridge. The Smooth

SEDIMENT MOVEMENT, STEEP SLOPES, AND MARINE LIFE

Scientists have found that the erosion of sediments can support some types of marine life in Monterey Bay. Researchers originally thought that chemosynthetic biological communities, which consist of organisms that use methane and hydrogen sulfide to produce energy, would be more abundant along the many small fault lines that exist in Monterey Bay. The recent removal of sediments from the seafloor is now thought to be especially important for the support of these communities. The erosion and exhumation of sediments from the floor of the bay can release methane, which is the natural gas that is used for gas appliances. It is thought that Archaeabacteria (primitive, anaerobic bacteria) first produce hydrogen sulfide gas, by combining the newly released methane with sulfate in seawater. The hydrogen sulfide, released by the bacteria, can then support chemoautotrophic bacteria (which exist in microbial mats and use hydrogen sulfide as fuel), vesicomyid and solemyid clams, and vestimentiferan tubeworms (which include the *Lamellibrachia barhami* species at Tubeworm Slump).

The important point is that the seafloor tends to have been recently eroded beneath these communities, by landslides or tectonically driven erosion. Some of these communities exist along hydrothermal fluid vents that were produced by fault activity, but the heat and gases of hydrothermal vents are not necessary for these communities to develop. In Monterey Bay, hydrothermal activity is more or less absent. Additionally, the communities in Monterey Bay exist almost exclusively at sites that are deeper than 1,805 feet (550 m). Even in this cold water, only primitive bacteria and a fresh source of methane are required to support the communities.

Scientists also found that the communities of methane-dependent organisms tended to be most abundant on steep slopes. The steep slopes tend to be sites at which erosion has recently occurred. Some of the erosion is driven by activity along fault lines, but the fault lines themselves do not appear to provide reliable supplies of these substances to the organisms. Some of the layers of organic sediments in Monterey Bay and in the walls of Monterey Canyon were converted into natural gas by tectonic forces.

Ridge is a topographical section of the canyon wall. Scientists think that the movement of sediments into Monterey Canyon at Tubeworm Slump is strongly influenced by tectonic activity. One part of Tubeworm Slump is being uplifted with respect to another, and this produces both fluid seeps and sediment movement.

It is important to note that the fluid seeps do not drive the sediment movement. If the uplift is like a series of intermittent earthquakes, the sediment movement is like an avalanche. The seeps are a by-product of the movement along the fault, but the seeps do not drive the avalanches. Some of the motion that occurs along the fault systems in Monterey Bay is oblique-slip motion, in which uplift accompanies the side-to-side motion of a strike-slip fault. The Pacific plate is converging with the North American plate at a slight angle, and this oblique convergence is reflected in the oblique motion that occurs along faults in the transform boundary.

LAYERS OF SEDIMENTS IN THE CANYON WALLS

Monterey Canyon has been cut out of at least two overall sets of sedimentary rock layers, and these sets are the Monterey Formation and the Purisima Formation. The Purisima Formation consists of sandstone and was deposited more recently than the Monterey Formation. The layers of the Monterey Formation were deposited during the *Miocene epoch* of the *Tertiary period*, an epoch that refers to the interval between 23.7 million and 5.3 million years ago. The layers of the Purisima Formation were first deposited toward the end of the Miocene and were also deposited during the *Pliocene epoch*, which occurred between 5.3 and 1.6 million years ago. The older layers of rock that are beneath the Monterey Formation are generally granite or granitelike and are between 66.7 and 144 million years old. Relatively thin layers of sediments were also deposited on the floor of Monterey Bay during the last 1.6 million years, which is the Quaternary period.

These sedimentary layers were not deposited in uniform patterns of distribution across Monterey Bay, and the sediments have been completely eroded away from some areas. In some parts of the bay, the layers of the Purisima Formation are not present. In these areas, the layers of the Monterey Formation are uppermost. The layers of the Monterey Formation are as thick as 2,100 feet (640 m) in some areas but are absent from other sites. The layers of the Purisima Formation vary in thickness between zero and 689 feet (210 m). It is important to note that in some parts of the bay, layers of the Monterey Formation may have either never been deposited or have been eroded before the Purisima Formation was deposited. The sites that contain layers of the Purisima Formation may or may not contain layers of the Monterey Formation beneath them. Some sites contain both, other sites may contain neither, and some sites contain only one or the other.

INCISION OF CHANNELS AND TERRACES IN THE CANYON

The walls of upper Monterey Canyon form an overall channel that is V-shaped, but significant portions of this channel have been filled with sediments. The walls of upper Monterey Canyon are composed primarily of sediments that were deposited between 1.6 million years ago and 10,000 years ago, during the *Pleistocene epoch* of the Quaternary period. These layers of sediments are collectively known as the Aromas Sand.

TRANSPORT OF SEDIMENTS THROUGH MONTEREY CANYON

In spite of the fact that rivers transport sediments from land to the ocean, remarkably small amounts of these sediments actually build up on the continental shelf. The continental shelf simply does not usually contain thick layers of sediments that have been recently deposited and recently delivered from land. Even on portions of continental shelf that receive sediments from rivers and do not contain submarine canyons, most of the sediments are transported across the shelf and into deeper water. Monterey Canyon does contain channel-fill sediments that are relatively young and that form terraces. However, enormous volumes of sediments are transported through the canyon each year. Most of these sediments are transported through the canyon and off the continental shelf. The continental shelf off the coast of central California, which includes the shelf beneath Monterey Bay, is between 6.2 miles (10 km) and 9.3 miles (15 km) wide. The width of the continental shelf can strongly influence the magnitudes of longshore currents, which move sediments in directions that are generally parallel to the coastline.

Until recently, the mechanisms by which sediments are transported from rivers to the deep ocean have been somewhat elusive to scientists. Scientists have been able to study these avenues of sediment transport by measuring the salinity, or salt concentration, sediment concentration, and temperature at different depths in Monterey Canyon.

Scientists recently found direct evidence of sediment transport plumes in Monterey Canyon, and these high-velocity currents transport relatively fresh water and sediments into the deep ocean. Researchers refer to these plumes of moving sediments as *turbid underflows,* and this rather loose nomenclature distinguishes the underflows from more strictly defined phenomena. The turbid underflows transport water that is low in salinity, warm, and heavily laden with sediments. For the sake of discussion, a plume can be regarded as the physical dimensions and features of a turbid underflow event. An underflow that takes the form of a low-salinity, sediment-laden plume is often referred to as a hyperpycnal flow. However, many of the underflow events in Monterey Bay are thought to be smaller than hyperpycnal flows. Additionally, the turbid underflows that are carried through Monterey Canyon may not show all of the characteristics that one would expect to see in a hyperpycnal flow. For these reasons, scientists distinguished the low-salinity plumes and turbid underflows from the larger-scale hyperpycnal flows. For example, hyperpycnal flows may only occur every 10 or more years.

HIGH-ENERGY FEATURES OF PLUMES

Some aspects of these plumes may initially appear paradoxical. The plumes are between 131 feet (40 m) and 164 feet (50 m) thick and move 32.8 feet (10 m) or more above the floor of the canyon. One plume, which passed through Monterey Canyon in 1995, began at a depth of 492 feet (150 m) and extended down to 623 feet (190 m). The bottom of Monterey Bay, at the point of measurement, was 755 feet (230 m). The plumes carry water that is lower in salinity and also less dense than the surrounding water. Their water is warmer than the temperatures that would be predicted for their depths, and they are less buoyant than the water above them. To understand these characteristics, it is helpful to ask: What factors prevent the plume from rising to the surface, and what factors maintain the low salt concentration in the plume?

Simply put, the high concentration of suspended sediments is responsible for maintaining both the negative buoyancy and the low salinity of the plume. The negative buoyancy of this type of plume is thought to result from the high concentration of sediments. If one were to begin with perfectly fresh water and gradually deliver sediments into the water, the sediment-laden water would eventually be dense enough to maintain neutral buoyancy in the saltwater of the ocean. Freshwater that contains between 2.67 ounces per gallon (20 g/L) and 4.01 ounces per gallon (30 g/L) of suspended sediments is of roughly the same density as seawater. The water does not necessarily have to be more dense than the seawater at a given depth. The sediments and freshwater are injected into the ocean by the river, and the plume simply has to "not rise." In other words, the plume does not really have to begin at the surface and sink to a given depth. But scientists found that the plume was characterized by a decrease in density of the seawater. The suspended sediments make the plume more dense than freshwater but less dense than seawater at the depth of the plume. This is most likely possible because of the inertia, or momentum, that was created in the plume by the force of the floodwaters in the river. Scientists refer to the underflows in Monterey Canyon as "high-energy" events. A forward, pulling motion can cause an inflatable tube, pulled behind a motorboat, to be initially dragged underwater. This transiently overcomes the positive buoyancy that would cause it to float. If a river is flooding or is delivering sediments into the ocean with enough force, the sediment-laden water can be slightly less dense than seawater and still maintain negative buoyancy.

The higher temperature of the water in the plume may also influence the threshold concentration of suspended sediments that is required to maintain negative buoyancy. The movement of sediments may also maintain the temperature, creating a kind of self-perpetuating phenomenon. Scientists have found that gravity is not the major factor that is responsible for the downhill and forward motion of this type of plume. Given that inertia is responsible for the motion, this stored energy also maintains the temperature and salinity gradients.

The sediments also allow the plume to appear to cheat the kinds of osmotic forces that might equalize the salinity difference. One might ask why the relatively fresh water in the plume does not rush outward in all directions, to equalize the different salt concentrations and apparent osmotic gradient. A nontechnical answer is essentially that the sediment behaves like a "salt substitute." The technical answer has to do with the electrical conductivities of the sediments and the salt that is dissolved in the surrounding water, but an exploration of this is beyond the scope of this book.

The turbid underflows through Monterey Canyon tend to occur and produce plumes at the times that the Salinas River floods. Researchers estimated that a turbid underflow may carry as much as half of the total amount of sediments that the Salinas River delivers into Monterey Bay. During those times that the Salinas River is flowing at normal levels, Monterey Canyon helps to guide and transport large amounts of sediments into the deeper ocean, down the continental slope. The turbid underflow events are remarkable in the rapidity with which a large fraction of sediments are shuttled from the shore to the deep ocean. An underflow can function as a release valve that allows a marine shelf environment to respond to changes in the sediment discharge of a river.

It is also noteworthy that the plume of an underflow current is a high-energy process. The movement of sediments in a plume is relatively slow, but large amounts of energy are required to maintain the reversal of an osmotic gradient. In the human body, for example, about a third of the overall chemical energy production is used to maintain reverse osmotic gradients in cells, such as by transporting potassium into cells and sodium out of cells. The maintenance of a reversed salinity gradient in the ocean or a reverse osmotic gradient in the human body may appear mundane, but the amounts of energy involved in the process are remarkably large. The energized state of a plume, moving beneath a mile of ocean water, can be seen as analogous to a tornado moving through a vat of molasses. If the river and the downhill slope of the undersea canyon did not put energy into the plume, the temperature and salinity gradients within the plume would be forcefully dissipated. There is a tendency to imagine an underflow current as a spontaneous process of moving sediments, a mild process of gradual sinking. The underflow could also be viewed as being similar to a dam break in slow motion. It is as if the downhill energy of a dam break were harnessed and somehow used to slow the dam break.

INTERACTIONS OF SEDIMENTS FROM MULTIPLE SOURCES

Monterey Canyon also receives sediments from several smaller avenues. Some turbidity currents exist in Monterey Bay and may deliver sediments to the canyon from different directions. Sediments are also delivered into Monterey Bay through onshore waterways that are distinct from the Salinas and Pájaro Rivers. The Elkhorn Slough, an estuary that delivers sediments from north of Moss Landing Harbor, feeds into Moss Landing Harbor and appears to contribute some of the sediments that are delivered to the head of the canyon. These sediments would be directed toward the canyon from the east, along with sediments from the Pájaro River. An active slump, also known as a complex slump, is another site at which sediments are delivered to the canyon head from the north. This slump is a broad and relatively flat area that slopes into the main channel of Monterey Canyon. The slump appears more like a wide cliff, one that might accommodate a waterfall into a terrestrial canyon, than a narrow tributary. Scientists have recently mapped and studied Monterey Canyon in relatively great detail, and a number of processes related to sediment transport have been identified. Researchers found that gravity flows occurred in the canyon for three years in a row, in the fall, and were essentially undersea landslides. Given that these gravity flows occur in the fall, a period that corresponds to seasonal rainfall and sediment delivery from the land, they are likely to occur in concert with seasonal flushing events. These flushing events serve to transport sediments down along the axis of the canyon. This moves sediments off the margin of the continental shelf, which serves to maintain the depth of Monterey Bay. Some of the gravity flows and low-energy sediment movements may also be driven by the artificial dredging of Monterey Bay, an artificial deepening of the water that moves sediments around, near the edge of the Moss Landing Harbor.

The flushing events serve to transport sediments off the margin of the continental shelf. The continental shelf can generally be envisioned as a precipitous ledge or slope, a line along which the water becomes

Trees and grasses can be seen growing on the rim of the Grand Canyon, in the foreground, and sedimentary rock layers are visible, in the walls of the opposite rim, in the distance. *(Christina Tisi-Kramer/ShutterStock, Inc.)*

The walls of the Grand Canyon extend to the horizon and cast long shadows. *(Mike Hamm/ShutterStock, Inc.)*

In this picture, taken from the Toroweap overlook in the western end of the Grand Canyon, the Colorado River flows toward the camera. *(National Park Service)*

Crown Point, which points west and is on the Oregon side of the gorge, is the site of Vista House and the point at which the Priest Rapids Channel, carrying water up from the southeast, joins the Columbia River. *(Natalia Bratslavsky/ShutterStock, Inc.)*

A section of the Three Gorges in which the walls, covered with vegetation, are exceptionally steep. *(Taolmor/ShutterStock, Inc.)*

The Alcanadre River flows through lower Peonera Canyon, a rock tunnel that may have, in part, been shaped by thermal springs. *(Guara-Canyoning)*

This photograph shows the terrain of the Sierra and Canyons de Guara Natural Park, within which Peonera Canyon is located. *(© Marco Cristofori/Age Fotostock)*

In Windjana Gorge, trees survive along the ephemeral Lennard River. *(© John Noble/CORBIS)*

Each set of vertical lines, shown here in the walls of Windjana Gorge, may indicate that a reef structure shifted landward or seaward in response to some change, such as a change in the sea level or the growth of the reef. (*Lonely Planet Images*)

This picture shows Monterey Bay and some of the coastal mountains in the distance. Since the time that Monterey Canyon was first discovered, people have noted that the coastal mountains are lower and less numerous along Monterey Bay. To the extent that rivers have carved out valleys and delivered sediments into the bay, the onshore topography can be regarded, subjectively, as an extension of Monterey Canyon. (*Natalia Bratslavsky/ShutterStock, Inc.*)

This picture, taken from the Angel's Landing overlook, reveals the mountainous scale and topography of Zion Canyon. *(Jim Lopes/ShutterStock, Inc.)*

The water of the Virgin River is low enough to make the Narrows of Zion Canyon, shown here, accessible to a hiker. *(Tomas Kaspar/ShutterStock, Inc.)*

This picture shows the vast scale of Fish River Canyon and the dry bed of the Fish River, winding along the left edge of the image. *(Allan Montaine/Getty Images)*

This picture shows a car, in the upper lefthand corner, parked near the rim of Fish River Canyon. *(Frans Lemmens/Getty Images)*

The remains of Anasazi dwellings can be seen here, adjacent to the outer wall of Chaco Canyon. *(Tim Davis/Getty Images)*

The Arizona Meteor Crater is near the winding channel of Canyon Diablo, visible on the left side of the photograph. *(National Geographic/Getty Images)*

SEASONAL FLUSHING EVENTS

The flushing events that occur each fall in Monterey Canyon are driven by increases in the outputs of rivers, but the events are not really the result of seasonal floods. Flushing events occur most years or every year and are not as energetic as true hyperpycnal flows, which may occur once or twice a decade. Some researchers argue that hyperpycnal flows should not really be regarded as unusual events, even in other river-sea systems with submarine canyons. In this sense, there is a spectrum of processes that can move sediments through submarine canyons. The flushing events in Monterey Canyon serve to move sediments off the continental shelf. Sediments that have been recently deposited in the head of the canyon, which is part of the continental shelf, are transported along the axis of the canyon. On the floor of Monterey Canyon, sediments are currently being deposited slightly more quickly than they are being incised or eroded away. Thus, a seasonal flushing event is essentially a mechanism for maintaining the status quo in a submarine canyon. The process does not have a great deal of energy behind it and does not strongly drive incision.

deeper. Monterey Canyon has been cut out of the shelf, however, and the heights of the canyon walls may not increase in proportion to the depth of the water.

WAVE-CUT PLATFORMS, MARINE TERRACES, AND UPLIFT

Tectonic activity in the Santa Cruz Mountains, especially within the coastal mountains that are just north of Monterey Bay, appears to have influenced sediment delivery to Monterey Bay. Some of the uplift that has occurred in the Santa Cruz Mountains has been driven by the vertical motion along the Loma Prieta Fault, the San Andreas Fault, and the San Gregorio Fault. These fault systems are all located within the transform boundary, inland of the offshore subduction zone in the Pacific Ocean, and are generally classified as transform faults. This produces motion that is primarily side-to-side, along the horizontal axis of the fault. This means that one side of the fault is not usually pushed upward in relation to the other side. The aforementioned transform faults do exhibit some reverse-slip motion, meaning that there is both vertical and side-to-side motion. This reverse-slip motion has produced fault-associated uplift of the Santa Cruz Mountains.

The uplift of the Santa Cruz Mountains has probably helped to maintain the delivery of river-borne sediments, from the north, to the head of Monterey Canyon. Over the last 200,000 or more years, uplift has primarily occurred on the peninsula that defines the northern margin of Monterey Bay. The uplift in the Santa Cruz Mountains has also helped to maintain the gradient of the drainage pathways that feed land-based sediments from the north. The land to the south has been more stable and has not undergone recent uplift. Tributary canyons feed sediments into Monterey Canyon from both the north and south, but the major source of land-based sediments is the Salinas River. This river flows roughly north and delivers sediments to the canyon head from the south. Thus, streams and rivers will not necessarily transport more sediments from uplifted land. The high sediment load of the Salinas River has persisted, even in the absence of *active uplift*.

The uplift of the Santa Cruz Mountains, north of Monterey Bay, could still have helped shape the marine terraces and wave-cut platforms that are north of Santa Cruz. They extend along the coast, particularly north of Santa Cruz. The Highway 1 Platform and several other wave-cut platforms have been cut out of an offshore portion of Ben Lomond Mountain, an onshore mountain that is on the coast of California and is just north of Monterey Bay. The mountain is also immediately north of the city of Santa Cruz, California. The Ben Lomond Dome is a moniker that can be used to refer to the onshore and offshore portions of the mountain. Ben Lomond Mountain is closely associated with the Ben Lomond Fault. Over the 125,000 years that the Highway 1 platform has existed, the Ben Lomond Dome has been subjected to about 108 feet (33 m) of uplift.

A wave-cut platform is one type of offshore platform. Wave-cut platforms are offshore platforms that have been shaped by the actions of waves and that tend to slope, downward, in the offshore direction. The mechanisms that are responsible for this seaward slope can be complex. It makes intuitive sense that the depth of the ocean should increase as the distance from shore increases, but waves and ocean currents can carry sediments in multiple directions. Waves generally produce more erosion as they move into the shallow water, close to the shoreline. Sediments that are agitated and moved by waves can also be deposited, however. Scientists have actually found that suspended sediments, at least those that are near the shoreline, are often not transported in any overall direction by waves.

Uplift that is produced by fault activity or *orogenic* deformation events can also interact with wave actions, causing a wave-cut platform to develop into a marine terrace. Waves can interact with uplift to create cliffs along parts of wave-cut platforms. These cliffs tend to be cut out of bedrock and older, underlying layers of sedimentary rock. If layers of sedimentary rocks accumulate above these foundational layers of bedrock, uplift can cut terraced structures out of the overlying, solidified layers of marine sediments.

The influence of uplift on these marine terraces may also have influenced sediment delivery to Monterey Canyon. Longshore currents could be affected in different ways by the evolution of a wave-cut platform. These changes in the longshore currents, which transport sediments along the shoreline, could also have impacted the delivery of sediments to Monterey Canyon.

◇◇◇◇◇◇◇◇◇◇◇◇◇◇◇◇◇◇◇◇◇◇◇◇◇◇◇◇◇◇◇◇◇◇ **7** ◇

Zion Canyon

Southwestern Utah, the United States

Zion Canyon is located in southwestern Utah, in the High Plateaus region that encompasses portions of southern Utah. The Markagunt Plateau, out of which Zion Canyon was *incised*, and its neighboring plateaus are part of the western portion of the Colorado Plateau. These plateaus also occupy the only region in which the Colorado Plateau, east of Zion Canyon, overlaps with the Great Basin, which is west of Zion Canyon and is a portion of the Basin and Range Province. Zion Canyon is also relatively near the Mojave Desert to the south and the Sevier Desert to the north. The elevation of the Markagunt Plateau is roughly 2.1 miles (3.3 km), or 10,827 feet (3,300 m), above sea level in some places, and the walls of Zion Canyon are as high as 1,181 feet (360 m) in some places. The highest elevation in Zion National Park is approximately 8,590 feet (2,618 m) above sea level.

The North Fork Virgin River incised Zion Canyon out of thick layers of sandstone and other *sedimentary rocks*, some of which are more than 245 million years old. As labeled in the map on page 114, the North Fork Virgin River flows south and meets the westward-flowing East Fork Virgin River. In the vicinity of the confluence of the two branches, the rivers become the southwestward-flowing Virgin River. A section of the East Fork Virgin River flows through Zion National Park.

In the walls of Zion Canyon, the Navajo Sandstone is an especially thick set of sedimentary rock layers. The layers of the Navajo Sandstone were deposited during the *Jurassic period*. Some layers of the Navajo Sandstone formation, which is up to 2,198 feet (670 m) thick in some places around Zion Canyon, contain solidified cross-bedding, providing the appearance of rippling, that was formed by the actions of wind.

During the Jurassic period, 144,000 square miles (372,960 km²) of land in the southwestern United States was covered by an actively shifting area of sand dunes. In much the same way as sedimentation in an inland lake is influenced by wave actions and wind storms, the layering

113 ◇

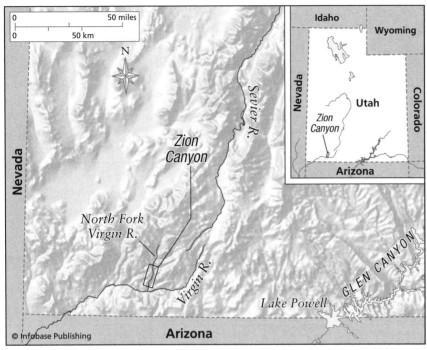

This diagram displays an outline of the main section of Zion Canyon, with the North Fork Virgin River and East Fork Virgin River joining into the Virgin River.

of sandstone *sediments* in the Navajo, Aztec, and Nugget Sand Seas was strongly driven by wind and avalanches of sand dunes. These actively shifting and moving sand dunes comprised a large *erg*, which is a portion of desert that contains actively moving sand dunes. During the Jurassic period, Zion National Park was located at the western margin of the Page erg and the eastern shore of the Carmel Seaway. Scientists estimated that the average daily wind speed across the sand dunes in this area was 51.5 miles per hour (82.3 km/hr), and the average height of the dunes was about 108 feet (33 m).

During the *Cretaceous period*, the area around Zion Canyon was located on a so-called coastal plain and accumulated coastal marine sediments. During this time, Zion Canyon and southeastern Utah were bordered by newly uplifted mountains on the west and a marine *basin* on the east. The mountains were formed during the Sevier Orogeny, a mountain-building event that is discussed below, and the coastal plain around Zion Canyon became a *foreland basin*. (The upper color insert on page C-6 illustrates Zion Canyon's topography.)

Different types of sediments accumulated in this Sevier foreland basin, both during and after the Sevier Orogeny. After the mountain building of the Sevier Orogeny ceased, in the Late Cretaceous, extensive activity along *fault* lines began to occur. This *fault activity* in southern Utah is essentially regarded as having been a result of the fold-thrust deformation, and mountain building, of the Sevier Orogeny. This *fault-associated uplift*, which occurred over various times and in numerous places, influenced sediment deposition and drainage around Zion Canyon.

Although this post-thrust, or post-orogenic, fault activity is mainly relevant in the context of land elevations and sedimentation, it is also notable that fault activity can be related to orogenic activity in certain ways. Activity along faults does not necessarily come "out of the blue," so to speak. *Volcanic arcs* and *volcanic activity* can also interact with fault activity, as discussed in other chapters.

INTERACTIONS OF RIVER WATER AND GROUNDWATER

Like the climates around other canyons discussed in this book, the climate around Zion Canyon is semiarid and characterized by seasonal rainfalls. The annual rainfall is about 15 inches (38 cm) per year.

Zion Canyon contains a remarkably diverse range of landforms, and the canyon has been a popular destination for tourists and canyoneering climbers. In the section of the canyon known as the Narrows, for example, the walls are extremely steep and form a so-called slot canyon. In the Narrows, tourists cannot hike along the Virgin River; they must walk or boat within the actual river (as shown in the lower color insert on page C-6). The walls of the Narrows are largely composed of the Navajo Sandstone, which is more permeable and easily incised. A similar degree of uplift occurred elsewhere in Zion Canyon, but the canyon tends to be wider outside of the Narrows and tends to contain layers of more *resistant rock*. This may seem counterintuitive, but the wider and more U-shaped portions were eroded by a specific type of groundwater phenomenon.

The erosion that was produced by this process, known as groundwater sapping, occurred in areas where the resistant shales of the Kayenta Formation are present below the Navajo Sandstone. The groundwater percolates downward to the Kayenta Formation and then tends to flow out and over it, rather than primarily incising downward. The Navajo Sandstone tends to weaken and collapse in what amount to rockslides, whereas the Kayenta Formation is less severely eroded. There tends to be a sharp transition from steep, V-shaped walls to wider, U-shaped walls at places where groundwater channels and layers of resistant rocks are present.

Although sapping is something of a rare phenomenon on Earth, scientists have noted evidence of sapping in the topography on Mars. This and other water-mediated processes in Utah, which was part of a vast desert for long periods of time, have been compared to processes that are thought to have occurred on Mars. When liquid water was present on Mars, for example, the planet was likely to have been a kind of vast and cold desert. The liquid water may have existed primarily as subsurface groundwater. Some scientists think that water probably flowed over the surface at least some of the time. Other scientists think rainfall may have once occurred on Mars.

Scientists working on the Mars Explorer Rover project have found many similarities between iron concretions photographed on Mars and concretions found in Utah. Iron concretions can be found throughout the arid regions of the western United States, regions that include portions of Montana, Utah, Arizona, and elsewhere. The iron concretions appear as small, spherical, reddish-brown rocks that may be scattered across the ground or fixed to the face of a larger rock. Some of the iron concretions that have been photographed on Mars, at Endurance Crater and at the Berry Bowl site in Eagle Crater, on *Meridiani Planum*, are roughly four millimeters in diameter and show many morphological similarities to iron concretions in Utah.

The comparison of terrestrial and Martian iron concretions helps scientists to piece together the geological history of Mars, particularly with regard to water-related phenomena. Liquid water has probably not existed on Mars very recently, but there is strong evidence that the Martian iron concretions were formed by the deposition of dissolved iron oxide.

RED IRON OXIDE IN UTAH AND ON MARS

Iron concretions do not form on an iron-containing rock surface without the addition of another source, from outside the rock, of dissolved iron. The growth of concretions occurs when the reduced iron (Fe^{2+}, or ferrous iron) that is dissolved in water is oxidized to ferric iron (Fe^{3+}). The oxidation causes the iron to precipitate out of solution in the solid form of iron oxide. Concretions simply cannot form by delivering an oxidizing agent, by itself, over an iron-containing rock. The growth of iron concretions on Earth requires "two solutions," meaning moisture on the iron-containing rock and a second source of water, containing dissolved iron, running over the rock. This tells scientists that iron dissolved in liquid water must have been present to form the Martian concretions. Additionally, the rock outcrop to which the so-called blueberries are fixed is not very rich in iron oxide, but the Martian iron concretions themselves are 50 percent iron oxide. Given what is known about the formation of iron concretions, this suggests that the iron concretions were not simply formed by the abrasion or erosion of a rock outcrop of nonuniform composition. Scientists also noted that the Martian concretions were generally uniform in size, which suggests that the rock outcrop is roughly uniform in composition.

With regard to weathering by wind and dust, the preservation of the Martian iron concretions is also interesting. The iron concretions were found on a rock outcropping that juts out of the sloping wall of a crater, and scientists think this has protected the concretions from physical weathering by windstorms.

THE SEVIER FORELAND BASIN AND CORDILLERAN ARC

The Sevier Foreland Basin of southwestern and central Utah can also be viewed as part of a larger system, the Cordilleran Foreland Basin. The term *cordillera*, pronounced cor-dee-YAIR-a, is a general term that can refer to a mountain range or the mountain range on a continent that is more extensive than the other ranges. The term was derived from the Spanish word *cordilla*, which means a cord or small rope. In the context of the western United States, researchers attach the term to geological events and phenomena that relate to the Cordilleran Orogeny.

The Cordilleran Orogeny, which created the Rocky Mountains and resulted from *plate* convergence, can actually be viewed as a complex cascade of geological events. The beginning of the Laramide Orogeny coincided with the end of the Sevier Orogeny, and both events resulted from the presence of the Cordilleran Arc and the occurrence of Cordilleran mountain-building processes.

The Sevier Foreland Basin is known as a *retroarc foreland basin*, which is part of the *backarc zone* and backarc thrust belt that are often created during plate convergence. The Sevier Orogeny, which refers to the processes that occurred along the Sevier Fold-Thrust Belt, resulted from the *subduction* of the Farallon plate beneath the North American plate. The Cordilleran Arc was created inland, or east, of the convergent plate boundary, the zone at which the two plates converged. This boundary extended from north to south. The forearc basin, part of the forearc zone, was formed cratonward, or east, of the plate boundary. The backarc zone, or retroarc zone, was inland, or east, of the arc. The most important point is simply that the Sevier Fold-Thrust Belt, the Sevier Foreland Basin, and the extensional faulting and volcanism occurred as a result of the plate convergence.

TECTONIC HISTORY OF SOUTHWESTERN UTAH

Another event that shaped the regional topography was the Sevier Orogeny, a mountain-building cycle that occurred to the northwest of Zion National Park. The Sevier Orogenic Belt is a fold-thrust belt that deformed the landscape of southwestern Utah during the Cretaceous period and early *Tertiary period*. The deformation of land along the Sevier Fold-Thrust Belt was directed to the northwest, and the Sevier Foreland Basin was created to the southeast of this line.

In the context of Zion Canyon, the relevant portion of the Sevier Fold-Thrust Belt is the southern Nevada–southwestern Utah segment. The fold-thrust belt is quite long and extends northward in multiple segments, which are further divided into multiple thrusts. The Sevier Foreland Basin was equally vast. During the Cretaceous period, the

ZION CANYON AND UPLIFT OF THE COLORADO PLATEAU

The activity along the Sevier Fold-Thrust Belt ended as the Laramide Orogeny began, and researchers have proposed various mechanisms to explain this general interaction. The uplift of the Colorado Plateau was crucial to the formation of the Grand Canyon, as discussed in chapter 1, but some aspects of the early Colorado Plateau have been confusing for researchers. The Colorado Plateau was at sea level during the interval between 100 and 70 million years ago, but the *crust* beneath the plateau is presently too thick to be consistent with a sea-level elevation. The crust of the Colorado Plateau is presently about 28 miles (45 km) thick, and essentially, no portions of continental crust are known to exist at sea level and also be this thick.

To maintain the surface of this thick crust at sea level, the *mantle lithosphere* would have to be extraordinarily thick. This is because the mantle lithosphere is negatively buoyant and tends to pull the crust down into the *asthenosphere.* A portion of a *continental plate* is maintained at neutral buoyancy, a sort of isostatic equilibrium, by virtue of the balance between the upward push, of the crust, and the downward pull of the *mantle lithosphere.* Something must have either thinned the mantle lithosphere beneath the Colorado Plateau, thereby lessening the downward pull, or increased the upward buoyancy of the crust. The problem is that, depending on the context, uplift can result from either the thinning or thickening of the crust. If the crust is thickened with low-density crustal material, the crust might only be weighted down a little bit. The result can be a net uplift of the surface, with *isostatic uplift* balanced by some erosion. If the crust is thinned by *erosional exhumation* of surface rocks, the crust will ultimately become more buoyant and undergo isostatic uplift. Mountain building, of course, tends to produce both uplift and localized thickening of the crust. The crustal rock is compressed and pushed up, like the hood of a car that has undergone a fender bender.

One group of scientists proposed that a portion of crustal material, one that was buoyant and of relatively low density, was transferred from the "Sevier Plateau" to the middle crust beneath the Colorado Plateau. This transfer of crustal material that was about 8.7 miles (14 km) thick could help explain the present-day thickness of the crust, beneath the Colorado Plateau, and some of the eastward "migration" of the Sevier Fold-Thrust Belt. This belt is known to have migrated eastward, and extensional fault activity subsequently occurred in the Basin and Range Province. In essence, the process can be imagined as an eastward extrusion of part of the crust that was beneath the land near the Sevier Fold-Thrust Belt. The process is thought to have ultimately been connected to changes in the subduction angle of the Farallon plate. The effects of changes in this subduction angle are discussed in chapter 1. Scientists have referred to the high elevations that existed in and around the Sevier Fold-Thrust Belt, 80–100 million years ago, as the Sevier Plateau. In this context, the Sevier Plateau has been viewed as a proto–Colorado Plateau that was flattened and morphed, from a visual standpoint, into the Colorado Plateau. Even after the Sevier Orogeny and any crustal transfer process had ended, the area around Zion Canyon was still at high elevations. Parts of southwestern Utah were even uplifted during parts of the Laramide Orogeny.

Sevier Foreland Basin reached east, across central and southern Utah, into southern Colorado.

The Virgin Anticline and the Pintura Fold, another anticline, are other nearby portions of land that were folded during the Sevier Orogenic Cycle. These anticlines are parallel to the Sevier Fold-Thrust Belt and are oriented from the southwest to the northeast. The Pintura Fold is located in between two segments of the Hurricane Fault and also intersects the Hurricane Fault in one area. West of the Pintura Fold is the Virgin Anticline, which intersects the Washington Fault. Both the Hurricane and Washington Faults are west of Zion National Park and are oriented in roughly north-south lines. So the orogenic deformations are oriented from southwest to northeast and are parallel, and the fault systems extend in parallel lines from north to south.

A number of fault lines are in closer proximity to the Sevier Fold-Thrust Belt and have produced complex landforms. Spring Canyon, for example, is adjacent to extensional fault lines that partially flattened, in a localized fashion, the mountains that the Sevier Orogeny had built up. This extension occurred during the *Cenozoic era*, more recently than the Sevier folding and thrusting. About 140 million years ago, the Sevier Fold-Thrust Belt began to gradually migrate inland. The Sevier Foreland Basin, east of the Sevier Fold-Thrust Belt, also migrated inland and accumulated sediments at different times. Post-thrust fault systems are common in association with this type of Fold-Thrust Belt, produced on a continental plate that is overriding a subducting oceanic plate, and the fault systems that are in the vicinity of Zion Canyon are examples of this.

The accumulation of sediments in the Sevier Foreland Basin was therefore initiated by orogenic processes and then sustained by the post-thrust fault systems. Many sites within Zion National Park are at very high elevations today. For a long time, however, the site of Zion Canyon was at lower elevations than the land to both the east and the west.

FAULT SYSTEMS, UPLIFT, AND DRAINAGE

Zion National Park is located in between two significant fault systems, the Sevier and Hurricane Fault Systems. The Hurricane Fault System is located to the west of Zion Canyon, and the Sevier Fault System is located to the east. These fault lines, which extend essentially from north to south, are "systems" in the sense that they form branches and may be moving in different ways along different portions of the faults. These fault systems began to show significant activity, producing different combinations of uplift, extension, and localized *subsidence*, during the Cenozoic era. The activity along these faults occurred after the end of the Sevier Orogeny and was essentially the "result" of the Sevier mountain building. Again, the Sevier Fold-Thrust Belt was located to the west and northwest of the Sevier Fault System. The activity along the Sevier and Hurricane Faults began during the Cenozoic era, and some of the fault systems in the vicinity of Zion Canyon are still active.

The activity along the Hurricane Fault, which is still active and extends from southern Utah into Wyoming, has been complex and has varied over different portions of the fault. The fault is generally a normal and dip-slip fault, meaning that one side is moving downward as the other is being pushed upward. In the vicinity of Zion National Park, however, at least two sections of the the fault have also exhibited dextral, or right-handed, motion in recent times.

The activity along the Hurricane Fault has generally been producing uplift on the eastern side of the fault, and Zion National Park is largely confined to the eastern side of the fault. This fault-associated uplift occurred between 5 and 6 million years ago, during the Tertiary period, and lifted the eastern side of the fault roughly 6,890 feet (2,100 m) in relation to the western side. The uplifted eastern side is regarded as having been the *footwall* of the Hurricane Fault, and the western side is known as the *hanging wall*. Both sides of the fault accumulated some lava during this fault activity and during fault activity that occurred, more recently, during the Quaternary period.

A small portion of the Hurricane Fault System extends into Zion National Park, near the visitor center. The Hurricane Cliffs, which extend roughly from north to south and were formed as a result of uplift along the Hurricane Fault System, form part of the topography that is roughly parallel to Zion Canyon.

Fault-associated uplift along the Hurricane Fault System could have contributed to recent intervals of incision at Zion Canyon. Near Hurricane Utah, the major fault of the Hurricane Fault System extends from north to south. The Virgin River flows west and crosses this fault at an almost perpendicular angle. At various times, the eastern and upstream side of the fault was *upthrown* with respect to the western and down-stream, and downthrown, *fault block*. This would have locally increased the *gradient*, a short distance downstream of Zion Canyon, of the Virgin River. This could have contributed to recent incision, given the large magnitudes of the uplift along the Hurricane Faults. Incision of the canyon probably began between 6 and 5.5 million years ago, as discussed below. This incision would have occurred before the fault-associated uplift and any resulting incision occurred. Displacement, producing some uplift, along different parts of the Hurricane Fault was occurring as early as 3–4 million years ago. Fault-associated uplift along this fault system has also occurred over the last 850,000 years.

THE LARAMIDE OROGENY AND BLEACHED SANDSTONE

Zion National Park is located at one of the westernmost sites that was subjected to some uplift and deformation by the Laramide Orogeny. The Laramide Orogeny produced more concentrated deformation to the east of Zion Canyon, such as in the Circle Cliffs Uplift and Kaibab Upwarp, and in other states in the four corners. Zion Canyon is sometimes regarded as being part of the Colorado Plateau and occupying a site at which the Colorado Plateau overlaps with the Basin and Range Province. In Zion Canyon and other parts of southern Utah, the Laramide Orogeny did create anticlines, synclines, and fault activity. These cracks and deformations are thought to have allowed methane, which is natural gas, and other hydrocarbons to be released and migrate through the Navajo Sandstone. The anticlines, synclines, and faults are thought to have acted as conduits for the upward migration of hydrocarbons. The hydrocarbons produced bleaching of the upper layers of the Navajo Sandstone. As recently as 6 million years ago, the erosional exhumation of the Colorado Plateau and the site of Zion Canyon are thought to have released large amounts of these hydrocarbons.

The bleaching pattern of the Navajo Sandstone can be seen in the Great White Throne and in other parts of the walls of Zion Canyon. The layers of Navajo Sandstone that were deposited during the Jurassic period extend across much of central and southeastern Utah and contain high concentrations of quartz. By itself, quartz is essentially white. At different places in Utah and Colorado, however, iron oxide was deposited in various patterns and sub-layers of the Navajo Sandstone and stained the quartz to a reddish-orange color. Even the 1 percent or 2 percent content of iron oxide that is found in some parts of the Navajo Sandstone, which is about 98 percent quartz, is enough to redden the layers of sandstone. Some scientists have argued that oil and other hydrocarbons, which include natural gas, were moved as a result of the Laramide Orogeny and were responsible for the bleaching patterns.

In areas near Zion Canyon, such as at the White Cliffs of the Grand Staircase, the lower layers of the Navajo Sandstone have been stained with iron oxide, and the upper layers have been bleached to white. The concept of upper and lower does not explicitly refer to the timing of the layers' deposition but to the relative physical height of the layers, such as they would appear on a cliff face. This bleaching of the upper layers may have occurred when oil and natural gas, when in a liquid phase or gas phase, were released and allowed to migrate upward. This bleaching pattern can also be seen in the Great White Throne, a rock formation in Zion Canyon.

Other scientists have proposed that groundwater removed the iron, and the cooperation of groundwater and hydrocarbons cannot be ruled out. The methane that is the main component of natural gas is lighter than air and will accumulate at the top of a room, and other hydrocarbons are known to separate out to the surface of a portion of liquid water. Just as oil sits on the ocean surface after an oil spill, hydrocarbons tend to rise above groundwater. This is because the hydrocarbons are of lower densities than water. Because oil and natural gas

In this picture of the Great White Throne, at Zion Canyon, the uppermost layers of the Navajo Sandstone have been bleached. *(Alysta/ShutterStock, Inc.)*

are reducing agents, they reduce the ferric iron (Fe^{3+}) to ferrous iron (Fe^{2+}) and allow it to be washed away by water. This is essentially the reverse of the process that allows iron concretions, discussed earlier in this chapter, to form.

RELEVANCE TO THE TIMING OF INCISION

The bleaching of the Navajo Sandstone may have been largely complete, and probably had at least begun, at the time that Zion Canyon was incised. Around 6 million years ago, fault activity in the Basin and Range Province helped to cause changes in the drainage of the Colorado Plateau. There is evidence that a relatively sudden increase in the global sea-surface temperature, of up to 1.8°F (1°C), also occurred about 6 million years ago. Researchers think that the rapid exhumation of near-surface hydrocarbons from "anticlinal reservoirs" and other stores in the Navajo Sandstone may have contributed to this. A similar, sudden release of hydrocarbons, elsewhere in the world and at the beginning of the *Eocene epoch*, is thought to have produced a larger increase in sea-surface temperature.

The bleaching of the Navajo Sandstone had probably been largely complete by 6 million years ago, when erosional exhumation opened up the hydrocarbon reservoirs. Rock layers had been deposited above the Navajo Sandstone, and these layers were eroded down after the Laramide Orogeny. The Navajo Sandstone was highly permeable, and this allowed natural gas to accumulate in the upper layers of the Navajo Sandstone. A large part of the incision of Zion Canyon probably began between 6 and 5.5 million years ago, in response to changes in drainage pathways. Thus, much of the incision of the canyon is likely to have occurred after the bleaching process.

Beginning about 5.5 million years ago, the Virgin River produced numerous intervals of incision in and around the Mesquite Basin. This basin is just north of Lake Mead, and the Virgin River still flows through the basin. Thus, incision by the Virgin River coincided significantly with incision by the Colorado River. The Mesquite Basin is far downstream from Zion Canyon, but the incision at this site would have helped increase the gradient of the river at Zion Canyon.

OTHER LAYERS OF SEDIMENTARY ROCKS

Immediately above the Navajo Sandstone are the Temple Cap Formation and the Carmel Formation, which consist of sandstone, siltstone, and volcanic ash. The sediments in the Temple Cap and Carmel Formations were deposited when the eastern and central portions of southern Utah were part of a kind of tidal shoreline. The ash in the Temple Cap Formation was deposited between 170 and 171 million years ago, and the ash in the Carmel Formation was deposited between 162 and 168 million years ago. The volcanic eruptions that released these different portions of ash occurred during periods of extensional fault activity.

Some of this volcanic ash accumulated along the edges of intraccontinental seaways that covered large portions of Utah, California, and Nevada. When the ash of the Carmel and Temple Cap Formations were being deposited, the site of Zion Canyon was located on the edge of the submerged Arapien Basin. The major sites at which ash accumulated in ash beds, in southern Utah and northern Arizona, are located along the shores of this so-called Carmel Seaway. Large sand dunes were also still present in portions of southeastern Utah, and these dunes were also located along the tidal ash beds that make up the Carmel and Temple Cap Formations. Later, during the Cretaceous period, the borders of the Carmel Seaway were shifted into the vast western Interior Seaway, which effectively split North America into two islands.

8

Fish River Canyon
Namibian Highland, Southern Namibia

The area of land that is occupied by Fish River Canyon, which is located on the Namibian Highland of southern Namibia, is thought to make it the second-largest canyon (second to the Grand Canyon) in the world. As shown in the upper color insert on page C-7, the climate at the site of the canyon is arid, largely because the canyon is a short distance east of the hyperarid Namib Desert. The land around the canyon was influenced by *orogenic* events, *volcanic* eruptions, *fault activity*, and *rifting*. The Fish River has formed the walls of the canyon by *incising* through layers of *sedimentary rock*, some of which are more than 500 million years old.

The Fish River has cut down through rocks that are considerably older than Fish River Canyon. The layers of gneisses, near the lower walls of the canyon, are up to 1.5 billion years old. Namibia was once near the center of the Gondwana supercontinent, a portion of lithosphere that included Africa, South America, and Antarctica. As Gondwana broke up, the South Atlantic Ocean began to form off the coast of Namibia. This geological event had only an indirect effect on the formation of Fish River Canyon. Geomorphological remnants of the event are, nonetheless, still evident in Namibia and South Africa. Perhaps to commemorate the importance of this event to the landscape of Namibia, the land that surrounds Fish River Canyon is known as Gondwana Cañon Park.

The Fish River probably began incising parts of Fish River Canyon at about 2.7 million years ago, during the late *Pliocene epoch*. Some of the incision was indirectly facilitated by the high elevations in Namibia, such as at the headwaters of the Fish River. The development of the drainage pathway of the Fish River was partially determined by the erosion, as in the *erosional exhumation*, of the Namibian escarpment, part of the Great Escarpment. The escarpment is a structural component of a *passive continental margin*, formed as a result of a rifting event. Some of the incision of the canyon may have been driven by a change in the climate of the Namib Desert. Specifically, the Benguela *upwelling* system began to consistently deliver dry air and winter rainfall to Namibia and South Africa.

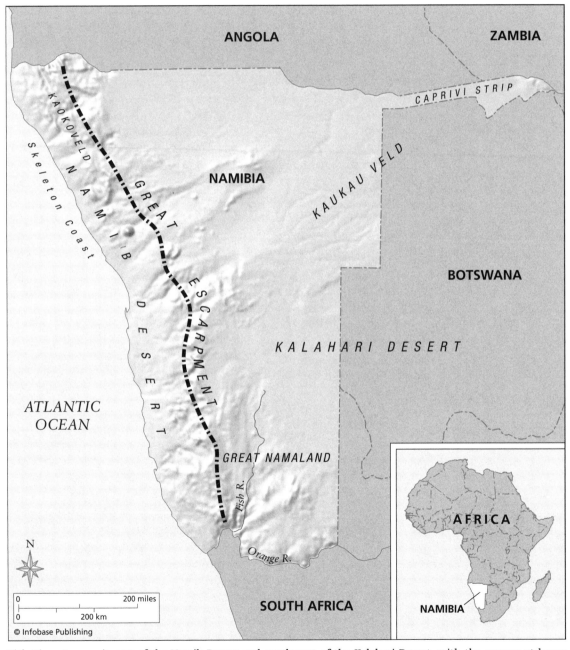

Fish River Canyon is east of the Namib Desert and southwest of the Kalahari Desert, with the canyon at lower elevations than much of the southern Namibian Great Escarpment.

In the figure on page 126, the Namibian portion of the Great Escarpment can be seen to the west of Fish River Canyon. The Namib Desert is depicted along the South Atlantic coast. The Great Escarpment is viewed as defining the eastern margin of the Namib Desert, even though the coastal Namib Desert is the most intensely arid. Thus, Fish River Canyon is a relatively short distance from both the escarpment and the desert. The Kalahari Desert can be seen to the northeast of the canyon.

The Benguela Upwelling System is the set of factors that produces upwelling off the coasts of Namibia and South Africa. The term *upwelling* refers to the upward movement of cold water from deeper depths. The upwelling process results from complex interactions among seasonal wind patterns and the Benguela Current, an ocean current that flows along the coastline from south to north. North of Namibia, the Benguela Current veers to the west, away from the coast, and crosses paths, near the westward divergence area, with another current that is directed to the south. In this context, the term *upwelling* refers to a process in the ocean. Beneath a *hot spot*, the upwelling process is occurring in the *mantle* and not the ocean.

Even during the middle of the *Miocene epoch*, between 5 and 10 million years ago, Namibia began to experience some of the climatological effects of the upwelling process. Other scientists have estimated that the Namib Desert may have existed, in some form, for 10–15 million years. This age corresponds to the middle of the Miocene Epoch. Between 2.2 million years and 1.3 million years ago, much of Namibia became profoundly and consistently dry. Some parts of the Namib Desert receive almost zero annual rainfall, and 70 percent of this rain falls during the winter months. Along with the dry climate, the winter rainfall pattern tends to limit vegetation. Vegetation grows in response to rain, but winter is colder and less conducive to plant growth than summer is.

THE FISH RIVER AND THE CLIMATE OF NAMIBIA

Some scientists have noticed that deserts can often be found on the western coasts of continents in equatorial regions, and the Namib Desert is an example of this. It is noteworthy that canyons can also exist for long periods of time in semiarid regions that are not deserts, and desert can certainly exist on land that is not on the western edge of a continent. Canyons require at least some moving water to form, however, and a full-blown river cannot usually be found in the middle of a desert.

Although the Fish River was not always small and narrow, it is now known as an *ephemeral river*. Because of the relatively arid climate and also because of a dam, a significant distance north and upstream of Fish River Canyon, the Fish River is often completely dry in Fish River Canyon. Something that is ephemeral is something that is highly transient and is

This photograph shows the channel of the Fish River, winding through Fish River Canyon, carrying some water. *(Getty Images)*

fleeting or vanishing. The Fish River is a *tributary* of the Orange River and flows in a southward direction, into the westward-flowing Orange River.

In contrast to an ephemeral river, a perennial river has at least some water in it at all times. A perennial river might carry more water during the spring or another period of time that occurs perennially, much as perennial flowers bloom every summer. But a river that only carries water for a few days, or in some cases hours, every year is ephemeral.

Although some scientists think that the site of the Namib Desert may have been fairly arid for as long as 80 million years, the Namib Desert is probably about 10–15 or 20 million years old. The Namib Desert extends up and down the entire coast of Namibia and ends along the northern coast of South Africa, Namibia's neighbor to the south. The desert has sometimes been separated into five major portions, including the Namib Sand Sea and the Skeleton Coast. Fish River Canyon is east of the southernmost, Sperrgebiet section of the Namib Desert. The soil in much of Namibia is generally also very dry, very thin, and poor for growing crops. Almost no vegetation grows on the dunes of the Namib Sand Sea.

The Namib Desert is a subtropical desert, and canyons can often be found in or around these arid regions. Subtropical deserts or arid regions tend to begin at the western coasts of continents and tend to be found at latitudes between 20 and 30 degrees north or south of the equator. In fact, each of these deserts is part of a larger area of dry air that extends to the west, out over the ocean. A large area of the South Atlantic Ocean to the west of the Namib Desert, extending almost to South America, is very "dry" and receives less than 9.8 inches (250 mm) of rain per year. Similar portions of dry air can be found, for example, above the Pacific Ocean, to the west of southern California and the Baja Peninsula, and above the Indian Ocean, off of the western coast of Australia.

Researchers think that arid conditions in Namibia may have been partially maintained by changes in the amounts of Antarctic sea ice. Major fluctuations in Antarctic sea ice do not occur on an annual basis. The seasonal, winter rainfall pattern of the Namib Desert is therefore not driven by seasonal fluctuations in sea ice. Rather, the seasonal pattern is driven by seasonal changes in the wind patterns above the South Atlantic. Suffice it to say that the sea surface temperature off the coast of Namibia varies seasonally, and the variation is driven by the upwelling of colder, nutrient-laden water from depths of about 656 feet (200 m). The amount of ice around Antarctica has primarily increased during intervals of glaciation. During these intervals, an increase in the amount of ice was accompanied by an increase in the amount of winter rain in coastal, Southern Namibia.

The Namibian Highland and central plateau on which Fish River Canyon is located are less arid than the Namib Desert but are still part of a desert climate. The site of Fish River Canyon receives between 7.9 inches (200 mm) and about 9.8 inches (250 mm) of rain. This low amount of annual rainfall makes the climate, technically, arid and part of a desert. Most of southern Namibia is arid, and most of the other parts of Namibia are semiarid. Most of the Namib Desert receives less than two inches (50 mm) of annual rainfall. The high evaporative capacity of the air also makes the Namib Desert part of a hyperarid climate: The aridity index is as high as 100. An aridity index of 100 means that the air can evaporate, over the course of a year, 100 times the annual rainfall. This evaporative capacity is measured with an evaporation pan, which contains water that is continuously replenished. This type of measurement fails to take wind and other factors into account. The measurement has been criticized by researchers, but the index highlights the magnitude of the aridity.

Even though the winter rainfall zone and Namib Desert are technically confined to the coastal zone, west of the Great Escarpment, the climate of the Namib Desert has been important for the formation and preservation of Fish River Canyon. The margins of the winter rainfall

THE NAMIB DESERT AND ANTARCTIC SEA ICE

The amounts of winter rainfall appear to have increased during intervals of glaciation. During intervals of glaciation over the last 45,000 years, large portions of the ocean around Antarctica were frozen over. This caused an atmospheric phenomenon in the South Pole, the Polar Vortex, to expand northward. The polar frontal zone and subtropical fronts, which deliver winter rainfall to Namibia and South Africa, also expanded toward the equator. This intensification of winter rainfall was ultimately tied to the increased moisture that can occur in the atmosphere above glacial ice. A large amount of Antarctic sea ice can also influence subtropical weather by decreasing the water temperature of the ocean, such as in the Weddell Sea of Antarctica.

There is evidence that sea ice in Antarctica may have influenced winter rainfall in the Namib Desert for 128,000 years or longer. In portions of eastern Australia that receive winter rainfall, Antarctic ice may have influenced rainfall amounts for 500,000 years. According to the estimates of other researchers, Namibia may have been subjected to some extent of seasonal upwelling for 12 million years. Interestingly, researchers think that an early form of the Namib Desert may have existed for 10–15 million years.

Over the last 2.2 million years, the winter rainfall appears to have helped maintain the hyperarid conditions of the Namib Desert. If the winter rainfall zone expanded inland during glacial intervals, in addition to intensifying, the winter rain could also have contributed to the incision of Fish River Canyon. Winter rain could have driven incision, by the Fish River, and helped limit the growth of vegetation. Plants tend to grow more abundantly in areas that receive summer rainfall. Without vegetation, the incisional effect of flooding may have been intensified. If the Antarctic sea ice continues to melt, such as in response to the effects of greenhouse gases, the Namib Desert may become even more arid. The sea around Antarctica is known to have frozen and melted over very short periods of time. Vast portions of glacial ice, around Antarctica, are known to have frozen and melted within an interval of only 2,000 years. From a geological standpoint, this is very dynamic. If a reduction in Antarctic sea ice warms the ocean, researchers think that the winter rainfall pattern could expand across significant parts of southern Africa. This could maintain Fish River Canyon but interfere, for example, with agriculture.

zone are thought to have expanded and contracted at different times, and Fish River Canyon is quite near the Great Escarpment. Another subtropical desert, the Kalahari Desert, is also a short distance northeast of the canyon. The important point is that the climate of Fish River Canyon has been, for a long time, strongly tied to the climate of the Namib Desert. The climate of the Namib Desert, in turn, has partially been maintained by winter rainfall.

In contrast to the eastern portions of southern Africa, the seasonal rainfall pattern in the Namib Desert and in the western portion of South Africa are not driven by the Indian Ocean monsoonal system. A discussion of the mechanisms that drive seasonal wind patterns and seasonal ocean currents is beyond the scope of this book. For the sake of discussion, it is only relevant that, during intervals of glaciation, the Benguela Current was more heavily influenced by the climate and oceans of Antarctica than the current is today. For example, the upwelling appears to have been more heavily influenced, during the last glacial maximum, by the movement of cold water along the Drake Passage. Now, ocean currents from the Indian Ocean influence the Benguela Current.

The water off the coast of Namibia is now part of a kind of intermediate zone, in terms of ocean temperature. The water is warmer than the ocean to the south and cooler than the ocean to the north. Along the coast of South Africa, the northward path of the Benguela Upwelling System intersects the westward path of the Agulhas Current. Around this zone of intersection of the ocean currents, the ocean is able to support some unique types of red algae and phytoplankton. The area has also been described as the Benguela Marine Province.

The relatively low temperature of the ocean surface, off the coast of South Africa and southern Namibia, apparently helps to limit precipitation in the Namib Desert. Less water evaporates from cooler water, and the decrease in evaporation is thought to help reduce precipitation in the Namib Desert. The Benguela Current transports water that is both cold and rich in nutrients. These nutrients support the phytoplankton and algae that are part of the Benguela Marine Province. These forms of marine plant life can use up carbon dioxide, but they also have deposited carbonate debris off the coast of Namibia.

In the eastern portions of South Africa and the land that is east of the Great Escarpment, the pattern of seasonal rainfall is reversed. These areas receive 60 percent of the annual rainfall in the summer months. On the surface, the Namib Desert is similar to the Sahara Desert and other subtropical deserts. Like other subtropical deserts, the position of the Namib Desert is on the western coast of a continent.

SUBTROPICAL DESERTS AND ATMOSPHERIC CONVECTION CURRENTS

Researchers think that the arid climates of subtropical deserts, such as the Namib, are maintained by so-called atmospheric convection cells. The air is consistently hot at equatorial latitudes, and heated air tends to rise. In the case of the air that is west of Africa and above the Atlantic Ocean, the heat at the equator causes the air to both rise and move away from the equator. If two torus-shaped innertubes were affixed above and below the equator of a spherical globe, like belts around the midsection of the globe, the air would tend to move along the circular innertubes, in a direction roughly north or south, away from the equator. This tends to cause moisture to be evaporated from the air that is near the equator.

However, the wet air that is rising and moving away from the equator tends to cool as it approaches the latitudes that are 20 or 30 degrees north or south of the equator. Because cool air holds little water vapor, the water condenses out and falls as rain. This direction of convection accounts for the band of dry air above the South Atlantic, given that the moisture tends to arc over it and fall at more southerly latitudes.

The direction of the convection cell is reversed, however, in the air over Namibia and South Africa. Over Namibia and Southwest Africa, some of the moist air tends to move toward the equator and descend over the rain forests in central Africa.

The north-south direction of convection currents, driven by equatorial heat, causes rain to fall in places other than Namibia. This determines the position of the desert along a west-east line. However, the Namib Desert could be regarded as both a subtropical desert and a "supra-polar desert." Antarctica creates north-south differences in the air and water temperature. These thermal differences help to drive the winter rainfall pattern of the Namib Desert. The Antarctic ice may also contribute to the overall aridity of Namibia.

SEDIMENTARY ROCK LAYERS IN THE CANYON WALLS

The walls of Fish River Canyon generally contain layers of the Nama Group, which sit above the older layers of gneissic rocks. In some parts of the canyon walls, *dikes* of basalt lava extend through the gneiss and into the layers of the Nama Group. Many of the dikes appear as cube-shaped chunks and consist of dolerite.

The land that is in and around Fish River Canyon was once part of a shallow water, marine environment. In this environment, layers of dead organisms gradually accumulated on the shore or seafloor. These layers were gradually converted into limestone and other carbonate-containing sedimentary rocks. These rocks make up some of the layers of the Nama Group.

After the land was high enough to be above sea level, the rivers that drained into the ocean were able to cut downward through the layers of sedimentary rocks. A number of the canyons discussed in this book, canyons in many different parts of the world, were in shallow marine environments. Canyons can, however, also be cut out of granite and other highly resistant rock layers. If the land around a canyon was once part of a coastal or tidal marine environment, the land was in a position to accumulate thick layers of sediments.

EARLY DEVELOPMENT OF THE NAMA BASIN

The present-day site of Fish River Canyon is located on the extreme southwestern margin of the Nama Basin, a *peripheral foreland basin*. The Nama Basin was created during the Pan-African Brasiliano Orogeny, which amounted to a joining of Africa to South America. The actual event was a joining, by a mixture of *subduction* and suturing, of three *cratons*. These were the Río de la Plata Craton, the Kalahari Craton, and the Congo Craton. The result was the closure of the Adamastor Ocean, also known as the proto–Atlantic Ocean, that had previously separated Namibia and South Africa from the southern arm of present-day South America. Along with the Sao Francisco Craton, the four cratons comprised the western portion of Gondwana.

For at least 300 million years, Namibia and the rest of Africa were part of the Gondwana supercontinent. As part of Gondwana, Africa was joined to South America, Antarctica, and India. Scientists think that Gondwana was located near the South Pole from 500 to 320 million years ago, and that different parts of South America and Africa occupied the geographical South Pole at different times. North America and the continent known as Eurasia then gradually joined with Gondwana to form, by about 225 million years ago, the larger supercontinent of Pangaea. It is apparent from any map of the present-day world that South America and Africa could "fit together" in this way.

The Nama Basin was created as a result of the orogenic upwarping, a type of uplift, that occurred along two orogenic belts. These orogenic belts were the Gariep Belt, which was west of the Nama Basin, and the Damara Belt, which extends along the northern margin of the Nama Basin. These orogenic events, which formed the Nama Basin, occurred at a site that was inland of a continental *subduction zone*. The site of the present-day canyon is located immediately inland of the Gariep Belt, near the southern border of Namibia. The Damara Belt deformed the land, in a line extending roughly from west to east, that corresponds to northwestern Namibia.

The land beneath South Africa and Namibia were part of the Kalahari Craton, an early plate. Like present-day *plates*, cratons were plates that consisted of *lithosphere*. These cratons are now part of the stable and central portion, the craton, of the African *continental plate*. The Kalahari Craton was shaped like the southern half of present-day Africa. The orientation of the Damara Belt was the result of a collision between the Kalahari Craton and the Congo Craton, which was shaped like the northern half of present-day Africa. After this collision, the Kalahari and Congo Cratons were similar in shape to the land mass of present-day Africa. Suffice to say that present-day Namibia was on a portion of crust that was subducting beneath the Río de la Plata Craton, which was shaped like the southern half of the South American continent.

Although scientists refer to these portions of rock as cratons, they behaved like continental plates and were essentially immature versions of the present-day plates. The South American plate that exists today is larger than the South American continent, but the eastern coast of South America now occupies the central core, or craton, of the plate. Thus, these early cratons became enlarged, by extensional faulting and other mechanisms, to form the present-day continental plates.

SUBDIVISIONS OF THE NAMA BASIN

The Nama Basin has been divided into subbasins, and Fish River Canyon is part of the Witputs Subbasin. The Osis Arch separates the Witputs

Subbasin, in southern Namibia, from the more northern Zaris Subbasin. It is not clear if the *orogenic uplift* of the Damara Belt has had any lasting influence on the drainage pathways. It is likely that the Damara Orogen and Gariep Orogen occurred too long ago to even have an indirect influence on the drainage network of southern Namibia. For example, the north-south directionality of the Fish River cannot be attributed to the orogenic uplift, in northern Namibia, of the Damara Belt. Instead, it appears that the path of the Fish River is likely to have been influenced by the erosion of a passive rift margin. The erosional retreat, inland from the coast, of the Great Escarpment, the erosional "ghost" of the horst that existed during the active rifting, appears to have contributed to both the topography and to *passive uplift*. The layers of sedimentary rocks that accumulated in the Nama Foreland Basin are, however, present in the walls of Fish River Canyon.

The Nama Group consists of the Fish River Subgroup, the Schwarzrand Subgroup, and the Kuibis Subgroup. In the Witputs Subbasin of the Nama Basin, and in the walls of Fish River Canyon, the layers of rock in the Schwarzrand and Kuibis Subgroups are more abundant than the layers of the Fish River Subgroup. The Kuibis Subgroup is part of the so-called lower Nama Group, and the layers of the Kuibis Subgroup were deposited beneath the layers of the Schwarzrand Subgroup. The uppermost layers of the Nama Group are the layers of the Fish River Subgroup. In some areas of land, the layers of the Fish River Subgroup were never deposited in very significant amounts. In other areas, the layers of sedimentary rocks in the Fish River Subgroup have been eroded. Some of the layers of sedimentary rock in the Nama Group are up to 590 million years old, and the youngest layers are between 521 and 539 million years old. This means that layers of sediments were deposited within this time frame, often in reefs or shallow marine environments. The sediments were then converted, by the heat and pressure that resulted from their burial beneath overlying rock layers, into sedimentary rocks. Researchers have dated the Nama Group layers by looking at the ages of basalt lava layers, layers of lava that were deposited in between various layers of carbonate sediments.

EXTENSION, RIFTING, AND THE SOUTH ATLANTIC OCEAN

During the late Carboniferous period, during the interval of 310–286 million years ago, and early *Permian period*, between 286 and about 255 million years ago, Africa began to extend away from South America. This separation ultimately occurred along a rift axis, and the Atlantic Ocean did not open until about 131 million years ago. Some extensional faulting did, however, occur in Namibia during these earlier intervals.

This preceded the actual rifting process. The distinction between the two processes has, however, been discussed in somewhat nebulous terms. The rifting of Africa from South America, on the western coast, and Antarctica, on the eastern coast, was driven by hot spots and mantle upwelling. The *mantle plume* that was ultimately responsible for the hot spot that influenced southern Namibia, which in turn was responsible for the rifting, had become active as early as 200 million years ago. Thus, the process that allowed the hot spot to develop or migrate might have been involved with the earlier extensional faulting. This earlier faulting, as discussed above, occurred during the Carboniferous and Permian periods.

In Namibia, the early phase of rifting caused a series of extensional basins, which have been loosely referred to as rift basins, to develop along the western coast of Namibia. Fish River Canyon is now located on the area between the Karasburg Basin and, immediately north, the Aranos Basin. These basins were depressions of land that were produced by extensional movement. In terms of directionality, rifting can be viewed as extension at an intracontinental site that is separated from the existing plate margins. Rifting is not equivalent to extension, however. Rifting, for example, tends to be driven by upwelling of the mantle. This upwelling occurs within mantle plumes. Mantle plumes may be highly localized or line up along a rift axis. Various details about mantle plumes, details related to their origin and movement, are still an area of controversy.

As the rifting began, approximately 250 million years ago, the site of Fish River Canyon was still part of the Nama Basin. In other words, the margins of the Nama Basin overlap with the margins of the Karasburg and Aranos Basins. These basins are extensional because they were pushed downward, and filled in with marine sediments, during extension and as a result of extension.

This rifting began some 200–230 million years after western Africa had become joined to South America. This rifting and the rifting on the eastern coast of Africa, which opened the Indian Ocean, occurred within the continent of Gondwana. South America did not simply collide and slide past Africa. The rift between South America and Africa did end up roughly lining up with the border of the collision, or convergence, of the two landmasses. But Africa and South America had been fused, or sutured, together as part of Gondwana, for some 200–230 million years. Gondwana was a single, continuous, supercontinent.

RIFTING, UPLIFT, AND THE TRISTAN DE CUNHA PLUME

Portions of basalt lavas were delivered to Namibia, before the Atlantic Ocean opened, as part of the Etendeka flood-basalt eruptions. These eruptions were part of the magmatic activity that occurred during the rifting between western Africa and South America. The eruptions of lava were especially intense in northern Namibia. The hot spot that straddled the South American Paraná Basin and Northern Namibia, to which the Paraná Basin was still attached, had been produced by the Tristan da Cunha plume. The upwelling of the mantle, resulting from this mantle plume, drove the rifting that opened the South Atlantic. The plume produced a hot spot, and the hot spot produced an area of intense magmatism. This area was known as the Paraná-Etendeka igneous province. This was a volcanically active area that included northern Namibia and portions of eastern South America. The Etendeka *lava flows* were deposited on the Namibian side, but the South American Paraná Basin was also buried beneath basalt lava.

Some researchers proposed that the overall drainage pattern in present-day Namibia was driven by the indirect effects of the Tristan da Cunha plume. The researchers suggested that the plume may have produced at least some crustal underplating, implying an active component to the uplift. As a result of rifting, escarpments and the lithosphere beneath them can be tilted over long periods of time. This long-term tilting can be sustained by complex mechanisms, even after the rift zone has cooled and become a passive margin. The Namibian portion of the Great Escarpment is also likely to have led, by its erosional exhumation, to *isostatic uplift* in parts of Namibia. Researchers estimate that the plume produced, by whatever combination of active or passive mechanisms, between 1,641 feet (500 m) and 3,281 feet (1,000 m) of uplift in Namibia. There is reason to think that much of this was isostatic uplift, produced by the erosion of the escarpment. This escarpment was part of the passive margin of a rift axis, the failed arm of a rift.

UPLIFT AND ESCARPMENT RETREAT

The drainage pathway of the Fish River appears to have been influenced by uplift, but researchers are not sure if the uplift was passive or active. The topography of Namibia was heavily influenced by the opening of the Atlantic Ocean. The rifting event that opened the Atlantic Ocean continued for long enough to allow water to fill in, but the rift zone in Namibia then became the passive margin of the rift. The Great Escarpment, which extends from north to south in parts of Namibia and South Africa, is the present-day remnant of the passive margin of that rift. The escarpment is between 1,641 feet (500 m) and 3,281 feet (1,000 m) higher than the coastal land of the Namib Desert. This difference in elevation is rather striking in some parts of Namibia. The escarpment appears as a long, linear cliff that extends almost to the horizon and is very high. Along other sections, the escarpment appears more like a mountain range. The escarpment also follows a gentler slope that extends inland from the "cliff." As a result, the escarpment is higher than most of the Namibian Highland (shown in the lower color insert on page C-7). For a long time, the Great Escarpment has caused significant portions of water and sediments to be directed inland and to the east. The Fish River then carried sediment-laden water south, through Fish River Canyon.

Essentially, the rift zone gradually cooled and became a passive margin. The graben, a low-lying valley, was formed along the rift axis and ultimately expanded considerably. The low-lying area could then be regarded as a rift basin, and this basin accumulated sediments. When a rift is formed by a mantle plume, such as the Tristan de Cunha plume, the rifting event tends to produce significant changes in the properties or thickness of the lithosphere. As Namibia became more and more distant from South America, to which it had been originally connected, the cooling along the rift axis was accompanied by seafloor spreading. The continental plate margin, between southern Africa and South America, is now in the middle of the Atlantic Ocean. The original rock structures that formed the horst, which was the rift flank or rift margin, have never moved from Namibia. The rift flank, or passive rift margin, is essentially like a mountain range that was formed along the rift axis. These uplifted rocks, like a mountain range that was formed along the active rift axis, are referred to as an escarpment. It is helpful to discuss uplift, in the context of escarpment retreat, in terms of familiar processes.

The isostatic uplift that results from escarpment retreat is very much analogous to the uplift that results from erosional exhumation. An obvious question, however, remains. How could the erosion of a 130-million-year-old escarpment have continued for 130 million years and produced relatively recent uplift? The answer is that passive margin development, and the uplift that accompanies it, is a remarkably prolonged process. In Namibia, the cooling process, a process that was associated with the original rifting at 130 million years ago, was still continuing between 80 and 60 million years ago. There was also ongoing reactivation of fault activity, producing uplift, along parts of the escarpment. As new *fault blocks* were uplifted, the rocks were subjected to ongoing erosional exhumation. Scientists think this type of long-term process can help explain the long-term maintenance of an uplifted escarpment. In the case of the rift flank that was maintained along the North Atlantic Ocean, the periodic fault activity essentially kept the isostatic uplift, resulting from ongoing erosional exhumation, going for something on the order of 100 million years. This is analogous to a mountain range that is eroded and then gradually regenerated by another phase of orogenic uplift. In an escarpment, fault-associated uplift is followed by erosional exhumation and then isostatic uplift.

In Namibia, the escarpment appears to have gradually migrated in an inland, or eastward, direction. This escarpment retreat process is thought to have produced isostatic uplift, a form of passive uplift, in different parts of Namibia. For the most part, the retreated escarpment is a kind of "migrated horst." The actual rocks that formed the horst might have been partially eroded away, but the relatively higher elevation of the horst would persist.

The passive uplift produced by escarpment retreat would have been similar to the uplift produced by erosional exhumation, such as in a sedimentary basin. In other words, some remnant of a rift basin was left over along the passive margin. The escarpment was persistently higher than neighboring areas, and the relative elevation persisted during the escarpment retreat. In Namibia, for example, this created a drainage divide. The drainage divide determined the direction in which eroded rocks were transported away from the escarpment. If sediments were eroded from the drainage divide and deposited in the adjacent lowlands, the drainage divide would be lighter. This denudation, or erosion, of the drainage divide would have contributed to its isostatic uplift. The sediments in the lowlands would eventually be eroded, and the lowlands would be subjected to isostatic uplift.

Chaco Canyon

Northwestern New Mexico, the United States

Chaco Canyon is located in northwestern New Mexico, within the Chaco Culture National Historical Park. The canyon was formed relatively recently, probably within the last 5.3 million years, but the layers of *sedimentary rocks* that are visible in the canyon walls were deposited as many as 80 million years ago. The canyon is largely composed of sandstone that was either deposited at the bottom of a marine seaway, the *Cretaceous* Western Interior Seaway, or blown in during more recent times. The Western Interior Seaway is sometimes referred to as the Cretaceous Interior Seaway or Cretaceous Epeiric Sea, and part of this seaway covered the Western Interior Basin. The San Juan Basin, out of which Chaco Canyon has been *incised*, was once submerged beneath the western portion of this seaway. The floor of the *arroyo channel*, which has been cut out of the canyon floor, also contains *alluvial sediments* that were deposited, during fluctuations in the climate, within the last 1,000 years.

The layers of sedimentary rocks in Chaco Canyon are located on part of the Colorado Plateau, and the formation of the canyon was influenced by the development and *uplift* of the plateau. The Chaco River carved the larger features and cliffs of Chaco Canyon, but the inner arroyo channel was shaped by more complex mechanisms. A stream carries water, intermittently, through the canyon in the present day. This stream system or channel system is known as the Chaco Wash, the streambed that follows part of the path of the older Chaco River.

The Chaco River originates southwest of Chaco Canyon, near the Continental Divide. Within New Mexico, the Continental Divide extends along a southwest-northeast line and crosses through the central portion of the state. The Chaco River first flows northwest, away from the Divide, and then flows essentially north. After flowing through Chaco Canyon, the Chaco River reaches a site near the northern border of New Mexico and joins the San Juan River. The Chaco River is a *tributary* of the San Juan River. The San Juan River originates in southeastern Utah, flows southwest into northern New Mexico, and then flows slightly northwest into southern Utah. The San Juan River, carrying the water from the Chaco River, ultimately flows into the Colorado River in southern Utah.

The area of the drainage basin of the Chaco River is 4,363 square miles (11,300 km²), an area of land that essentially corresponds to a portion of land on each side of the river. The river begins at elevations as high as 7,481 feet (2,280 m) above sea level and joins the San Juan River at 4,905 feet (1,495 m) above sea level. The concept of the drainage basin refers to a topographical depression of land that directs water and sediments to the river and its tributaries. In contrast to the term *foreland basin*, the term *drainage basin* does not refer to the *tectonic* forces that shaped the area of land around the river. In the case of the Columbia River, there is overlap between the area of the Columbia Basin and the drainage basin of the Columbia River. Scientists have noted that the terms are often used interchangeably, even though the terms are not equivalent.

The formation of the outer canyon walls by the Chaco River appears to have mainly been driven by *isostatic uplift* of various parts of the Colorado Plateau. The isostatic uplift of the Colorado Plateau served to increase the *gradient* of the Chaco River, which flows into the San Juan River. The inner arroyo channel has partially been shaped by other forces, as discussed below.

Chaco Canyon was also the home of early Native American people, and some of the most recently deposited alluvial layers contain important archaeological items and remnants. As seen in the upper color insert on page C-8, there is evidence that the Anasazi people lived in and around Chaco Canyon during the period A.D. 1–950. The Anasazi constructed *pueblos*, a term that refers to the "great houses" that were several stories high, and probably constructed dams and other water-management systems in Chaco Canyon. The three uppermost layers of unconsolidated sediments in the inner arroyo channel contain fragments of pottery and fragments of the great houses themselves. The uppermost alluvial layer is known as the Bonito channel fill, previously known as the "Post-Bonito sediments," and was named for the large series of structures known as the Pueblo Bonito.

The reference to the sediments being "post-Bonito" may have been based on an erroneous assumption. Scientists originally believed that the flooding of the arroyo channel, around A.D. 900, produced an end to the existing structures and farmland that the Anasazi had created. Researchers now think the Anasazi may have developed methods for controlling the flow of water through the arroyo channels, thereby decreasing the impact of floods. Not surprisingly, this human element in the historical sediments has complicated the interpretation of the alluvial layers in the arroyo channel. These complications only apply to the inner channel at Chaco Canyon.

Beneath these historical sediments are other layers of sediments that were deposited during the latter half of the *Holocene epoch*. The present-day arroyo channel, which is separated from the canyon walls, has been cut out of sediments that were deposited during the late Holocene. In the walls of the arroyo channel, between 13 feet (4 m) and 23 feet (7 m) of these unconsolidated Holocene sediments are visible. The present-day shape and depth of the arroyo channel has only existed for about 200 years. During the interval between about 5,000 years ago and 200 years ago, the arroyo channel has been repeatedly filled in and re-incised in cycles. These cycles of cutting and filling are characteristic of arroyo systems.

EARLIER INCISION OF THE OUTER WALLS

The reworking of the sediments on the arroyo valley floor occurred within the last 7,000 years, but the incision of the canyon walls occurred earlier. Scientists have primarily studied the times at which the inner arroyo channel was cut out or filled in, and the arroyo channel has often been studied as a kind of isolated system. When the arroyo channel, valley floor, and canyon walls are viewed together, it is possible to separate Chaco Canyon into nine overall terraces. The ages of the alluvial sediments on the flatter portions of the upper terraces, which are part of the canyon walls and were cut out of the Cretaceous sandstone, have nonetheless not been determined. Scientists have, however, studied the histories of other rivers and drainage pathways in the vicinity of Chaco Canyon. Scientists have found that many of the rivers in the southeastern portion of the Colorado Plateau, which Chaco Canyon is located within, produced significant incision between 5.3 and 1.6 million years ago. This interval is known as the *Pliocene epoch*, and the outer walls of Chaco Canyon were probably incised during, and perhaps also before, this interval of time.

The younger sediments that cover the arroyo channel and valley floor are still immediately above the layers of Cretaceous sandstone and shale. First, the shale of the Menefee Formation and the Cliff House Sandstone were deposited, during the interval of 83.5–71 million years ago, in the San Juan Basin. During the interval between the end of the Cretaceous period, at 66 million years ago, and the beginning of the *Miocene epoch*, at 23.7 million years ago, other layers of sediments were deposited throughout the San Juan Basin. These post-Cretaceous sediments were, subsequently, entirely eroded from the vicinity of Chaco Canyon. During the Pliocene epoch or perhaps before, the Chaco River then cut through these Cretaceous sediments and formed the canyon. The incision of the

Chaco River is likely to have been driven by intervals of uplift and climate change, probably induced by the melting and forming of glaciers.

The exposed floor of the early canyon was composed of the same Cretaceous sedimentary rocks of which the canyon walls consist. Between 1.6 million and 10,000 years ago, the canyon floor is thought to have become covered by relatively flat layers of gravel and other sediments. These *Quaternary* sediments are still present in the valley floor of Chaco Canyon, and the Cretaceous Cliff House Sandstone is immediately below them. Above the Quaternary sediments are the Holocene sediments, which include the sediments deposited within the historical time frame.

Thus, even the relatively deep portions of the arroyo channel were incised within the last 10,000 years. The walls of the arroyo channel are also composed of unconsolidated sediments that were deposited within the last 10,000 years. In contrast, the canyon walls were incised between 1.6 and 5.3, or more, million years ago and are composed of 71–83-million-year-old sedimentary rocks. The formation of these sedimentary rocks was the result of their long-term burial—burial that provided the necessary heat and pressure for rock formation by other sediments.

UPLIFT AND MARINE SEDIMENTS

The tectonic events that caused sediments to accumulate in northwestern New Mexico are also unusual and have led to controversy among geologists. Chaco Canyon was cut out of the sediments of the San Juan Basin, a sedimentary basin that was part of the Western Interior Basin. The San Juan Basin and other portions of the Western Interior Basin were then uplifted and deformed by the Laramide Orogeny. The Laramide Orogeny produced uplift and deformation and played a major role in the shaping of the present-day Colorado Plateau. The uplift that occurred during the Laramide Orogeny temporarily halted sediment accumulation in the San Juan Basin, especially in the southern portion of the basin. After the Laramide Orogeny ended, newly uplifted land surrounded the San Juan Basin. These high elevations, around the margins of the basin, contributed to the delivery and deposition of sediments to the basin.

Between the end of the Laramide Orogeny, about 40 million years ago, and the more recent uplift of the Colorado Plateau, which occurred between 5 and 6 million years ago, the topography of New Mexico was heavily influenced by *fault activity*. The first stage of the Laramide Orogeny occurred in a roughly eastward—or slightly northeastward—direction, deformed the older basement rocks of the crust, and was amagmatic. Amagmatic tectonism refers to those processes that are not driven by or accompanied by the movement of magma within the crust. These processes are generally orogenic events or certain types of uplift.

Toward the end of the Laramide Orogeny, however, the entire Colorado Plateau began to be deformed in a clockwise, rotational manner that is one type of wrench tectonism. Along with the clockwise rotation of the plateau, fault activity and magmatic activity tended to migrate around the periphery of the plateau.

Many of these tectonic events in New Mexico can also be traced back to the Cordilleran Orogeny, which set the stage for the Laramide Orogeny and initially caused magmatic activity to migrate eastward. Around 80 million years ago, as the Farallon *plate* was undergoing *subduction* beneath the North American plate, both the mountain-building processes of deformation and the *volcanic activity*, or arc magmatism, migrated to the east. After the Laramide Orogeny had ended and the magmatic activity had reached the vicinity of Colorado and New Mexico, the most intense magmatic activity migrated back to the west and southwest. The fault activity that followed this migration is thought to have contributed significantly, by shaping the topography, to the delivery of sediments into the San Juan Basin. The magmatic activity first migrated east, was then put on hold across much of the Colorado Plateau, and then was essentially rotated, along the curved margin of the Colorado Plateau, back to the west and southwest. The San Juan Basin was near to the curve that the magmatic activity followed, as the activity was wrenched into a reverse of its direction.

The formation of Chaco Canyon was also influenced by the uplift of the Colorado Plateau that occurred more recently than the Laramide Orogeny. Between 5 and 6 million years ago, the Colorado Plateau underwent isostatic uplift. The uplift increased the elevation of the Colorado and Chaco Rivers above sea level. This uplift also drove the incision of the Grand Canyon by the Colorado River. Finally, the uplift increased the gradient of the Chaco River. The Chaco River is a tributary of the San Juan River, which itself is a tributary of the Colorado River.

ARROYOS, CHANNEL INCISION, AND FLOODPLAINS

The rock structures that are present at Chaco Canyon were formed as a result of channel incision, but some of the land in and around Chaco Canyon is also essentially an alluvial floodplain. The central system of channels that exists in the vicinity of Chaco Canyon is known as the Chaco Wash, which flows into the San Juan River. Within Chaco Canyon, the Chaco Wash is about 15.5 miles (25 km) long. The wash consists of both a central channel and some small springs or channels that feed into it. These channels have been incised into the floor of the arroyo valley, which is between the two canyon walls. An arroyo is like a small canyon within a canyon, and the arroyo channel is separated from the walls of the larger canyon. Given that the distance between the walls of the canyon is very large in some areas, the floor of Chaco Canyon can almost be regarded as a small, alluvial floodplain.

Some forms of vegetation, either planted or occurring naturally, exist in Chaco Canyon and may help to limit the erosion of the outer canyon walls. On the floor of the canyon, vegetation may buffer changes in the depth to groundwater and thereby limit erosion of alluvial sediments. The streambed of Chaco Wash is completely or mostly dry for significant portions of the year, but large rainfalls can occur during the summer months. Plants and trees draw up moisture from the underground aquifer, which is essentially the water table. This can limit the erosion of the canyon walls by the smaller drainage sites, known as seeps, that feed into Chaco Canyon.

Researchers have counted roughly 50 seeps within the Chaco Canyon National Historical Park, and most of these seeps are located just outside the main portion of the canyon. The outside margins of Chaco Canyon contain smaller canyons, which have been referred to as either box canyons or *rincóns*. The seeps that are present in these *rincóns* essentially feed water into the canyon. When moisture is rapidly drawn up by plants, water from seeps may produce less weathering of canyon walls.

Plants can also slow the movement of sediment-laden water, thereby limiting the mechanical erosion of soil and alluvial sediments. If water is moving more slowly through the canyon, the dry air may evaporate it and leave the sediments behind. During the 1940s, workers planted cottonwood trees and other trees near an aquifer. The aquifer is the groundwater table. The depth to groundwater varies at different points along Chaco Wash. If the depth to groundwater is not too large, surface water may be able to persist in pools for considerable periods of time. Small pools exist in the area at which Chaco Wash empties into Escavada Wash, and trees are able to grow nearby. These trees can help to buffer changes in the groundwater level, but the groundwater table still fluctuates significantly. At one site in Chaco Canyon, for example, scientists were able to install equipment to monitor changes in the depth to groundwater. Scientists found that the groundwater level has undergone significant and daily changes, and these changes were attributed to the actions of trees and plants. The groundwater level beneath Chaco Canyon varies in a very dynamic way, and the buffering effect of plant life appears to be more than theoretical.

NATURALLY OCCURRING DAMS AND ALLUVIAL SEDIMENTS

The role that dams may have played in the development of the present-day arroyo channel system is still being researched. There is evidence,

DAMS AND DIFFERENT TYPES OF SEDIMENTS

There is evidence that the Anasazi people used dams and other structures to influence the flow of channels, probably for agricultural purposes, in Chaco Canyon. Some locations in Chaco Canyon contain larger amounts of the remains of Anasazi habitation structures, which include the great houses. The alluvial sediments tend to be shored up, in thicker layers, in the sites at which the remains of habitats have been found. Scientists have hypothesized that the Anasazi first diverted the channel network for agricultural purposes and then built houses in parts of the canyon that were free from erosion. There is evidence that the diversion of stream flow by the Anasazi artificially flooded the parts of the canyon that were not being used for housing or agriculture.

Scientists think that the Anasazi may have shaped the drainage patterns by removing vegetation from specific sites or deepening existing channels. The Anasazi may have used fire, for example, to locally remove vegetation. The absence of vegetation would have increased the erosion induced by a large rainfall.

Some of the lines of evidence that support these hypotheses are based on the locations and properties of different types of sediments. The layers of floodplain sediments tend to alternate with layers of sediments that were deposited by alluvial processes, perhaps as part of an *alluvial fan.* The floodplain sediments tend to be shale or gypsum and are comparable to other *lacustrine* sediments, meaning that they were deposited by relatively stagnant or unmoving water. The alluvial-fan layers tend to be composed of sandstone and were deposited as water entered the broad valley floor of Chaco Canyon. By studying the locations of these types of sediments in relation to the archaeological sites of Anasazi buildings, researchers can determine the extent to which the accumulation of Holocene sediments was influenced by the Anasazi.

for example, that sediments deposited in a sand dune environment acted as a naturally occurring dam at the downstream end of Chaco Canyon. These *eolian* dams, which were layers of sediments that were deposited under the strong influences of wind, may have been deposited in the context of the *erg* environment that dominated the southwestern United States over different geological intervals. An erg is an actively shifting sand dune system that can produce cycles of sediment deposition. There is also evidence, as discussed in the sidebar, that the Anasazi may have created some sort of dam or influenced the flow of water around a naturally occurring eolian dam.

Some of the younger layers of sediments in the arroyo channel were not deposited at higher elevations than the eolian dams. This may indicate that the Anasazi were still having to deal with some flooding from the naturally occurring eolian dams. It is clear, however, that the arroyo channel in Chaco Canyon has been higher than the floor of the Escavada Wash for some time. To the extent that the Anasazi were able to divert the arroyo channel or manipulate existing dams, the downward slope of the arroyo channel would have worked in their favor. In other words, Escavada Wash would have provided an effective outlet for drainage.

This photograph shows the ruins of Pueblo Bonito, in the foreground and to the right of the outer wall of Chaco Canyon. The arroyo channel extends along the right edge of the photograph. *(Ira Block/Getty Images)*

Apart from any interventions by the Anasazi, dams can have complex effects on sediment transport and incision. One of the most reliable effects of a dam is to increase sediment accumulation, or *aggradation*, upstream of the dam. Sediments do not usually accumulate immediately adjacent to the upstream wall of the dam. Rather, the sediments tend to accumulate a short distance upstream of the dam. This accumulation at one upstream site can then influence sediment transport and accumulation at other sites farther upstream. If the water that is upstream of the dam becomes loaded with sediments and flows more slowly, the river may produce less incision and allow more sediment buildup.

ARROYOS SUSTAINED BY CYCLES OF CUTTING AND FILLING

Another aspect of an arroyo system that limits chemical weathering and erosion is that the arroyo channels tend to be higher than the level of the groundwater in the surrounding area. This helps to distinguish an arroyo system from a karst environment, in which groundwater can erode the walls of the canyon and form subsurface caves. In Chaco Canyon, the walls and floor of the canyon are above the level of the groundwater. Arroyos tend to be self-reinforcing systems. Seasonal or episodic flooding of the land surrounding the arroyo channel can deposit sediments, thereby lowering the effective depth to groundwater. The depth to groundwater is the vertical distance, straight down, from the surface of the arroyo valley floor to the groundwater level. The arroyo valley floor is the floor of Chaco Canyon and is at the level of the uppermost point, or rim, of the walls of the arroyo channel.

After a large rainfall, the water that is left over in ponds on the arroyo valley floor will tend to evaporate rapidly and leave behind large amounts of sediments. This deposition of alluvial sediments raises the height of the rim on each side of the arroyo channel. This serves to lower the depth to groundwater and effectively deepens the arroyo channel. The rainfall might also produce incision along the floor of the arroyo channel. It is unclear if incision has a consistent effect on the depth to groundwater.

Some of the plants that are able to survive in the environment around Chaco Canyon may extend their roots down to between 13 feet (4 m) and 29.5 feet (9 m) to reach groundwater. This allows them to survive during annual fluctuations, or longer-term fluctuations, in the depth of the groundwater. Arroyos are often discussed in terms of cycles of cutting and filling, and some arroyo channels in the American Southwest have incised on a significant scale over the last 100 years. Some scientists think that the precipitation patterns in the Colorado Plateau region may be very sensitive to environmental changes. The Chaco Wash channel system has recently been relatively dry and filled in, with alluvial sediments and perhaps also windblown sand. This dessication leaves archaeological sites in the Chaco Canyon area more vulnerable to damage by flooding.

LAYERS OF EXPOSED SEDIMENTS

The sedimentary rocks that are exposed in the outer walls of Chaco Canyon can be divided into two overall sections. The upper section consists of layers of sandstone, and the underlying section comprises layers of shale and solidified silt. In contrast to other forms of sandstone, such as the highly permeable Navajo Sandstone in Zion Canyon, the Cliff House Sandstone at Chaco Canyon is *resistant*. The walls of Chaco Canyon are primarily composed of Cliff House Sandstone, which is between 492 feet (150 m) and 525 feet (160 m) thick and extends to the highest points on the canyon walls. Some of the walls also contain up to about 65.6 feet (20 m) of the Menefee Formation, which is below the Cliff House Sandstone and is at the lowest portions of the walls.

The Cliff House Sandstone and Menefee Formation are both part of the Mesa Verde Group. The layers of rocks comprising the Mesa Verde Group were deposited, originally as sediments, over an area that extends far outside Chaco Canyon. At Chaco Canyon, for example, the Chaco River has only incised through, at a maximum, the uppermost 65.6 feet (20 m) of the Menefee Formation. Additional layers of the Menefee Formation are buried beneath Chaco Canyon and have not been exposed by incision. Up to 1,739 feet (530 m) of the rock layers of the Menefee Formation are buried under some portions of the San Juan Basin.

The sediments of the Mesa Verde Group were deposited primarily at the bottom of the Western Interior Seaway, and the borders of this seaway shifted over time. The most abundant layer of marine sediments at Chaco Canyon is the Cliff House Sandstone, and this type of sandstone was deposited in relatively shallow portions of the seaway. The site of Chaco Canyon was generally at a more landward than seaward location. Some of the layers of the Cliff House Sandstone display slight patterns of curvature and were primarily deposited in a shoreface environment, meaning that the layers were deposited at depths that were below the level of low tide. As shoreface sediments, these layers were deposited during constant wave activity and tended to be low in the mud that accumulated in deeper water.

The nature of this shoreface environment was important for the formation of Chaco Canyon. The Cliff House Sandstone is low in mud and finely grained, and it is also less resistant than the mud-laden layers of shale that comprise the Menefee Formation. If the Cliff House Sandstone had not been more resistant than the Menefee Formation and had not been deposited above it, the walls of Chaco Canyon might have been shaped differently.

CHANGES IN SEA LEVEL

The Mesa Verde Group was deposited between 70–71 and 83.5 million years ago, corresponding to the late part of the Cretaceous period. Within this time frame of between 12.5 and 13.5 million years, the Mesa Verde Group was deposited over an interval of between 3 and 4 million years. A rise in sea levels occurred while sediments of the Mesa Verde Group were being deposited, and this caused the shoreline of the Western Interior Seaway to push westward, or inland to the west, by about 40 miles. It is important to note that this seaway essentially separated the central United States from California and other western, coastal land. If someone had stood on the portion of the coast that was nearest to present-day Chaco Canyon, the person would be facing east. This could be regarded as the "eastern coast" of the seaway, and the water off the coast would be part of the western half of the seaway.

The sea-level rise that helped to deposit sediments was evidently not driven by tectonic events. This may seem to be an unremarkable fact, given that few tectonic events could influence sea levels on a global or regional scale. However, changes in the topography induced by fault activity can create large tidal pools and gradually alter the coastline. Thus, the movement of the coastline inland and toward the west caused the fine sandstone of the Cliff House Formation to be deposited in a specific area. This landward expansion of the seaway did interact indirectly with subsequent tectonic events, given that tectonic events contributed to the closing of the seaway.

After the Laramide Orogeny, the Cliff House Sandstone in the San Juan Basin was covered over by almost 3,937 feet (1,200 m) of sediments. During the late portion of the *Tertiary period* and parts of the Quaternary period, these sediments were eroded away in the vicinity of Chaco Canyon and in other parts of the basin. As a result of this relatively recent erosion, the layers of the Cliff House Sandstone are physically the highest sediments that are present in the walls of Chaco Canyon. By the time Chaco Canyon was cut out, the sediments that had been deposited during the Paleocene epoch and Eocene epoch were largely absent from the site of Chaco Canyon.

THE CHACO SLOPE AND TERTIARY ROCKS

The San Juan Basin, as a whole, is generally regarded as a site at which thick layers of Tertiary sedimentary rocks accumulated, but these Tertiary layers have been eroded from Chaco Canyon. Just as the area around the Grand Canyon was eroded down to *Permian* sediments, with more removal of *Mesozoic* sediments than on other portions of the Colorado Plateau, the site around Chaco Canyon has been more heavily eroded of

MAGMATIC INTRUSIONS AND COAL IN THE SAN JUAN BASIN

The San Juan Basin contains large deposits of economically important coal, and volcanic processes are likely to have contributed to the formation of the coal. When the San Juan Basin was submerged beneath the Western Interior Seaway and was accumulating mud, silt, and sand, dead organic matter fell to the floor of the seaway. This organic matter became trapped and solidified between the layers of sandstone and shale.

Between 20 and 40 million years ago, an interval that corresponds to a portion of the *Oligocene epoch*, heat from the mantle is thought to have contributed to coal formation in the San Juan Basin. This heat source may have been a batholith, which is an intrusion of magma that has cut upward through preexisting layers of sediments. The source of heat may have been north of the San Juan Basin or within the northern portion of the basin itself. Layers of Cretaceous sandstone in the vicinity of the heat source were heated by both convection and conduction, and the heating participated in the maturation of the organic matter into coal.

Volcanic eruptions also occurred around the San Juan Basin during the Oligocene epoch, but lava that reached the surface did not participate in coal formation. These volcanic eruptions occurred along the northern margin of the San Juan Basin, in the vicinity of the San Juan Mountains. Uplift also occurred along the northern margin of the San Juan Basin, both before and during the Oligocene epoch. Most of the sediments that were deposited in the San Juan Basin after the Eocene epoch, which ended 36.6 million years ago and preceded the Oligocene epoch, have been eroded. Scientists nonetheless think that more than 2,461 feet (750 m) of sediments, in the form of lava or ash that had been combined with water and debris, may have been spread over the entire San Juan Basin during the early Oligocene. Other scientists think that layers of volcanic material may have been carried into the San Juan Basin later and accumulated to thicknesses of over 4,922 feet (1,500 m). In either case, however, most of these sediments have since been eroded from the San Juan Basin.

Tertiary sediments than northern San Juan Basin. The Chaco Slope is a subsection of the San Juan Basin, as shown in the figure on page 150.

The Continental Divide curves along a line that is slightly south of the San Juan Basin. Within the Chaco Slope, the land slopes downhill from the south to the north. The rest of the basin is more flat. The Chaco Slope is analogous to the Mogollon Slope, which will be discussed in chapter 10.

Another process that occurred over much of the San Juan Basin—a process that would normally not coincide with canyon formation—was a relatively recent phase of *subsidence*. When sediments are delivered rapidly and are also eroded to a relatively limited extent, the net effect can be to lower the relative elevation. This is like the reverse of isostatic uplift. During much of the *Cenozoic era*, the San Juan Basin underwent subsidence. This can occur when the input of water and sediments to a sedimentary basin, such as the San Juan Basin, exceeds the capacity of drainage pathways to export the sediments. The San Juan Basin was like a very deep pit that had been dug out of a mountaintop. The elevation

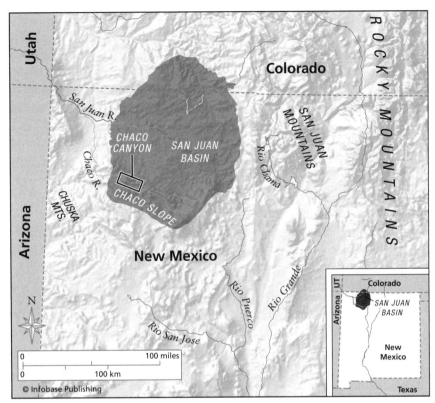

This diagram displays an outline of the San Juan Basin, the Chaco River and Chaco Canyon, and the relatively high elevations of the Chaco Slope.

above sea level was high, but all of the water and sediments were building up in the pit. After the pit had been completely filled, the entire mountain could be subjected to erosional exhumation. The subsidence therefore set the stage for subsequent canyon incision. The elevation upstream of Chaco Canyon, in the southern San Juan Basin, was higher than the elevations in the northern San Juan basin. Chaco Canyon can be seen as a site of intermediate elevation, meaning that the elevation is just downstream of the Continental Divide and slightly higher than other parts of the San Juan Basin.

GLACIERS, UPLIFT, AND INCISION OF TERRACES AND CANYONS

Scientists do not know the exact times at which the outer walls of Chaco Canyon were incised, but nearby rivers have cut out terraces at specific times. The Animas River, for example, flows south, from the San Juan Mountains in southern Colorado, and feeds into the San Juan River in northwestern New Mexico. The Animas River cut one of its upper terraces—terraces cut at relatively high elevations—at 2.43 million years ago. Taking place during the interval from 2.43 million years ago, a time point within the late Pliocene epoch, to 425,000–430,000 years ago, the incision by the Animas River was exceptionally rapid. The same pattern applies to other rivers that flow into the southeastern Colorado Plateau from higher elevations, typically originating near the Continental Divide.

This is somewhat relevant to incision produced by the Chaco River, given that the formation and melting of glaciers are likely to have driven the incision by the Animas River and other rivers. If the San Juan River incised a terrace at a particular time, downstream of the Chaco River and the Animas River, the timing of the incision could not simply be translated upstream and applied to Chaco Canyon. Scientists have nonetheless noted that the melting of glaciers has repeatedly delivered coarse, gravelly sediments to many of the valleys and low-lying basins across the southeastern Colorado Plateau. The portions of the Colorado Plateau that have been studied in the context of these drainage events are the Navajo section, which corresponds to the area around the San Juan Basin and Chaco Canyon, and the Acoma-Zuni section, which extends from southern New Mexico into southern Arizona. Several rivers flowing into the Navajo and Acoma-Zuni sections of the Colorado Plateau are known to have produced rapid incision during the late Pliocene, and the Chaco River is likely to have produced some of the same pre-Pleistocene incision at Chaco Canyon.

FAULTS AND UPLIFT AROUND THE SAN JUAN BASIN

The San Juan Basin was originally formed as an orogenic, foreland basin, but several intervals of uplift have also occurred around its margins. These geological events have occurred at different times throughout the history of the basin, have raised the land on almost all sides of the basin, and have helped deliver sediments to the basin from different directions. The Nacimiento Uplift and Sangre de Cristo Uplift have helped to deliver sediments from the east; the San Luis Uplift delivered sediments from the northeast; the San Juan Uplift delivered sediments from the north; and the Defiance and Zuni Uplifts have, respectively, delivered sediments from the southwest and south.

Around 60–65 million years ago, the San Juan Uplift occurred to the north of the San Juan Basin and caused sediments to be transported into the basin from the north. Both the San Juan Uplift and the Sangre de Cristo Uplift were part of the Laramide Orogeny. The layers of sediments that were delivered into the San Juan Basin during the San Juan Uplift are collectively known as the Ojo Alamo Sandstone, and most of them have been eroded away from the San Juan Basin. Some of the layers of shale that make up the Kirtland Formation, which is present in some portions of the San Juan Basin but is not present in Chaco Canyon, contain dinosaur fossils. In the parts of the San Juan Basin that still contain layers of the Kirtland Formation, deposited during the late Cretaceous, the Kirtland Formation is immediately below the Ojo Alamo Sandstone.

Canyon Diablo and Meteor Crater

Northern Arizona, the United States

Canyon Diablo is located in northeastern Arizona. The Canyon Diablo Wash, a relatively dry channel that is the remnant of a more powerful stream, now delivers some surface water through the canyon. The channel that defines the most downstream portion of Canyon Diablo is downstream of the point at which San Francisco Wash feeds into Canyon Diablo Wash. For the sake of discussion, the Canyon Diablo Wash will be referred to as Diablo Wash. On some maps, there appear to be two canyons, separated by a short distance, with the name of Canyon Diablo. In fact, these are different portions of a single canyon. Canyon Diablo has no real canyon walls between these two sections, and so there is really only a channel. For the purposes of this book, the discussion refers to the section of Canyon Diablo that is north of Interstate-40. The Meteor Crater is a few miles north of I-40. The relevant portion of Canyon Diablo is north of the Arizona Meteor Crater and is immediately downstream of the Little Colorado River.

The Diablo Wash, which flows north through this portion of Canyon Diablo, provides the primary drainage pathway for the land around the Arizona Meteor Crater. As is apparent in the diagram, Canyon Diablo is only about 2.5 miles (4 km) from Meteor Crater. Thus, the canyon receives some drainage, in the form of surface water, from the Meteor Crater. Diablo Wash is dry much of the time but nonetheless carries some surface water, which is carried into the Little Colorado River. The Little Colorado River is a *tributary* of the Colorado River. Thus, much of the surface water that flows through Canyon Diablo will ultimately flow into the Colorado River.

Scientists think that the overall drainage patterns in the vicinity of Canyon Diablo have existed for between 500,000 years and a few mil-

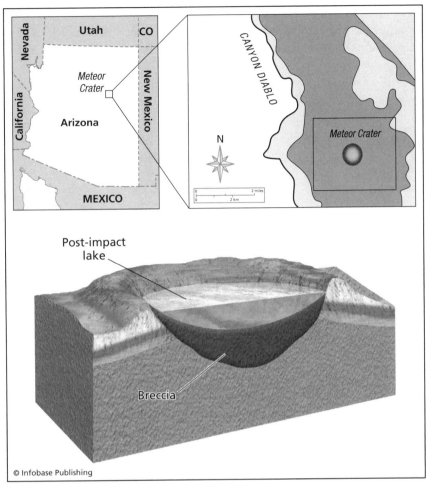

This diagram shows the location of Meteor Crater and the overall shape of the crater itself, with the breccia consisting of multiple, layered subdivisions.

lion years, and, as seen in the lower color insert on page C-8, the meteor impact produced the Meteor Crater at some date between 49,000 and 50,000 years ago. Even if one considers the margin of error in dating the meteor impact and uses a conservative estimate that would date the impact between 46,000 and 52,000 years ago, it is clear that the drainage patterns predated the impact. Thus, the meteor impact imposed various forces on the existing drainage patterns and modified the geomorphology of the area.

The study of terrestrial *impact craters* has traditionally been an area of controversy in the geological sciences, in part because of the number of unanswered questions. For example, the Arizona Meteor Crater was originally thought to be a volcanic cone. During the first decades of the

20th century, Daniel M. Barringer argued that the site had been formed by a meteor impact. He was eventually credited for his hypothesis, and Meteor Crater is sometimes referred to as the Barringer Crater.

The influence of the meteor impact on Canyon Diablo appears to have been somewhat subtle, but the degradation of the Meteor Crater may have influenced the delivery of *sediments* to the canyon. The impact caused dust and fragments to be ejected, and Canyon Diablo was located within this debris radius. Additionally, the layering sequence of *sedimentary rocks* has been inverted on the walls of the impact crater. Some of the underlying sediments are now uppermost, and the younger layers are physically beneath the older layers. The impact event would also have temporarily destroyed any vegetation, however minimal, that existed on the walls and plateau around Canyon Diablo. This could be expected to have temporarily accelerated the delivery of sediments into the canyon, such as during seasonal rainfalls. The crater and ejection fragments have been degraded by *fluvial* and *eolian* mechanisms.

There is also evidence that the meteor crater has produced some modifications in the inputs of subsurface water to Canyon Diablo. The meteor crater has interacted with pre-impact fissures and underground *karst* features. The ejecta blanket that immediately surrounds the crater may have provided an "armoring" effect against erosion. This may have intensified, locally, the already predominant role that subsurface water plays in the formation of karst features. *Alluvial fans* and alluvial terraces have been formed on the outer wall of the crater, an area that also contains active sinkholes. These relatively mild influences on karst formation and groundwater provide a framework for the discussion of other "crater-canyon" systems. For example, groundwater and fluvial processes can strongly participate in the degradation of impact craters. On Mars, groundwater sapping may erode the ground beneath craters, thereby causing the craters to sink downward.

Other meteor impact craters have produced greater influences on the topography than the Meteor Crater has. By looking at a canyon that has been influenced in small ways by a meteor impact, it is possible to consider the effects of larger meteor impacts on other canyons. With regard to those meteor impacts that appear to have produced dramatic changes in the local or regional topography, the impact sites have often been eroded. In other cases, the relationship between the impact crater and a true canyon, formed by *fluvial incision,* is nebulous. For example, there is evidence that the Upheaval Dome in southern Utah is a complex crater and that the impact caused rings of deformation in the land. Upheaval Canyon appears to have been formed by the fluvial incision of a channel, originating at the center of the impact crater and following a path to the Green River. In a sense, this channel was incised as part of the erosional degradation of the crater. The fluvial channels that radiate outward from a crater could therefore be regarded as extensions of the crater walls. Meteor Crater in Arizona is a simple crater that has been superimposed upon an existing drainage slope, one with relatively established drainage pathways.

HISTORY OF THE MOGOLLON RIM AND CANYON DIABLO

Researchers estimate that the walls of Canyon Diablo are several hundred thousand years old, meaning that the canyon has existed in its present form for that amount of time. The heights of the canyon walls tend to be about 131 feet (40 m) high or slightly higher. The *incision* of the canyon walls is thought to have begun in the late *Pliocene epoch*, between 2 and 3 million years ago. The incision may have begun slightly earlier than that time frame. The incision continued until some time between 500,000 and 200,000 years ago. Some of the weathering patterns in the walls of Canyon Diablo have been growing in size and depth for at least the last 200,000 to 300,000 years. The incision of the rock faces is thought to have occurred before the weathering patterns were formed.

Canyon Diablo and the Meteor Crater are located on a morphological feature known as the Mogollon Slope. The Mogollon Slope is north of the Mogollon Rim, which is located near the southwestern margin of the Colorado Plateau. The rim blends into the Mogollon Slope, which is roughly parallel to the Little Colorado River. The elevations on the Mogollon Slope decrease from the south to the north and northeast. This directionality first serves to direct water toward the north and slightly to the northeast. The Little Colorado River then flows to the northwest, carrying water from the Mogollon Slope to the Colorado River. The Little Colorado River joins the Colorado River at a site that is slightly upstream of the Grand Canyon.

Recently, from a geological standpoint, lava was deposited on the land around Canyon Diablo and the Meteor Crater. Between 3 million years ago and 200,000 years ago, *lava flows* from the San Francisco Mountains deposited lava across the Mogollon Slope. The land surrounding Canyon Diablo and the Meteor Crater was part of the San Francisco Volcanic Field. Interestingly, the overall directions of the drainage pathways were fairly well established by the time the eruptions began. Additionally, researchers think that the drainage pathways were not drastically changed by the lava flows.

The overall directions of drainage pathways appear to have existed on the Mogollon Slope for about 2–3 million years, but some of the incision by the Little Colorado River has been fairly recent. Researchers recently found metallic spherules, spherical rocks that appear to have been formed by the impact at Meteor Crater, on a flat portion of land that is near the Little Colorado River. The site at which these spherules were found is higher than the Little Colorado River and is almost 49.7 miles (80 km) from Meteor Crater. Given that particles were ejected by the impact within a radius of 6.2 miles (10 km) or less, researchers suggested that the spherules were transported by rivers or streams. The researchers suggested that some of the incision by the Little Colorado River may have occurred after the impact that produced Meteor Crater, and that the spherules were transported and deposited, much as coarse gravel and other *alluvial sediments* would be, before the river incised down to a lower elevation. This is not an unreasonable suggestion, given that some of the incision within the Grand Canyon has occurred within the last 200,000 years.

THE IMPACT EVENT

Most meteors do not have the requisite mass, density, and velocity to survive the entry into the atmosphere. Atmospheric entry is like a collision and is quite destructive to any object. This tends to either vaporize or incinerate objects or break objects apart, by a kind of crushing pressure or drag. Some meteors are slowed down by the atmosphere, but others are slowed down very little. These meteors can produce hypervelocity impacts. The term *hypervelocity* refers to the general range of velocities at which asteroids and other extraterrestrial debris travel. Some meteors hit the Earth, and thereby become meteorites, when the orbit and position of the Earth cross into the paths of asteroids or other debris. The meteor that produced the Arizona Meteor Crater was originally thought to have been massive enough to lose less than 1 percent of its velocity and less than 1 percent of its mass upon entry into the atmosphere of the Earth. Other researchers think that the velocity decreased more significantly upon entry. Even in this model, the meteor is thought to have been large enough to retain 71 percent of its extraterrestrial velocity.

Researchers think that the meteor was once part of the core of an asteroid. Scientists think that two or more asteroids collided about 500 million years ago, a collision that was suggested to have taken place in the primary asteroid belt of the solar system. This belt is between Mars and Jupiter. The collision then sent the fragments of the asteroid core off in different directions. One fragment was set on a course that ultimately led to its collision, at about 50,000 years ago, with Earth. Researchers estimate that the diameter of the meteor was between 64 feet (19.5 m) and 108 feet (33 m). The preponderance of the evidence indicates that the diameter was probably between 98 feet (30 m) and 108 feet, but the lower estimate of 64 feet cannot be ruled out. Scientists estimate that the mass of the meteor was, however, somewhere between 300,000 and

400,000 tons. The meteor contained mostly iron and nickel but also contained some palladium, silicates, and other substances.

The meteor that produced the Arizona Meteor Crater hit the surface with an impact velocity of between 26,844 miles per hour (43,200 km/hr) and 29,082 miles per hour (46,800 km/hr). The meteor was composed of nickel and iron and was fairly small, in its dimensions of length and width and height, in relation to other terrestrial meteorites. The meteor was, however, very dense and was therefore heavy.

The entry of the meteor into the atmosphere may have caused some small pieces to break off. These pieces would have immediately slowed down. Scientists can say with confidence that these smaller pieces hit the Earth at much slower velocities than the main meteor.

The kinetic energy of the meteor, an energy value that depends on the mass and velocity, was translated into other forms of energy upon impact. Two hemispheric shock waves were created by the impact. One was directed into the ground, producing *shock metamorphism* of rock in the ground, and another was directed outward and into the surrounding air. The impact was originally thought to have produced effects that were comparable to the detonation of a 20–40 megaton nuclear bomb. The detonation of a 20–40 megaton nuclear bomb produces an explosive energy that is equivalent to the detonation of 20–40 million tons of TNT, a conventional explosive. Researchers would also refer to these impact energies as 20 or 40 megatons of TNT equivalent. Other estimates suggest that the impact energy would have been as small as 2.5 megatons of TNT equivalent. Another group of scientists estimated the total energy of the impact and found a range of possible numbers. The number in the higher range of the estimate is comparable to the strain energy of the San Francisco earthquake of 1906, which registered approximately 8.25 on the Richter scale. In the context of the aboveground effects, much of the energy of the meteor impact was translated into light and heat and other forms. The impact energy of either the Arizona impact or a similar impact event is still viewed, by scientists, as being comparable to the energy released by a major earthquake.

The meteor itself was melted by the impact and was not vaporized to a significant extent. Some of the molten fragments of iron that were directed into the ground became fused with existing sedimentary rocks in the ground. The melted pieces of iron formed impact melt particles with the sedimentary layers of the Kaibab Formation. These impact-melt particles were only formed by an interaction of the iron with the Kaibab Formation. The sedimentary rocks of the Coconino Sandstone and Moenkopi Formation did not form significant amounts of impact melted rocks.

The impact sent out small fragments of sedimentary rock layers and very small droplets of iron, and these fragments were scattered over the land around the crater. The dry streambed that feeds into Canyon Diablo, which is northwest of Meteor Crater, passes very near to the Meteor Crater site. Researchers found a number of large fragments of the main meteorite in Canyon Diablo, some of which have been given the numerical designations of Canyon Diablo 1, 2, and 3. These fragments are thought to have been deposited, at low velocities, directly into Canyon Diablo. As the original meteor entered the atmosphere, some small pieces evidently broke off. Given their small sizes, they would have immediately been slowed and melted down by the atmosphere.

Stream systems may also have delivered some smaller pieces of iron into Canyon Diablo by gradual, fluvial transport. Large fragments of iron are too heavy to have been carried by fluvial transport. Some of the droplets of iron that were scattered during the impact, droplets that cooled and solidified, are only a couple of millimeters in diameter. Some of these could have been carried into Canyon Diablo during floods.

The magnitude of the actual earthquake produced by the Meteor Crater impact was estimated to have been 5.0–5.5 on the Richter scale. The rest of the energy was translated into melting portions of the meteorite, moving sediments and boulders, and producing the aforementioned light and heat.

Other impact events have produced much more profound geological changes. The Chicxulub Crater is between 103 miles (165 km) and 112 miles (180 km) wide and is located on the coast of the Yucatán Peninsula, in Mexico. The impact produced complex deformations of the rocks, an effect that complicates measurements of the dimensions of the crater. The meteor that produced the crater is thought to have been 9.3 miles (15 km) wide, at impact. The Chicxulub impact event is thought to have led to the extinction of the dinosaurs, during the Cretaceous-Tertiary boundary, at 66 million years ago. The first evidence to suggest that a meteor impact had caused the extinction was based on relatively traditional geological evidence. Researchers found that something had caused a layer of ash to be deposited at different sites around the world, and the ash was 65 million years old. The ash was very high in iridium, a rare element that is generally delivered to the Earth from meteor impacts. Scientists later discovered the morphological evidence of the crater off the coast of Mexico, during work related to deep-sea drilling for oil. Researchers also found evidence that shock-metamorphism had produced a modified form of quartz at the impact site.

The meteor impact was comparable to the explosive energy of 100 million megatons of TNT equivalent. This is the energy that would be released by the detonation of 100 million nuclear bombs, each providing a one-megaton yield, simultaneously in one location. The impact is thought to have triggered earthquakes of about 10.0 magnitude, as

GEOLOGICAL EFFECTS OF THE CHICXULUB METEOR IMPACT

The Chicxulub impact did not produce a blast wave and fireball that was 100 million times as large as the blast wave, and mushrooming fireball, produced by the surface detonation of a one-megaton nuclear bomb. Based on nuclear bomb tests, it is known that the atmospheric shock wave of an airburst, produced by a meteor that "explodes" in the upper atmosphere, is much larger than the shock wave produced by a surface impact or surface detonation. Only about 3 percent of the energy of the Chicxulub impact was translated into the actual blast wave, which created a blinding fireball and heated the air. This was still an explosion of 3 million megatons of TNT equivalent, an explosion that was up to 30,000 times larger than the explosion of a large hydrogen bomb.

Interestingly, a much larger percentage of the energy was translated into the slow heating of the air and of the rocks around the impact site. An analogous effect would occur if a giant, metal pot of water were heated rapidly by, for example, a blowtorch. The energy transfer would be rapid, but the cooling pot of water would very gradually release heat and steam into the air. This type of effect could be relevant to canyon formation, given that the Chicxulub impact produced *geothermal activity* and hydrothermal activity that lasted more than a million years. This is discussed later in the chapter.

Based on computer models, researchers think that the Chicxulub meteor caused vertical upwarping of the ground within a radius of 4,350 miles (7,000 km) from the impact site. The vertical movement of the land within 62 miles (100 km) of the impact event is thought to have been over 49 feet (15 m). Within the radius of 4,350 miles from the impact site, computer models suggest that the vertical motion was 3.28 feet (1 m). The ground motion evidently caused sediments to be dumped and displaced in a large-scale manner along the entire North American continental margin. Sedimentary rock movements from this mass wasting extended from Puerto Rico to parts of Canada.

The Chicxulub impact site was on the continental crust, but some evidence of the impact was found in the ocean. At two points on the ocean floor, points that are 1,591 miles (2,560 km) and 1,759 miles (2,830 km) from the impact crater and are near Bermuda, scientists working on drilling projects found Cretaceous chalk. The chalk had been dredged up by the impact. This type of chalk tends to be buried far beneath the ocean floor. The chalk was probably not transported across the entire distance from the impact site. Rather, the chalk may have been dredged up by indirect mechanisms.

The impact appears to have also caused small fragments to be ejected, ballistically, from the ground to the upper atmosphere. Upon reentry into the atmosphere, the ejecta is thought to have skidded, by "postballistic skidding," across the upper atmosphere and thereby crossed the Pacific Ocean. The fragments would only have had to be ejected from the impact site at 10,067 miles per hour (16,200 km/hr), rather than at the higher, gravitational escape velocity.

measured on the Richter scale. The resulting tsunamis crashed into coastlines around the world.

KARST FORMATIONS, JOINT FAULTS, AND SUBSURFACE WATER

In the land around Canyon Diablo and the Meteor Crater, scientists think that significant portions of water are transported through underground drainage pathways. Subsurface water has also created karst structures and sinkholes around the Meteor Crater. Many of these underground karst formations, which include caverns and fissures, appear to have been formed in close proximity to existing joint faults and fissures. Some true fault lines do exist in the land around Canyon Diablo. In the immediate vicinities of Canyon Diablo and Meteor Crater, the faults are not actively moving and are simply cracks, or joints, in the ground. Researchers think that water, from rain and surface streams, enters these joint faults and erodes some of the nearby sedimentary rock layers. This causes some of the underlying layers to collapse, a process that further widens the cracks. The widening of a joint fault allows more surface water to flow into the cracks after a rainfall or other event. Eventually, the collapses of the underlying rock layers can create subterranean holes and karst caverns.

Sapping is a process of erosion by subsurface water. In some forms of sapping, the erosion occurs because permeable layers of sediments have been deposited above sediments that are more resistant to chemical weathering. At least in the past, sapping appears to have contributed to the formation of canyons on the Colorado Plateau. Both Canyon Diablo and the Meteor Crater are now far above the water table, and sapping is not presently contributing to the erosion of either landform. However, there is evidence that another form of subsurface erosion is occurring in the walls of both the Meteor Crater and Canyon Diablo. This tafoni weathering appears to have contributed to rockslides in the walls of Canyon Diablo. Much as sapping tends to cause rockslides by eroding different layers of rock at different rates, tafoni weathering occurs more rapidly in some layers of rock than in others.

In the walls of Canyon Diablo and the Meteor Crater, the sandstone layers of the Moenkopi Formation have been more rapidly weakened by tafoni weathering than the underlying limestone layers of the Kaibab Formation have been. Along some parts of Canyon Diablo and the land that is west of the canyon, the overlying layers of the Moenkopi Formation have been entirely eroded away. Researchers found that tafoni weathering is occurring in the walls of both the Meteor Crater and Canyon Diablo. The tafoni in the walls of Meteor Crater began forming shortly after the impact. Thus, they are at most about 49,000 years old. The tafoni in the crater rim are likely to eventually contribute to the collapsing of parts of the crater rim. For now, however, they are not large enough to contribute to the erosion, by mass wasting, of the crater. In the walls of Canyon Diablo, however, the tafoni are much larger and are growing more rapidly on the upper portions of the walls. The tafoni in the Moenkopi Formation may eventually trigger mass wasting, which refers to erosion induced by rockslides, of the canyon walls. In other words, the upper portions of the wall would collapse first. Mass wasting of the canyon walls, in response to tafoni, could help to maintain a U-shape to the canyon walls.

TAFONI, KARST FORMATIONS, AND SAPPING

Tafoni weathering might therefore produce effects that are similar to sapping, but unpredictable effects can occur in canyon walls. The layers of the Moenkopi Formation may be eroded more rapidly than the underlying layers of the Kaibab Formation, but the Moenkopi Formation does not always extend to the rim of Canyon Diablo. It is not necessarily valid to say that the less resistant layers of the Moenkopi Formation are above the more resistant layers of Kaibab limestone. The layers of the Moenkopi Formation might be more or less resistant than the layers that are above it. Similar issues can complicate the discussion of sapping, as discussed below.

Additionally, tafoni weathering appears to be especially dependent on the localized delivery of rainwater and other surface water. In the walls of Canyon Diablo, the small pits that have been formed by tafoni weathering are especially numerous along flat portions of rock. Researchers have suggested that water may percolate down and become, in a sense, pooled in the flat and straight parts of the sedimentary layers. This implies that tafoni are sustained by a rather passive process of groundwater movement. In contrast, spring sapping and other forms of sapping can be more active.

An important feature of tafoni weathering is that the pits do not form because of major irregularities in the rock itself. The rock layers at Canyon Diablo are more or less uniform and homogeneous in their composition. A uniform rock face has been subjected to tafoni weathering if multiple focal points of chemical weathering, each of which is an individual tafone, are distributed across the rock face in a pattern that is not uniform. Tafoni weathering is thought to be driven by salt that is dissolved in groundwater. Tafoni weathering can eventually cause portions of the rock to collapse.

The selective collapse of one set of layers in a canyon wall can alter the shape of the canyon in different ways. The walls of Canyon Diablo define a stream channel, which are the walls on either side of Diablo Wash, and tafoni may have contributed to the slopes of the channel walls. Just as the walls of a canyon can be sloped into a U-shape or V-shape, the walls of a drainage channel can be U-shaped or V-shaped. These shapes are known as the *channel profile*, a term that can also be used to describe the channel that is defined by canyon walls. The channel profile can be used, in conjunction with other morphological analyses, to understand the mechanisms by which a channel was formed.

Some forms of sapping produce U-shaped channel profiles, a characteristic of some channels and canyons on the Colorado Plateau. Canyon

Diablo may have been shaped by sapping in the past, but other ground-water effects may have also acted on the canyon. Researchers have suggested, for example, that karst features may exist around Canyon Diablo and beneath the floor of the canyon. Subsurface water began to exert a more and more prominent effect on the area around Canyon Diablo. The decrease in the amounts of surface water may have been driven by changes in climate, in the depth to the water table, or in the relative elevation of the Mogollon Slope. Unlike some portions of the Colorado Plateau, the Mogollon Slope is not in close proximity to the Continental Divide. Moreover, the delivery of sediments onto the Mogollon Slope would have been recently diminished. The drainage of water off the Mogollon Rim is still directed to the northeast, but sediments used to enter the Colorado Plateau are from the southwest. About 6 million years ago, the Mogollon Rim was cut off from this input. The same shift in the direction of sediment input was responsible for the recent incision of the Grand Canyon. Researchers think that as surface water became less abundant, the fluvial incision of Canyon Diablo dwindled. The erosive actions of water effectively moved underground. As a result, less vertical incision was possible in Canyon Diablo and other nearby canyons.

Intriguingly, tafoni weathering is thought to be driven by the effects of salt water. Scientists still do not understand the mechanisms that produce tafoni. Tafoni at Canyon Diablo and Meteor Crater are thought to have been formed by groundwater that is high in salt, but what is the source of the salt? Many of the individual pits in the rocks, each of which is a tafone, are formed fairly near the rim of the canyon wall. Thus, the tafoni form near the surface of the ground. The main aquifer, which exists beneath the land around Meteor Crater and Canyon Diablo, is the Coconino Aquifer. Across much of this area, the water table of the aquifer is between 394 (120 m) and 656 feet (200 m) below the surface. Researchers estimate that the water table was not much different at the time of impact. At 50,000 years ago, the water table was about 459 feet (140 m) below the surface. Interestingly, the aquifer does contain water that is high in salt. Moreover, researchers think that the salt water drives the formation of the underground, evaporite karst features on the Mogollon Slope. These karst features are thought to be part and parcel of the sinkholes around Meteor Crater. The salt in the groundwater, in the Coconino Aquifer, is derived from sedimentary rocks that are beneath the Coconino Sandstone.

Surface water and near-surface water tends to become more salty by repeated cycles of evaporation. Surface water might erode some salt from near-surface rock layers and then evaporate, leaving behind the salt. During the next large rainfall, the extra salt will make the surface rain-water more salty. The tafoni are near the surface and are therefore likely to have been formed by the downward percolation of salt-laden surface water. The salt water from the Coconino Aquifer almost certainly did not produce the tafoni in Canyon Diablo.

IMPACT BASINS, ELASTIC REBOUND, AND UPLIFT

Hypervelocity impacts can produce impact basins and other large-scale depressions of rock layers, but the initial depression can be followed by a phase of uplift. Some of this *elastic uplift* can result from elastic forces in the rock layers that were impacted. Large impacts can produce complex craters, in which land can be warped upward in concentric rings. The rings of upwarping surround the impact point and may be misinterpreted as being *anticlines* and *synclines*.

The impact that produced the Arizona Meteor Crater was not large enough to produce a complex crater, but fractures in the surface sediments do appear to be physically associated with the crater. The layers of sedimentary rock of the Coconino Sandstone are abundant in silica and extend far below the Meteor Crater. Researchers have found that the meteor impact caused cracks in a significant portion of the Coconino Sandstone beneath the impact site. This is a "zone" of the rock layers that contains fissures, known as shock damage. The fissures extend up to about 3,281 feet (1,000 m), or 0.62 miles (1 km), beneath Meteor Crater. This distance is the diameter of shock damage, a distance into the ground that increases in proportion to the diameter of an impact crater. The Chicxulub impact, for example, produced shock damage down to a depth of 6.8 miles (11 km). The shock damage extends only about 1.24 miles (2 km) beneath the Upheaval Dome impact crater in Utah. The depth of the shock damage also depends on the tensile strength of the rock that is impacted. The Coconino Sandstone beneath Meteor Crater is essentially quartz, very similar to the composition of glass. A meteor impact would have caused a combination of surface melting, subsurface cracking, and vibration. The shock wave would have interacted with the sandstone in the way that a tuning fork could interact with a wine glass. A tuning fork might resonate with a wine glass, producing a high-pitched buzzing sound, and then crack the glass as the pitch of the buzzing deepens. An analogous effect occurred beneath Meteor Crater.

INVERSION AND EROSION OF SEDIMENTS AT METEOR CRATER

Within a radius of three-quarters of a mile (1.2 km) from Meteor Crater, the layering pattern of sediments has been inverted. Before the impact, the layers of sedimentary rocks were deposited in an existing sequence.

About 32.8 feet (10 m) of the layers of the Moenkopi Formation were deposited above 262 feet (80 m) of the Kaibab Formation. Roughly 10 feet (3 m) of the Toroweap Formation was beneath the Kaibab Formation, and the Coconino Sandstone was beneath the Toroweap Formation. The meteor impact essentially served to excavate the crater to a level that was within the Coconino Sandstone. The Coconino Sandstone and the layers above it were thrown out onto the land around the crater.

A remarkable feature of the crater is that the inversion pattern primarily exists on the outer wall of the crater. A person who is standing inside the crater, looking at the inner wall, will see that the pre-impact layering pattern is mostly preserved. This is not the case on the rim of the inner wall of the crater, on the outer wall of the crater, or on the land that extends for 0.75 miles (1.2 km) around the crater. Across most of this ring-shaped portion of land surrounding the crater, the Coconino Sandstone and Kaibab Formation are above the pre-impact landscape. The ejected material is thickest on the land that is closest to the crater. This ejecta blanket forms a kind of rough crust, consisting of sizable boulders and smaller rocks.

The meteor impact initially caused a relatively uniform inversion pattern around the crater, with the Coconino Sandstone above the Kaibab Formation. The erosive actions of wind and water have washed much of the ejected Coconino Sandstone from the west, east, and north sides of the crater. On these three sides, the ejected ring is largely composed of layers of the Kaibab Formation. On the southern side of the crater, the Coconino Sandstone is still fairly abundant and is mixed in with chunks from the Kaibab Formation.

On the land around the outer wall of the southern crater rim, the presence of Coconino Sandstone as the uppermost layer has produced some small effects on vegetation. The Coconino Sandstone layers are permeable enough to allow some Piñon juniper trees to grow there.

EROSION OF THE EJECTED MATERIAL

The larger pieces and layers of debris have also been covered over by alluvial debris, some of which was washed down from the outer wall of the crater rim. Much of this was deposited during the last 10,000 years, which corresponds to the *Holocene epoch*, as alluvial fans and alluvial terraces. Significant portions of these alluvial sediments were delivered along radial gullies, which are small fluvial channels that have been carved out of the outer wall of the crater rim. These alluvial sediments are most abundant on the north and northeastern portions of the rim, extending away from the outer wall. On the southern and southwestern portions of the rim, the alluvial deposits of Holocene age are not as abundant on the surface.

Scientists estimate that 30–50 percent of the erosion of the Meteor Crater has been produced by the actions of surface water. The rest of the erosion has been driven by wind and mass wasting. Scientists think that only somewhere between 3.3 feet(1 m) and 98 feet (30 m) of the uppermost layers of sediments, which are primarily parts of the Cococino Sandstone, have been eroded from the rim of the crater. The 3.3 feet of erosion corresponds to the amount that has been eroded from the flatter parts of the inner and outer walls of the crater. This is a very small amount of erosion. Scientists often note that the Meteor Crater is "pristine" and has been almost perfectly preserved in the very arid climate of central Arizona. The thickness of eroded sediments, the number that is between 3.3 feet to 98 feet, represents the total thickness of sediments that has been removed from the crater rim in 50,000 years.

It is important to recognize that the long-term impact of the crater on Canyon Diablo, in terms of the delivery of sediments, has probably not yet occurred. Many of the large rocks and other ejecta are still scattered over different points around the crater. If the annual precipitation increased significantly, for example, the degradation of the crater by fluvial mechanisms might significantly impact the shape or depth of Canyon Diablo. If the climate had not been arid during much of the time since the impact, the crater might now be much smaller.

Wind has also contributed to the degradation of the crater. The prevailing wind pattern causes fine sediments and dust to be blown in a northeastern direction. This has created a pattern of eolian sediments, deposited under the actions of wind, extending over the land that is northeast of the crater. Over the last 10,000 years, the alluvial fans and terraces were initially deposited in a relatively uniform ring around the outer wall of the rim. The blowing of wind to the northeast has become stronger over the last 8,000–10,000 years. This has blown sediments in from the southwest of the crater, thereby covering over some of the alluvial deposits. This is important because both the wind patterns and drainage patterns are directed to the northeast.

The southern rim of the crater displays several unique features, and these have been influenced significantly by wind. Diablo Wash approaches the crater from the south, passes by the western rim, and flows roughly north through Canyon Diablo. The overall direction of water flow is north and northeast, toward the Little Colorado River. The land only slopes one or two degrees to the northeast. This means that water and sediments will, in fact, be capable of flowing down the crater and toward the streambed that feeds into Canyon Diablo. Some of the fissures that are west of the crater appear to direct water, both on the surface and underground, toward Canyon Diablo. Some of the fissures and joint faults appear to interact with actively expanding sinkholes, karstlike features that are formed by subsurface water. The unique aspects of the southern rim can therefore not be attributed only, or even primarily, to differences in fluvial erosion.

The inner portion of the crater has also been filled with thick layers of alluvial debris. Shortly after the impact, the crater was much deeper than it is now. Some of this debris was deposited by landslides and rockslides, which are examples of erosion by mass wasting. Much of the debris consists of alluvial deposits, however. About 98 feet of alluvial sediments are deposited inside the crater. A thin layer of dust and volcanic material, some of which was blown in from the San Francisco Mountains, has been deposited above the thick alluvial layers.

Some of the alluvial material is thought to have been deposited under *lacustrine* conditions. The Meteor Crater contained a shallow lake for short periods of time, as is evident in the accompanying diagram. Most of these alluvial layers were, however, delivered by the fluvial channels in the inner wall of the rim. Thus, the sediments are consistent with a lacustrine environment that was also a kind of alluvial fan. Beneath the 98 feet of alluvium is 32.8 feet (10 m) of shocked quartz and other breccia, produced by the impact.

Below these layers of breccia is a thick portion of impact-melted material. The impact-melted material is about 525 feet (160 m) thick. This 525 feet of impact melt begins at 131 feet (40 m) below the surface of the crater interior and ends at 656 feet (200 m) below the surface. The meteor impact also cracked more deeply buried rock, below the rocks that comprise the impact melt. The cracked rock is most significant at points that are 820 feet (250 m) or more below the present-day surface of the crater interior. The impact did induce some fractures that extend as far as 3,281 feet (1,000 m) below the ground.

Importantly, the meteor impact did not induce the fissures and joint faults in the area around Canyon Diablo. The meteor impact induced new cracks in the basement rock, and these may have interacted with the underground fissure system. But the fissures and joints were present before the impact. After the crater was formed, some of the existing fissures influenced the shape of the crater. The crater has a square shape to it, and the squarelike quality has resulted from the actions of fissures. The fissures acted on the crater after its formation. A small scissor fault, for example, has caused part of the inner wall of the crater to be upthrown with respect to the adjacent, downthrown portion of the wall.

SAPPING AND THEATER-HEADED VALLEYS ON MARS AND EARTH

Scientists have repeatedly noted that canyons and valleys on the southern Colorado Plateau exhibit many similarities to valleys found on Mars. The fine dust and other rocks on the surface of Mars consist primar-

HYDROTHERMAL ACTIVITY INDUCED BY IMPACT EVENTS

The effects of very large meteors can be similar to the effects of fault-associated magmatism and other igneous processes. The Chicxulub impact that occurred 66 million years ago, on the Yucatán Peninsula, evidently heated the crust for long periods of time. Researchers originally estimated that the Chicxulub impact produced 100,000 years of hydrothermal activity, a heating of the crust. This thermal effect extended at least a few miles into the crust, beneath the crater. More recent estimates suggest that the hydrothermal activity lasted between 1.5 and 2.3 million years. The hydrothermal activity took the form of hot springs, geysers, and related phenomena. The Chicxulub impact was on the continental crust, which is thicker than the oceanic crust. Thus, the conductive heating that was induced by the Chicxulub impact was subjectively mild. Larger impacts on the oceanic crust could have produced hot spots and igneous provinces, discussed below.

Importantly, researchers think that the heated groundwater and surface water may have contributed to the persistence of heat at the Chicxulub site. Thus, the initial impact melting would have heated the rock and water, and the water may have slowed the loss of heat from the rocks. The water in a large cup of coffee will, for example, retain its heat and produce steam for a longer time than a small volume of water will.

ily of basalt lava that has been eroded in various ways. Thus, basalt lava flows and volcanic activity on Mars have been imposed upon an existing network of valleys and craters. Although the volcanic activity on the Mogollon Rim was also imposed on established drainage pathways, the structural features of valleys on the Mogollon Rim are more relevant to a comparison with Martian geomorphology. Many of the drainage channels on both Mars and the Colorado Plateau are thought to have been strongly shaped by groundwater erosion and groundwater sapping, and sapping tends to create channels with distinctive characteristics.

Groundwater sapping may also help degrade some impact craters. The Arizona Meteor Crater has not been degraded, in a significant way, by groundwater sapping. This may be due to the fact that the major aquifer is so far below the surface. Tafoni weathering and karst-related processes can cause rock walls to collapse and produce U-shaped channels, as discussed above. These are similar but not identical to sapping.

Sapping can also cause rockslides to occur at specific sites along a canyon or fluvial channel. If a fault or fissure cuts through a canyon wall at one point, springs or seeps may enter the canyon at that point. As a result, rockslides may selectively be induced at that point. The water table is influenced by the local topography and the elevation above sea level. The effects of sapping can therefore result from complex interactions of water and landforms.

Groundwater sapping tends to create wide canyons that may display boxlike heads, and the valleys surrounding the canyons are often very flat. These canyons, which are sometimes referred to as theater-

In this photograph of a section of Canyon Diablo, the walls of the canyon and the tributary channels, providing stream inputs without the streams, are reminiscent of the Martian landscape. *(Thomas Wiewandt/The Photo Gallery at Slide Canyon)*

headed canyons, may appear to have been formed without any discernible input from a stream. The most upstream portions, or heads, of the canyons are not tapered in comparison to the downstream portions of the channel. Someone flying at a low altitude over the Mogollon Rim, or over other parts of the Colorado Plateau, might observe a flat plateau and then suddenly see a sharply incised network of channels. The channel network might also appear to end abruptly, without feeding into a river. At the sites of intersection between two arms of this sort of channel, the angles may be sharp and appear like a trapezoid. Similar channel networks exist on Mars and may appear as self-contained canyons with no inputs or outputs.

Glossary

active uplift   UPLIFT of a portion of the CRUST, with respect to either sea
level or adjacent portions of land, that is produced by TECTONIC ACTIVITY;
includes FAULT-ASSOCIATED UPLIFT, OROGENIC UPLIFT, ANOROGENIC UPLIFT,
and volcanically mediated uplift, as in DOMING

aggradation   an increase in the GRADIENT of a river that results from the
deposition of ALLUVIAL SEDIMENTS; alluvial sediments are usually deposited
locally; often occurs at points along a river that receive large amounts of
SEDIMENTS from HILLSLOPES or other input sites

alluvial/alluvial sediments   SEDIMENTS that are deposited at the bottom of
a river or stream in the context of the FLUVIAL TRANSPORT of sediments;
sediments that are deposited as a river flows out onto a valley or flat portion of land; sediments that are deposited as part of an ALLUVIAL FAN

alluvial fan   a fanned-out pattern of SEDIMENTS that has been deposited, by a
river or stream, as a result of FLUVIAL TRANSPORT; a fanlike pattern of sediments deposited as part of a SUBMARINE FAN

angular unconformity   a physical and "rock-age" boundary, as in a canyon
wall, between slanted layers of SEDIMENTARY ROCK and younger, overlying,
horizontal layers of sedimentary rock; the underlying sedimentary rocks
have usually been slanted to one side or deformed by TECTONIC forces;
the age gap can occur when sedimentary rocks, above the slanted layers,
are deposited and then eroded

anorogenic uplift   UPLIFT that is not produced by OROGENIC ACTIVITY; sometimes applied in reference to DOMING

anticline   a fold in the rocks, generally produced by OROGENIC ACTIVITY along
a fold-thrust belt, that is CONVEX-UP; may or may not be apparent on the
surface; may appear as a mountain

asthenosphere   the lower two-thirds of the UPPER MANTLE; the ASTHENOSPHERE
is about 155 miles (250 km) thick and extends from about 62 miles (100
km) below the surface, of the water in the ocean or the land that is the
CONTINENTAL CRUST, to about 218 miles (350 km) below the surface; consists of slowly moving, soft rock that is still, technically, solid

asymmetrical meander a bend in a river and the channel that the river has INCISED, such that the walls on each side of the bend display different slopes; the degree of asymmetry is sometimes expressed as the ratio of the average slope on one side to the average slope on the other; includes INGROWN MEANDERS

axial drainage the multiple streams or channels that drain a mountain range and that exit the mountain range, such as by entering a FORELAND BASIN, along lines that are roughly, or at least partially, parallel to the axis along which the mountain range is oriented; characteristic of a mature drainage system, a drainage system that is draining a relatively old mountain range

axial zone a band of mountains that extend along an old or existing axis, as in an axis of deformation or an axis of a fold-thrust belt, of a mountain range; the main axis along which mountains exist and along which mountains were formed, such as during an OROGENIC event; sometimes applied to discussion of orogenic events that produce deformation along more than one axis, as in the South Pyrenean Axial Zone (see chapter 4) and North Pyrenean Axial Zone; can also be applied to oceanic ridges formed as a result of seafloor spreading between two portions of oceanic LITHOSPHERE, in which undersea "ridges" can be formed in the context of compressional, rather than extensional, forces

backarc basin a low-lying depression of land that exists on a CONTINENTAL PLATE that has been converging with another plate, cratonward of, and adjacent to, a VOLCANIC ARC; a BASIN that has been created as a result of this volcanic arc activity

backarc zone the land that exists cratonward of a VOLCANIC ARC, an arc that is produced along a CONVERGENT PLATE BOUNDARY; generally produced on the PLATE that is overriding the other SUBDUCTING plate; may contain one or more low-lying portions of land, known as BACKARC BASINS

basin a low-lying depression of land, often found adjacent to a fold-thrust belt or other area of uplifted, raised land; the depression of land is produced as a result of the nearby UPLIFT

Cenozoic era the most recent era, between 66.4 million years ago and the present day; characterized by the dominance of mammalian life on Earth

circular vent a point source at which magma breaks through the surface as lava; often surrounded by a volcanic cone, which is a volcano

colonnade the relatively homogeneous, vertically oriented COLUMNS that are found, below the ENTABLATURE and above the PILLOW PALAGONITE COMPLEX, in a solidified LAVA FLOW that displays COLUMNAR JOINTING; formed by the downward motion of water, moving through the MASTER JOINTS, through a lava flow that is still fairly hot and has only recently begun to cool

column a vertically oriented, pipe-shaped column that is part of a cooling or solidified LAVA FLOW; separated from other columns by JOINTS

columnar jointing   the pattern of vertically oriented COLUMNS, shaped like pipes, that can form as a LAVA FLOW cools and solidifies; found within numerous layers of a solidifying or solidified lava flow, including the ENTABLATURE and COLONNADE

compressional fault activity   FAULT ACTIVITY in which two FAULT BLOCKS collide along the axis of the FAULT; includes TRANSPRESSIONAL FAULT ACTIVITY

concave-up   refers to a bowl-shaped area of rock, such that the bowl shape is facing upward, vertically (a satellite dish that is pointing straight up, to the sky, is concave-up); often seen in the overall shape of a BASIN, SYNCLINE, or canyon with a U-shaped channel profile

continental margin   the zone along which the thick, continental CRUST thins and slopes into the thinner, OCEANIC CRUST; can take the form of a PASSIVE CONTINENTAL MARGIN, the margins of the plates along a DIVERGENT PLATE BOUNDARY

continental plate   one of the seven largest PLATES, out of 35 total plates; consists of continental LITHOSPHERE, which is a portion of continental CRUST, or CRUSTAL LITHOSPHERE, that is attached to underlying MANTLE LITHOSPHERE

continental shelf   the portion of the CRUST of a CONTINENTAL PLATE that is between the continental craton and the CONTINENTAL SLOPE; the portion of the continental plate that is seaward of the CRATON and landward of the continental slope; is still thick enough to be regarded as continental crust; extends a few miles offshore and is covered by relatively shallow water

continental slope   the portion of a CONTINENTAL PLATE along which the continental crust thins out and slopes down into the thin, OCEANIC CRUST; is still part of the continental crust; is covered by fairly deep water

convergent plate boundary   a line, as in an axis or zone, along which two PLATES interact; interactions along convergent plate boundaries can take the forms of collision, SUBDUCTION, or, in the case of convergence between two continental plates, suturing

convex-up   refers to a dome-shape (an indoor football stadium, with the white roof maintained partially by air pressure, is convex-up); may refer to a canyon wall that has been heavily smoothed by erosion or to a dome-shaped ANTICLINE that appears as a mountain; a hill that slopes down into a river is convex-up

coupling   the connection of one form of SEDIMENT transport to another; the processes by which a river responds to a change in sediment delivery and reestablishes some type of equilibrium

craton   the central and oldest portion of a PLATE or CONTINENTAL PLATE; the portion of a plate or continental plate that is farthest from the plate margins or CONTINENTAL MARGINS; tends to be TECTONICALLY stable

Cretaceous period   the interval of time that occurred between 144 and 66.4 million years ago and that is a subdivision of the MESOZOIC ERA; reptiles were dominant, and the first flowering plants appeared

crust   the outer layer of the Earth; consists of solid rock and varies between a minimum of about 5.1 miles (8.2 km) thick, in the case of OCEANIC CRUST, and a maximum of about 44 miles (70 km) thick, in the case of continental crust; can be subdivided into the continental crust and oceanic crust; equivalent to CRUSTAL LITHOSPHERE

crustal lithosphere   entirely equivalent to the CRUST; the upper portion of the LITHOSPHERE that exists above the MANTLE LITHOSPHERE; of lower density than the mantle lithosphere; the positively buoyant portion of the lithosphere that makes up each CONTINENTAL PLATE; the densities of the rocks in the crust increase as the depth, below the surface, increases; the rocks in the lower crust are generally more dense than the middle crust, and the rocks in the middle crust are more dense than the rock layers of the upper crust; all three subdivisions of the crust are positively buoyant, with respect to the ASTHENOSPHERE, and are being pulled down into the asthenosphere by the negatively buoyant mantle lithosphere (as if a steel plate had been glued to the bottom of an inflatable, rectangular raft, floating on water, and was pulling part of the raft below the surface of the water)

Devonian period   the interval of time, a subdivision of the PALEOZOIC ERA that occurred between 408 and 360 million years ago, during which fish species were dominant and during which some insects and amphibians first appeared

dextral   right-handed; directed to the right; derived, in part, from a Latin word, *dexter,* which refers to the direction of right and is the opposite of *sinister,* meaning left; the Latin word *rectus* also means right and has been used, in the sciences (as in organic chemistry), to describe right-handed directionality that is opposite to sinistral directionality; *rectus* refers to right in the sense of straight, as in the context of a person righting, or straightening, his or her balance or posture

dextral transpression   the interaction of two portions of LITHOSPHERE or CRUST, along either a FAULT line or fold-thrust belt, that is characterized by both compressional movement and clockwise, right-handed movement; the rock on the side of the fault or fold-thrust axis that is doing the pushing (such that the net direction of deformation or compression is away from this rock) is rotated to the right, or clockwise, with respect to the forward direction of compression; in dextral transpressional FAULT ACTIVITY, one fault block is uplifted with respect to the other

dextral transtension   the interaction of two FAULT BLOCKS, along a FAULT line, that is characterized by both extensional separation and clockwise rotation of one fault block; the rotation is the result of strike-slip FAULT ACTIVITY; may be accompanied by UPLIFT of one fault block with respect to another

dike   a solidified intrusion of magma into rock layers; may appear as a vertical segment, of solidified magma, in the wall of a canyon; the present-day remnant of a FISSURE-VENT SYSTEM

dike swarm a cluster of DIKEs that are localized in one area and are often parallel to one another

disconformity a physical and "rock-age" boundary, as in a canyon wall, between underlying, horizontal layers of SEDIMENTARY ROCK and younger, overlying, horizontal layers of sedimentary rock; often results from the net erosion of sedimentary rocks that were deposited during the age gap; can indicate that UPLIFT, in concert with minimal deposition of sedimentary rocks and EROSIONAL EXHUMATION of existing rock layers, occurred during the age gap

divergent plate boundary a line, as in an axis or zone, along which two plates are separating from each other; a DIVERGENT PLATE BOUNDARY usually begins as a RIFT; after the rift axis has been established, plates may move away from each other by divergence and seafloor spreading

doming the process by which rocks in the CRUST or the underlying MANTLE LITHOSPHERE are pushed upward into a dome; the resulting deformation may be similar to an ANTICLINE, and a structural basin, analogous to a SYNCLINE, is formed adjacent to the dome; may be produced by mantle UPWELLING, such as by a MANTLE PLUME or by convection currents in the MANTLE beneath a HOT SPOT; a dome produced by magmatic activity is not the same as a dome produced as part of a CIRCULAR VENT and VOLCANIC ARC

downthrown block the rock on the side of a FAULT, one in which the motion has some normal, or vertical, displacement, that has been pushed downward with respect to the rock, or FAULT BLOCK, on the other side of the fault; also applies to rock on one side of a JOINT FAULT

elastic uplift/elastic rebound the UPLIFT and upwarping, sometimes occurring as alternating rings of concentric SYNCLINES and ANTICLINES, of rock layers beneath and within a complex crater and in the portions of the IMPACT BASIN that surround the IMPACT CRATER; produced as a kind of elastic response that follows the formation of the impact basin; occurs as a result of the interaction of the impact shock wave, in the ground, with the surface rocks; magnitude determined by the interaction, and eventual cancellation, of the shock wave amplitude with the tensile properties and thicknesses of the surface rock layers; analogous to the upward ballooning of a trampoline, such as after a person bounces off the trampoline

embayment a bay-shaped indentation of a shoreline or coastline, with the indentation visible from above; the indentation is not a depression or valley in the ground but an indentation in an otherwise linear coastline, such as of a linear coastline that extends from north to south; a curved-in, scooped-out portion of an otherwise flat, and linear, coastline

entablature the layer, of a cooling LAVA FLOW, that is beneath the VESICULAR CRUST and above the COLONNADE; contains FANNING COLUMNS

Eocene epoch the interval of time between 57.8 and 36.6 million years ago; a subdivision of the PALEOGENE AGE of the TERTIARY PERIOD; characterized by the dominance of mammals and the appearances of the earliest camels, ancestors of horses, and large birds; also characterized by the formations of the Alps, Himalayas, and consistently thick polar ice caps

eolian produced by, modified by, or deposited under the influence of wind

ephemeral stream/ephemeral river a stream or river that transports water for less than 10 percent of the year, a percentage that corresponds to about five weeks out of the year

era an interval of time in geological history, with the boundaries of the interval corresponding to the beginning and end of the dominance of a given type of life-form; includes the PALEOZOIC ERA, MESOZOIC ERA, and CENOZOIC ERA

erg a portion of a desert that consists of actively moving sand dunes

erosional exhumation the erosion of layers of SEDIMENTARY ROCK, usually in a relatively uniform fashion, from a large area of land; applies to mountain ranges and the sedimentary rock layers in BASINS

fanning columns fan-shaped, slender columns that are produced within the ENTABLATURE of a LAVA FLOW; curved, fanlike COLUMNS that are formed, during the later phase of the cooling of a lava flow, by upwardly directed convection of water (up through the cooling layers of the lava flow)

fault a crack in the rocks of the CRUST; often extends to the surface but may be confined to the deeper layers of the crust or extend down through the MANTLE LITHOSPHERE

fault activity interactions that occur along FAULT lines and produce horizontal motion, vertical motion, as in FAULT-ASSOCIATED UPLIFT, or a combination of horizontal and vertical motion; can also be accompanied by magmatic activity; includes extensional fault activity, transtensional fault activity, COMPRESSIONAL FAULT ACTIVITY, and TRANSPRESSIONAL FAULT ACTIVITY

fault-associated uplift UPLIFT that occurs on one side of a FAULT; refers to NORMAL FAULT ACTIVITY; can occur when any FAULT ACTIVITY exhibits some normal character and produces some vertical motion

fault block the rock on one side of a FAULT

fault system a collection of FAULTs that are generally oriented along the same axis; individual faults within a fault system may display different types of motion at different times

fissure a crack in portions of rock, generally near the surface of the Earth; a site along which magma is delivered to the surface and erupted from, thereby forming LAVA FLOWS; a crack that is not a TECTONICALLY active FAULT but that may be widened by erosion or by the actions of groundwater

fissure-vent system a crack in surface rocks that defines a LINEAR VENT SYSTEM, from which LAVA FLOWS originate; a linear vent that, as a result of solidification at different points on the FISSURE, has one or more focal points of lava delivery

flexural subsidence the downward movement, or sinking, of a relatively large area of land, such that the downward movement is driven partially by active mechanisms; SUBSIDENCE that is partially guided or distorted by the actions of opposing, compressional forces on a portion of LITHO-SPHERE, as in an intermontane BASIN

flexural uplift   UPLIFT of a sedimentary BASIN or other portion of land that is not accompanied by deformation or cracking; often associated with compressional, tectonic forces that are acting on the basin from opposing directions, causing the land in the basin to be flexed or bent upward as a piece of paper would become curved (without being creased, folded, or torn); can largely take the form of ISOSTATIC UPLIFT, in response to the EROSIONAL EXHUMATION of a sedimentary basin and the mountains surrounding it, that is made slightly nonuniform (as a result of the distortion produced by mountain ranges surrounding the basin, etc.)

flood basalt lava   freely flowing lava that is often low in silica and low in viscosity; may also be high in magnesium oxide or other minerals and dissolved gases

fluvial incision   INCISION produced by a river or stream; the most common form of incision

fluvial transport   the transport of SEDIMENTS by a river or stream; refers to sediments that are suspended and are not dissolved in water

footwall   the rock, or FAULT BLOCK, that extends along a FAULT and that has been downthrown, or pushed downward, with respect to the rock on the other side of the fault; also referred to as the DOWNTHROWN BLOCK; found in a fault that displays some NORMAL CHARACTER

foreland basin   a depression of land that is formed, on the overriding PLATE, in the context of plate convergence and is adjacent to a fold-thrust belt; includes a RETROARC FORELAND BASIN, which can be formed on a CONTINENTAL PLATE that is overriding a SUBDUCTING, oceanic plate, or in the context of continental-continental plate convergence, and a PERIPHERAL FORELAND BASIN, formed on the extreme periphery, adjacent to the collision zone and subsequent suture zone, of a continental plate that is converging with another continental plate

geothermal activity   conductive heating of rocks, usually granite, in the crust; may be driven by magmatic activity or may occur when the crust beneath a newly formed mountain range, such as would be formed by OROGENIC ACTIVITY along a CONVERGENT PLATE BOUNDARY, is still cooling (see chapter 4); may produce THERMAL SPRINGS

geothermal formation   a layer of SEDIMENTARY ROCKS that has been modified, after its deposition and solidification, by the water of a THERMAL SPRING or by other effects of geothermal heat transfer

gradient   the downhill slope of a portion of land; usually refers to the downhill slope that a river or stream follows; often expressed, numerically, as numbers between 1.00, 2.00, 3.00, and so on; varies at different points along the river

groundwater incision   INCISION produced by an underground spring, THERMAL SPRING, seep, cold seep, or aquifer; may produce small channels, which include sapping channels, that are visible, in the walls of a canyon, at the site of intersection between a canyon and the groundwater source

hanging wall   the rock, or FAULT BLOCK, that extends along a FAULT and that has been upthrown, or pushed upward, with respect to the rock on the other side of the fault; also referred to as the UPTHROWN BLOCK; found in a fault that displays some NORMAL CHARACTER

hillslope   the land that surrounds a channel or canyon and that is capable of feeding surface water, which often contains suspended SEDIMENTS, into the channel or canyon

Holocene epoch   the most recent 10,000 years; a subdivision of the QUATER-NARY PERIOD; characterized by the dominance of humans and the absence of major intervals of glaciation

hot spot   a localized site of magmatic activity that is characterized by intermittently active VOLCANIC ACTIVITY, which refers to the eruption of lava from a LINEAR VENT SYSTEM or from CIRCULAR VENTS (point-source vents, as in volcanoes); the volcanic activity associated with a hot spot will often take the form of FLOOD BASALT eruptions; may be produced by a MANTLE PLUME or by a major hypervelocity impact event; a localized site of magmatic activity that is not produced as part of a VOLCANIC ARC and that is not the result of arc magmatism; includes IMPACT HOT SPOTS

impact basin   a depression of land that is produced by an impact event; the depression may be found within and around the IMPACT CRATER, but the impact basin is generally regarded as the broad depression that surrounds and encompasses the impact crater

impact crater   a crater produced by an impact event and not as a result of VOLCANIC ACTIVITY; a bowl-shaped crater (a simple crater) that is surrounded by one circular rim; a series of concentric rims that surround a central bowl or a central peak and that form a complex crater

impact hot spot   a HOT SPOT that may, in theory, be produced by a major impact event, such as by the impact of a large meteor, comet, or other object; characterized by magmatic activity, VOLCANIC ACTIVITY, and prolonged GEOTHERMAL ACTIVITY in the CRUST

impact melting   the process by which molten iron and other metals, derived from a meteor that is melted upon its impact with surface rocks, cause surface rocks to melt and become fused with metals from the meteor; may simply melt surface rocks or may form conglomerations of iron and, for example, the quartz of SEDIMENTARY ROCKS near the surface

impact plume   a MANTLE PLUME that may be produced as a result of an extraordinarily powerful, hypervelocity impact event; a site of UPWELLING, within the MANTLE, that may result from an impact event and may sustain an IMPACT HOT SPOT, which itself is a somewhat theoretical phenomenon

incised meander   a bend in a river, one that has INCISED a channel or canyon, such that the walls on each side of the bend are of roughly similar slopes;

an example of a SYMMETRICAL MEANDER; the canyon walls tend to be relatively vertical on both sides of an incised meander

incision/incised   the process by which a river, stream, or source of underground water erodes downward through rock layers; incision is enhanced and favored by anything that increases the GRADIENT of the river; the gradient of a river or stream can be increased by UPLIFT, AGGRADATION, or a decrease in sea level; includes FLUVIAL INCISION and GROUNDWATER INCISION

ingrown meander   an ASYMMETRICAL MEANDER in which the OUTER WALL of a meander is more gently sloped than the INNER WALL

inner core   the solid, innermost portion of the core of the Earth

inner wall   the canyon wall, at a MEANDER, or bend in the river, that is facing away from the overall axis along which the river is flowing; if a river is winding back and forth but is flowing along a north-south axis, the inner wall of a meander will be facing west

interbasaltic sediments   layers of SEDIMENTS or SEDIMENTARY ROCKS that are contained within the solidified layers or structure of a LAVA FLOW; generally formed as sediment-laden water carries sediments into a cooling lava flow, thereby depositing the sediments; sediments may have been deposited above layers, within a cooling lava flow, that solidified first; location in lava flow may also be determined by differences in the porosity or permeability of COLONNADE, ENTABLATURE, or other sections

intracanyon flow   a LAVA FLOW that flows through an existing canyon or gorge; the lava flow may or may not solidify immediately; the intracanyon flow may or may not completely, or permanently, divert the river that normally flows through the canyon

isostatic uplift   PASSIVE UPLIFT of the LITHOSPHERE that can result from EROSIONAL EXHUMATION of surface rock layers; a bobbing upward of the surface rocks, and the CONTINENTAL PLATE beneath them, that results from the unloading of dense, surface rock layers

joint   a vertical joint, as in a crack or as analogous to a grain in a piece of wood, that separates two or more COLUMNS of a cooling and solidifying, or cooled and solidified, LAVA FLOW

joint fault   a vertical or generally vertical crack in rock layers, such that rock on one side of the crack can be upthrown with respect to the rock layers on the other side of the crack

Jurassic period   the interval of time that occurred between 208 and 144 million years ago and that is a subdivision of the MESOZOIC ERA; reptiles were dominant, the first birds and flying reptiles appeared, and more early mammals appeared

karst formation   an underground cave, a subsurface channel, a sinkhole, or a portion of a canyon wall that was once underground that has been formed by subsurface water; subsurface water may move and erode rocks or may form karst features by evaporative processes

lacustrine   deposited at the bottom of a stagnant body of water, such as a lake or pool

laminar flow   lava that is moving relatively slowly and is moving in ordered layers or sheets, with limited splashing and mixing of different parts of the moving lava; a set of hydrological characteristics, one of which is velocity, of lava that is moving as either a PIPE FLOW or SHEET FLOW

laminar-to-turbulent transition   refers to the range of velocities, and the fluid properties that are associated with those velocities, of a LAVA FLOW that is moving more rapidly than a LAMINAR FLOW and more slowly than a TURBULENT FLOW; refers to a lava flow that is still a laminar flow but is almost moving rapidly enough to become a turbulent flow; both SHEET FLOWS and PIPE FLOWS can move with transitional velocities, but pipe flows and sheet flows exhibit different ranges of transitional velocities

lava dam   a dam, of a river or stream, that can occur when a lava flow enters a canyon

lava flowa portion of lava that has a relatively uniform composition and that has been delivered from a single source, usually a FISSURE-VENT SYSTEM or LINEAR VENT

linear vent system   a linear opening, generally along a FISSURE, from which lava erupts; a linear point of origin of a LAVA FLOW

lithosphere   consists of the CRUST and the MANTLE LITHOSPHERE, which is the uppermost 17 miles (27 km) to 50 miles (80 km) of the UPPER MANTLE; extends down to about 62 miles (100 km); PLATES consist of lithosphere

lower mantle   the portion of the MANTLE that is beneath the ASTHENOSPHERE; extends from about 218 miles (350 km) below the surface of the continental CRUST to about 1,802 miles (2,900 km) below the surface

mantle   consists of a lower portion of the LITHOSPHERE, the MANTLE LITHOSPHERE, the ASTHENOSPHERE, and the LOWER MANTLE; consists of the UPPER MANTLE and lower mantle

mantle lithosphere   the lower portion of the LITHOSPHERE that is beneath the CRUST; is generally between 17 miles (27 km) to 50 miles (80 km) thick; extends down to about 62 miles (100 km) below the surface of the crust

mantle plume   a convection current that originates in the ASTHENOSPHERE, or perhaps below, and that extends from below into the MANTLE LITHOSPHERE or even into the CRUSTAL LITHOSPHERE; the UPWELLING, at a relatively localized site, of molten rock into various portions of the LITHOSPHERE from a source in the LOWER MANTLE; may be the driving force of HOT SPOTS; may drive the formation of RIFTS at intracontinental sites

master joints   the widest and predominant JOINTS, formed in a cooling or cooled, and solidified, LAVA FLOW; avenues for the upward movement, by convection, and downward percolation of water within the lava flow

meander   a bend in a river or stream; a bend in the canyon or channel walls that has been carved by a river or stream

Mesozoic era   the interval between 245 and 66.4 million years ago, during which reptiles were the dominant life-forms on Earth

metamorphism   a change in the structure or composition of a rock that is produced without melting the rock; occurs as a result of heat, pressure, or other forces that do not actually cause the rock to undergo phase changes from solid to liquid and then back to solid; analogous to the conversion, without first melting the ice, of an ice cube to an orange juice cube; generally occurs during TECTONIC forces, such as continental plate convergence and suturing; includes SHOCK METAMORPHISM

Miocene epoch   the interval of time between 23.7 and 5.3 million years ago; a subdivision of the NEOGENE AGE of the TERTIARY PERIOD; characterized by the dominance of mammals and the appearance of large mammals; also characterized by the development of thick ice on Antarctica and the opening of the Red Sea

miogeocline   a portion of land, as in a cross between a BASIN and a large-scale SYNCLINE, that was once part of the low-lying depression of land that extends along a PASSIVE CONTINENTAL MARGIN; a passive continental margin that has been converted, as a result of plate convergence, into, essentially, a FORELAND BASIN; short for *miogeosyncline*; tends to have accumulated SEDIMENTARY ROCK layers, during the time the land was part of a passive continental margin (before plate convergence pushed the passive margin inland); an example is the Cordilleran Miogeocline (see chapter 1)

Neogene age   the interval of time that occurred between 23.7 and 1.6 million years ago and that is a subdivision of the TERTIARY PERIOD; characterized by the dominance of mammals and the appearances of whales, apes, and the earliest hominids; is subdivided into the MIOCENE EPOCH and the PLIOCENE EPOCH

nonconformity   a physical and "rock-age" boundary, as in a canyon wall, between old metamorphic and igneous rocks and younger, overlying, horizontal layers of SEDIMENTARY ROCK; often results from the net erosion of sedimentary rocks that were deposited during the age gap

normal fault activity/normal character   refers to vertical displacement along a FAULT line; refers to the upward, vertical movement of rock on one side of a fault; the upward motion occurs in relation to the rock on the other side of the fault; can occur along faults that display some NORMAL CHARACTER, or vertical displacement, but are still moving, predominantly, within the plane of the surface of the Earth, as in TRANSPRESSIONAL FAULT ACTIVITY or transtensional FAULT ACTIVITY

oceanic crust   the thin portion of CRUST that exists below the water of the oceans; is consistently about 5.1 miles (8.2 km) thick; is relatively homogeneous at different sites on the Earth; consists of about 656 feet (200 m) of marine sediments, which sit above 1.2 miles (2 km) of basalt rocks; the basalt rocks sit above 3.7 miles (6.0 km) of another type of rock

Oligocene epoch   the interval of time between 36.6 and 23.7 million years ago; a subdivision of the PALEOGENE AGE of the TERTIARY PERIOD; characterized by the dominance of mammals and the appearances of certain specific mammals; also characterized by various TECTONIC events

Ordovician period   the interval of time, a subdivision of the PALEOZOIC ERA that occurred between 505 and 438 million years ago, during which the first fish species appeared and marine invertebrates secured their dominance

orogenic activity/orogenic   the deformation of the CRUST that often produces UPLIFT, within an orogenic belt or fold-thrust belt; a type of TECTONIC ACTIVITY that often produces mountain ranges, by deformation and upwarping of the crust; includes OROGENIC UPLIFT

orogenic uplift   a type of ACTIVE UPLIFT that occurs, within an orogenic belt or fold-thrust belt, in response to OROGENIC ACTIVITY

orographic desert   an arid or semiarid region that is generally inland from, and downwind of, a coastal mountain range or other mountain range; also known as a rainshadow desert; is downwind of the rainshadow of a mountain range; often found at latitudes that are not subtropical and are more than 20–30 degrees north or south of the equator

outer core   the outermost portion of the core, consisting of liquid rock

outer wall   the canyon wall, at a MEANDER, or bend in the river, that is facing toward the overall axis along which the river is flowing; if a river is winding back and forth but is flowing along a north-south axis, the outer wall of a meander will be facing east

Paleocene epoch   the interval of time between 66.4 and 57.8 million years ago; a subdivision of the PALEOGENE AGE of the TERTIARY period; characterized by the dominance of mammals and the appearance of early primates; also characterized by the collision between India and Eurasia and by other TECTONIC events

Paleogene age   the interval of time that occurred between 66.4 and 23.7 million years ago and that is a subdivision of the TERTIARY PERIOD; characterized by the dominance of mammals, the appearances of early primates and early ancestors of horses, and the development of grasslands; is subdivided into the PALEOCENE EPOCH, the EOCENE EPOCH, and the OLIGOCENE EPOCH

Paleozoic era   the interval between 545 and 245 million years ago, during which invertebrates—which include marine invertebrates, various species of fish, and amphibians—were the dominant life-forms

passive continental margin   a CONTINENTAL MARGIN that was formed along a RIFT axis but is no longer especially TECTONICALLY active

passive uplift   UPLIFT of the LITHOSPHERE that is driven by the intrinsic properties of the asthenosphere; occurs, as ISOSTATIC UPLIFT, in response to EROSIONAL EXHUMATION of mountain ranges or layers of SEDIMENTARY ROCK; occurs when the crust is made lighter and more buoyant, such as in response to erosion or the melting of ice sheets; can be partially driven by horizontal forces in the MANTLE; includes and is roughly equivalent to ISOSTATIC UPLIFT

Pennsylvanian age   the interval of time that occurred between 320 and 286 million years ago and that is a subdivision of the Carboniferous period of the PALEOZOIC ERA; amphibians were still dominant, but the first reptiles and coal-creating swamps also appeared

peripheral foreland basin   a FORELAND BASIN that is produced on the extreme margin of a CONTINENTAL PLATE that is converging with another continental plate; exists between the convergence zone or suture zone and the more inland fold-thrust belt or belts that develop along an axis that is parallel to the convergence zone; cannot be formed by continental plate–oceanic plate convergence; is a continental-continental analogue of the forearc basin, which is formed, seaward of the VOLCANIC ARC, during continental-oceanic plate convergence

Permian period   the interval of time, a subdivision of the PALEOZOIC ERA that occurred between 286 and 245 million years ago, during which amphibians were dominant, the first forests began to diminish, and major intervals of glaciation occurred

Pillow Palagonite Complex   the lower layers of a LAVA FLOW that are solidified as the lava flow enters a body of water; solidified, pillowlike pattern is produced when LACUSTRINE conditions, meaning water existing above a given layer of lava, exist above or within parts of the cooling lava flow

pipe flow   refers to the relationship between fluid parameters in a moving liquid, as in a LAVA FLOW; refers to the theoretical model, or construct, in which the flow characteristics are modeled; pipe flow of lava is modeled in terms of the movement of a non-Newtonian fluid through a pipe; a non-Newtonian fluid, of which human blood is an example, is a fluid in which the physical parameters of the fluid vary in complex and dynamic ways; can be used to model the behavior of an INTRACANYON FLOW; some pipe flows of lava are examples of so-called Poiseuille flow

pipes   the vertically oriented, somewhat rounded COLUMNS that are formed, largely in the context of moving water or steam, as a LAVA FLOW cools; refers to columns or the shapes of columns in a solidifying lava flow

plate   a continuous block of LITHOSPHERE, consisting of both overlying CRUST and underlying MANTLE LITHOSPHERE, that moves across the ASTHENOSPHERE and interacts with other plates

Pleistocene epoch   the interval between 1.6 million and 10,000 years ago; a subdivision of the QUATERNARY PERIOD; characterized by the dominance of hominids

Pliocene epoch   the interval of time between 5.3 and 1.6 million years ago; a subdivision of the NEOGENE AGE of the TERTIARY PERIOD; characterized by the dominance of mammals and the appearance of early hominids; also characterized by the joining together of North and South America and by other TECTONIC events

Quaternary period   the most recent 1.6 million years of geological history, characterized by the dominance of hominids and humans; includes the PLEISTOCENE EPOCH and the HOLOCENE EPOCH

rainshadow effects   localized decreases or increases in precipitation that are found downwind of a mountain range and that occur as a result of the cooling effect of a mountain range; the rainshadow is immediately downwind of the range and receives abundant precipitation; farther downwind, an arid or semiarid rainshadow desert, also known as an OROGRAPHIC DESERT, can exist

resistant   refers to a type of rock that is not easily eroded or INCISED by FLUVIAL mechanisms

retroarc foreland basin   a FORELAND BASIN that is formed on the landward, or cratonward, side of a backarc fold-thrust belt (also known as a foreland fold-thrust belt or retroarc fold-thrust belt) of a CONTINENTAL PLATE that is overriding an oceanic plate (which is SUBDUCTING beneath the continental plate) or on a continental plate that is converging with another continental plate; the sequence of features, moving inland and therefore cratonward of a continental-oceanic convergence zone, are the coastal mountain range that is immediately inland of the subduction zone, the forearc basin, the VOLCANIC ARC, the BACKARC BASIN, the backarc fold-thrust belt (as in the Sevier Fold-Thrust Belt), and the retroarc foreland basin; part of the BACKARC ZONE that includes the backarc basin, backarc fold-thrust belt, and retroarc foreland basin

rift/rifting   a new PLATE boundary that has been formed, between two plates, at a site that is removed from the CONTINENTAL MARGIN; the process, as in rifting, that creates the new boundary; a rift is a crack that extends down through the CRUST and MANTLE LITHOSPHERE

sedimentary rocks   rocks formed by the actions of heat and pressure on SEDIMENTS that are deeply buried beneath other sediments, other rock layers, or glaciers; solidified, or solidified and otherwise modified, layers of sediments; includes limestone and other rocks that are based on carbonate, sandstone, and shales; includes rocks that contain conglomerations of calcium carbonate, silica, or another mineral with marine shell or plant debris, gravels, lava debris, or other material

sediments   the building blocks of SEDIMENTARY ROCK, such as carbonate and other mineral substances; refers to the dynamic, or implicitly dynamic, history of a layer of sedimentary rock; a canyon wall can be said to contain layers of sediments, meaning sediments that were dynamically deposited and that subsequently solidified into sedimentary rocks; refers to sedimentary rock layers, in the context of the conditions in which the rocks were deposited, eroded, or otherwise transported or modified, as in SHALLOW MARINE sediments or EOLIAN sediments

seepage   the delivery of water, usually from sources belowground, into a canyon, a subterranean KARST FORMATION, or a SUBMARINE CANYON by a seep

shallow marine   refers to the various shallow, ocean environments in which SEDIMENTS are deposited; a depositional environment for sediments that may subsequently be solidified into SEDIMENTARY ROCK layers; may include wavelike patterns or marine fossils in solidified rock layers

sheet flow   a set of hydrological, fluid characteristics that describe the movement of lava, especially FLOOD BASALT LAVA, in a LAVA FLOW; fluid parameters are modeled in terms of fluid movement in sheets, and a lava flow may not move in strictly defined, literal sheets; sheet flow movement can exhibit, depending on the velocity and other parameters, either LAMINAR FLOW characteristics or TURBULENT FLOW characteristics; can be applied in modeling the movement of lava over the rim of a canyon, down a hill, or over a relatively flat surface

shock metamorphism   a form of METAMORPHISM that can be produced by an impact event; formation of unique forms of quartz or other rocks, forms of metamorphic rock that are generally unique and characteristic of metamorphism that is driven by an impact-induced shock wave

Silurian period   the interval of time, a subdivision of the PALEOZOIC ERA that occurred between 438 and 408 million years ago, during which the fish species became especially dominant and some of the first plants appeared on land

sinuosity   refers to the total degree of curvature that a stream exhibits along its path between two points; defined as the ratio of the stream or channel length to the valley length, which is the shortest, linear, actual distance between two points on the stream; contextual definition: Suppose that a stream flows in an overall southward direction, an 80-mile (129-km) distance from City A to City B, but meanders back and forth along its axis (or even reverses direction or flows in a circular path). The valley length is the 80-mile distance along the straight line, from north to south, that is the axis of the flow of the stream. The stream length may be, in an extreme case, 800 miles (1,287 km) and may make a lot of MEANDERS. The degree of sinuosity might be quantified as 800 divided by 80, or 10, and would not have any units attached to it. However, one could express the units in miles per mile, or miles of angular length (or arc length) per mile of linear length. The stream length takes into account both the numbers of meanders and the windiness, or curvature, of the meanders. A stream with a high degree of sinuosity would make many meanders, and the meanders would tend to be very circuitous or serpentine

subduction/subducting   the downward motion, into the ASTHENOSPHERE, of an oceanic plate beneath a CONTINENTAL PLATE or another oceanic plate; occurs at a CONVERGENT PLATE BOUNDARY; driven by the larger density, in relation to the underlying asthenosphere, of the subducting plate

subduction zone   the line or axis along which one PLATE is undergoing SUBDUCTION beneath another plate

submarine canyon   a canyon that has been INCISED out of the CONTINENTAL SHELF or the CONTINENTAL SLOPE

submarine fan   an ALLUVIAL FAN that is formed in the vicinity of a SUBMARINE CANYON; a fanned-out pattern of SEDIMENTS, on the ocean floor, that usually extends seaward and away from the outermost end of a submarine canyon

submarine fan valley   the valley that allows SEDIMENTS to be funneled seaward and deposited as part of a SUBMARINE FAN

subsidence   the decrease in the positive buoyancy of the CRUSTAL LITHOSPHERE, such that the entire LITHOSPHERE is caused to sink downward into the ASTHENOSPHERE; may occur when thick layers of SEDIMENTARY ROCK accumulate in a BASIN; a sinking downward of crustal rocks with respect to adjacent crustal rocks, as in the subsidence of an IMPACT CRATER (in response to subsurface erosion by groundwater)

symmetrical meander   a bend in a river, one that has INCISED a channel or canyon, such that the walls are of nearly similar slopes on both sides of the bend; expressed as the ratio of the average slopes of the walls on each side of the MEANDER, such that the ratio is close to 1.0; includes INCISED MEANDERS

syncline   a CONCAVE-UP depression in the land that is adjacent to an ANTICLINE and is produced by folding of rock; generally formed along a fold-thrust belt, by OROGENIC ACTIVITY

tectonic activity/tectonic   the remodeling, cracking, or deformation of the CRUST, the MANTLE LITHOSPHERE, or both; includes FAULT ACTIVITY, OROGENIC ACTIVITY, MAGMATIC ACTIVITY, and VOLCANIC ACTIVITY

Tertiary period   the interval of time that occurred between 66.4 and 1.6 million years ago and that is a subdivision of the CENOZOIC ERA; characterized by the dominance of mammals, including early primates, whales, horses, and ultimately hominids; includes the PALEOGENE AGE, which is itself subdivided into the PALEOCENE EPOCH, the EOCENE EPOCH, and the OLIGOCENE EPOCH, and the NEOGENE AGE, which is itself subdivided into the MIOCENE EPOCH and PLIOCENE EPOCH

thermal spring   a spring whose flow is driven by hydrothermal convection, which results from temperature gradients in underground water sources; the temperature gradients that create hydrothermal convection, and that drive the movement of water in a thermal spring, are the result of GEOTHERMAL ACTIVITY

transpressional fault activity   COMPRESSIONAL FAULT ACTIVITY that is accompanied by strike-slip FAULT ACTIVITY (which is horizontal motion along the fault line); includes DEXTRAL TRANSPRESSIONAL fault activity and sinistral transpressional fault activity

transpressional orogenic activity   OROGENIC ACTIVITY that is characterized by both compressional, or convergent, deformation and side-to-side motion by the land on one or more sides of the fold-thrust belt; often described in terms of DEXTRAL TRANSPRESSIONAL orogenic activity, in which the land that is behind (the land that is pushing) the net direction of deformation is rotated clockwise with respect to the fold-thrust belt (can be applied to the clockwise rotation of the Colorado Plateau; see chapter 9), or sinistral transpressional orogenic activity, in which the land that is behind the net directionality of the deformation (for example, south of a northward-directed, or northward-vergent, fold-thrust belt) is rotated counterclockwise; can produce a transpressional FORELAND BASIN: During the late phases of the Qinling-Dabie Orogeny, the Sichuan Basin (see chapter 3) was a transpressional foreland basin and was rotated counterclockwise, during sinistral transpressional deformation along the Longmen-Shan Belt (the northwestern margin of the Sichuan Basin)

transverse drainage the multiple streams or channels that drain a mountain range and that exit the mountain range, such as by entering a FORELAND BASIN, along lines that are roughly perpendicular to the axis along which the mountain range is oriented; characteristic of an immature drainage system, a drainage system that is draining a relatively young mountain range

Triassic period the interval of time that occurred between 245 and 208 million years ago and that is a subdivision of the MESOZOIC ERA; reptiles became dominant, the first dinosaurs appeared, and some of the earliest mammals appeared

tributary a river or stream that flows and empties into another river

tributary canyon a channel or canyon that joins a second canyon, one that is usually longer or more extensive; a tributary canyon is a canyon that has been incised by a TRIBUTARY of the river that INCISED the second, larger canyon; a SUBMARINE CANYON or channel that feeds into another, usually larger, submarine canyon

tufa a deposit or conglomeration of calcium carbonate, sometimes consisting of spheres that appear as concretions, that are formed when the water evaporates from a carbonate-rich source of water; generally formed by an interaction of two water sources, such as the water in a stream and the surface water flowing into the stream; can also occur by the delivery and evaporation of groundwater from a spring; tufa are equivalent to tufa deposits; some tufa can form around plants; includes TUFA DAMS

tufa dam a collection of tufa that are built up on one or more sides of a stream channel; may limit the erosion, by the movement of surface water, of the banks of a stream

turbid underflow an event, often occurring as a result of a terrestrial flood, that transports SEDIMENTS from the shoreline to sites that are past the CONTINENTAL SHELF; characterized by low-salinity, sediment-laden water that moves in a plume; plumes, which are produced during turbid underflows, often move sediments through SUBMARINE CANYONS

turbulent flow a LAVA FLOW, which can be either a SHEET FLOW or a PIPE FLOW, that is moving very rapidly, is highly liquefied and may be splashing or frothing, and that is rapidly losing heat; a flow that is moving faster than the critical velocity required for the lava flow to exhibit turbulent characteristics; the critical velocity is different for a sheet flow and a pipe flow; a turbulent flow is moving much faster than a LAMINAR FLOW and slightly faster than a flow that is displaying characteristics of the LAMINAR-TO-TURBULENT TRANSITION

unconformity   a gap in the ages of rock layers, such as in a canyon wall or other context, that is physically apparent; often produced as a result of a phase of heavy erosion or cycles of erosion and deposition; can result from prolonged UPLIFT, in which there is minimal deposition and strong EROSIONAL EXHUMATION; can be informative when viewed alongside the ages and thicknesses of rock layers in other parts of a BASIN or region; includes ANGULAR UNCONFORMITY, NONCONFORMITY, and DISCONFORMITY

uplift   the vertical and upward motion of a portion of land; upward motion that serves to elevate the land above sea level or with respect to adjacent land; uplift that is accompanied by or that results from EROSIONAL EXHUMATION may produce no net elevation above sea level; includes ANOROGENIC UPLIFT, PASSIVE UPLIFT, ACTIVE UPLIFT, ISOSTATIC UPLIFT, OROGENIC UPLIFT, and FAULT-ASSOCIATED UPLIFT

upper mantle   refers to the ASTHENOSPHERE and the overlying MANTLE LITHOSPHERE, which is the lower 17 miles (27 km) to 50 miles (80 km) of the LITHOSPHERE

upthrown block   the rock on the side of a FAULT, a fault in which the motion has some vertical or NORMAL CHARACTER, that has been pushed upward with respect to the rock, or FAULT BLOCK, on the other side of the fault; also applies to rock on one side of a JOINT FAULT

upwelling   the upward movement, as in a current or plume, of liquid within a liquid or semiliquid medium; includes the upwelling of molten rock, moving in a direction from the LOWER MANTLE toward the ASTHENOSPHERE or MANTLE LITHOSPHERE, and upwelling of ocean water, as in the Benguela Upwelling System (see chapter 8); often driven by differences, between two sites in the liquid medium, in temperature, density, or combinations of various fluid properties

vesicular crust   the outer layer of a LAVA FLOW that is formed, at and beneath the surface of the flow, as the lava flow cools and solidifies; the first part of a lava flow to cool; can insulate the inner portions of the lava flow against heat loss; consists of vertically oriented COLUMNS, which are separated from one another by JOINTS and contain spherical, bubblelike vesicles; vesicles may appear as air pockets or pits; is a fraction of the total thickness of the flow; may be, at most, about one-third of the total height of the cooling lava flow

volcanic activity/volcanic   the eruption or delivery of magma to sites that are above the surface of the crust, thereby causing the magma to flow as LAVA; also, the actions of lava on the surface of the Earth, as in the creation of a VOLCANIC PLATEAU; can accompany FAULT ACTIVITY; may occur in the vicinity of a VOLCANIC ARC or HOT SPOT

volcanic arc   a band of volcanoes that is formed as a result of the SUBDUCTION of one PLATE beneath another; generally occurs on the plate that is not itself being subducted; as one plate subducts beneath a second plate, a volcanic arc will be formed on the second plate; generally forms slightly cratonward of the SUBDUCTION ZONE

volcanic plateau a plateau that consists of lava, generally in the form of FLOOD BASALT LAVA

Books

Chernicoff, Stanley, and Donna Whitney. *Geology: An Introduction to Physical Geology*. 3rd ed. Boston, New York: Houghton Mifflin, 2002. A good overview of concepts related to geology.

Erickson, Jon. *The Living Earth: Making of the Earth*. New York: Facts On File, 2001. A good overview of numerous aspects of geology.

———. *The Living Earth: Rock Formations and Unusual Geologic Structures*. Rev. ed. New York: Checkmark Books, 2001. A good discussion of some of the mechanisms by which surface formations were formed.

Levin, Harold L. *The Earth through Time*. Philadelphia: Saunders College Publishing, 1983. A good introduction to geology.

Time Almanac 2004. Needham, Mass.: Pearson Education, 2003. A compilation of useful data and facts.

World Atlas, Millennium Edition. New York: DK Publishing, 1999. Useful information that encompasses multiple disciplines.

Wyckoff, Jerome. *Reading the Earth: Landforms in the Making*. Mahwah, N.J.: Adastra West, 1999. An in-depth discussion of various types of surface processes, including the formation of mountains and the erosion of rocks by rivers.

Web Sites

Google Scholar

http://scholar.google.com.

*Allows anyone to search the full texts of journal articles, covering both the
sciences and humanities. Some of the full-text articles displayed in a
search result are available, for free, in PDF format. Many of the other
full-text articles may be accessible in PDF format, through computers
available for public use, at a library of a local university.*

ScienceDirect

http://www.sciencedirect.com.

*A powerful engine, run by Elsevier Science, Ltd., for searching the full texts
of more than 6 million journal articles. The advanced search feature
should be accessible in PDF format, through computers available for
public use, at a library of a local university. The PDFs may also be
accessible, such as on a site maintained by the author of the journal
article, by a Web search of Google or Google Scholar. Allows anyone to
conduct abbreviated, title and abstract searches on the Internet.*

Search GSA Journals Online

http://www.gsajournals.org/gsaonline/?request=search-simple.

*Allows one to search the full texts of journal articles, published in associa-
tion with the Geological Society of America, going back to 1973. The full
texts may be accessible in PDF format, through computers available for
public use, at a library of a local university.*

U.S. Geological Survey

http://www.usgs.gov.

*Includes articles, published by the U.S. Geological Survey, that provide
general overviews of various topics related to geology.*

Wiley Interscience: Advanced Search

http://www3.interscience.wiley.com/search/allsearch.

An engine for searching the full texts of journal articles, published by the journals division of John Wiley & Sons. The full texts may be accessible in PDF format, through computers available for public use, at a library of a local university. The PDFs may also be accessible, such as on a site maintained by the author of the journal article, by a Web search of Google or Google Scholar.

Journals

Note to readers: This list of journals includes many of the journals that were used as sources for this book. Many of these journal articles can be searched using one or more full-text search engines, engines that can be accessed through the Web sites listed above.

Australian Journal of Earth Science
Blackwell Publishing
Commerce Place
350 Main Street
Malden, MA 02148
http://www.blackwell-synergy.com/loi/aes
Includes articles on numerous aspects of geology, with special reference to the geology of portions of Australia

Basin Research
Blackwell Publishing
Commerce Place
350 Main Street
Malden, MA 02148
http://www.blackwell-synergy.com/loi/bre
Includes articles on numerous aspects of geology

Catena
Elsevier Science, Ltd.
The Boulevard
Langford Lane
Kidlington
Oxford OX5 1GB
United Kingdom
http://www.sciencedirect.com/science/journal/03418162
Includes articles on numerous aspects of geology

Earth and Planetary Science Letters
Elsevier Science, Ltd.
The Boulevard
Langford Lane
Kidlington
Oxford OX5 1GB
United Kingdom
http://www.sciencedirect.com/science/journal/0012821X
Includes articles on numerous aspects of geology

Earth-Science Reviews
Elsevier Science, Ltd.
The Boulevard
Langford Lane
Kidlington
Oxford OX5 1GB
United Kingdom
http://www.sciencedirect.com/science/journal/00128252
Includes articles on numerous aspects of geology

Earth Surface Processes and Landforms
John Wiley & Sons
111 River Street
Hoboken, NJ 07030
http://www3.interscience.wiley.com/cgi-bin/jhome/2388
Includes articles on the erosion and weathering of surface rocks and on geomorphology

Environmental Geology
Springer-Verlag New York
P.O. Box 2485
Secaucus, NJ 07096-2485
http://www.springer.com/journal/00254/about
Includes articles on numerous aspects of geology

Geological Society of America Bulletin / GSA Bulletin
P.O. Box 9140
Boulder, CO 80301-9140
http://www.gsajournals.org/gsaonline/?request=get-archive&issn=0016-7606
Includes detailed and interesting articles on geology, with many articles on geological events that occurred in North America

Geological Survey of Western Australia Annual Review /
    GSWA Annual Review
GSWA Kalgoorlie Regional Office
P.O. Box 1664
Kalgoorlie
Western Australia
6433
Australia
http://www.doir.wa.gov.au/gswa
Includes articles on numerous aspects of geology, with special reference to the
    geology of portions of Australia

Geology
P.O. Box 9140
Boulder, CO 80301-9140
http://www.gsajournals.org/gsaonline/?request=get-archive&issn=0091-7613
An informative monthly journal that publishes articles on the geological sciences

Geomorphology
Elsevier Science, Ltd.
The Boulevard
Langford Lane
Kidlington
Oxford OX5 1GB
United Kingdom
http://www.sciencedirect.com/science/journal/0169555X
Includes articles on numerous aspects of geology

GSA Today
P.O. Box 9140
Boulder, CO 80301-9140
http://www.gsajournals.org/gsaonline/?request=get-archive&issn=1052-5173
Includes research papers and review articles on numerous aspects of geology

Hydrogeology Journal
Springer-Verlag New York
P.O. Box 2485
Secaucus, NJ 07096-2485
http://www.springer.com/journal/10040/about
Includes articles on numerous aspects of geology

Journal of Geophysical Research
American Geophysical Union
2000 Florida Avenue, NW

Washington, DC 20009
http://www.agu.org/pubs/pubs.html#journals
Includes articles on numerous aspects of geology

Journal of Quaternary Science
John Wiley & Sons
111 River Street
Hoboken, NJ 07030
http://www3.interscience.wiley.com/cgi-bin/jhome/2507
Includes articles on numerous aspects of geology

Journal of the Geological Society
The Geological Society Publishing House
Unit 7 Brassmill Enterprise Centre
Brassmill Lane
Bath BA1 3JN
United Kingdom
http://jgs.geoscienceworld.org
Includes articles on numerous aspects of geology

The Journal of Geology
University of Chicago Press Journals
P.O. Box 37005
Chicago, IL 60637
http://www.journals.uchicago.edu/JG/home.html
Includes articles on numerous aspects of geology

Marine Geology
Elsevier Science, Ltd.
The Boulevard
Langford Lane
Kidlington
Oxford OX5 1GB
United Kingdom
http://www.sciencedirect.com/science/journal/00253227
*Includes articles on numerous aspects of marine geology, including informa-
tion on submarine canyons*

Palaeo / Palaeogeography, Palaeoclimatology, Palaeoecology
Elsevier Science, Ltd.
The Boulevard
Langford Lane
Kidlington
Oxford OX5 1GB

United Kingdom
http://www.sciencedirect.com/science/journal/00310182
Includes articles on numerous aspects of geology

Palaios
SEPM Society for Sedimentary Geology
6128 East 38th Street, Suite 308
Tulsa, OK 74135-5814
http://palaios.geoscienceworld.org
Includes articles on numerous aspects of geology

Precambrian Research
Elsevier Science, Ltd.
The Boulevard
Langford Lane
Kidlington
Oxford OX5 1GB
United Kingdom
http://www.sciencedirect.com/science/journal/03019268
Includes articles on numerous aspects of geology

Quaternary International
Pergamon Press, in association with Elsevier Science, Ltd.
The Boulevard
Langford Lane
Kidlington
Oxford OX5 1GB
United Kingdom
http://www.sciencedirect.com/science/journal/10406182
Includes research on geological processes that occurred during the Quaternary period or that were continuing to develop during the Quaternary period

Quaternary Research
Elsevier Science, Ltd.
The Boulevard
Langford Lane
Kidlington
Oxford OX5 1GB
United Kingdom
http://www.sciencedirect.com/science/journal/00335894
Includes research on geological processes that occurred during the Quaternary period or that were continuing to develop during the Quaternary period

Quaternary Science Reviews
Elsevier Science, Ltd.
The Boulevard
Langford Lane
Kidlington
Oxford OX5 1GB
United Kingdom
http://www.sciencedirect.com/science/journal/02773791
*Includes research on geological processes that occurred during the Quaternary
    period or that were continuing to develop during the Quaternary period*

Sedimentology
Blackwell Publishing
Commerce Place
350 Main Street
Malden, MA 02148
http://www.blackwellpublishing.com/SED
Includes articles on numerous aspects of geology

Tectonics
American Geophysical Union
2000 Florida Avenue, NW
Washington, DC 20009
http://www.agu.org/journals/tc
Includes articles on numerous aspects of geology

Terra Nova
Blackwell Publishing
Commerce Place
350 Main Street
Malden, MA 02148
http://www.blackwellpublishing.com/ter
Includes articles on numerous aspects of geology

U.S. Geological Survey Publications
508 National Center
12201 Sunrise Valley Drive
Reston, VA 20192
http://infotrek.er.usgs.gov/pubs
Includes articles on numerous aspects of geology

Index